A student's guide to international financial reporting standards

By Clare Finch

Third Edition

KAP

PUBLIS

British library cataloguing-in-publication data
A catalogue record for this book is available from the British Library.
Published by:
Kaplan Publishing UK
Unit 2 The Business Centre
Molly Millars Lane
Wokingham
Berkshire
RG41 2QZ

ISBN 978-1-85732-762-8

© Clare Finch

First edition published 2007
Second edition published 2008
Third edition published 2012

Printed and bound in Great Britain.

Contents

* In September 2007 the IASB amended the title of IAS 10 from Events after the balance sheet date to Events after the Reporting Period. The detail in the standard is unaltered.

3 For those interested in group accounts
– The 'blue' standards
203

4 For the seriously advanced!
– The 'red' standards
317

Index

About this book

Why do you need this book?

The most common reason for accountancy students failing exams is that they try to pass without learning their accounting standards. WHY? – they are soooo boring!!...... BUT it doesn't have to be like that.....

This book is essential reading for all students sitting accountancy exams to international financial reporting standards. Yes it's a "techie" subject... but the book is different because:

- it makes IFRS/IAS accessible for you, the student
- it is the first book to 'colour code' and group the standards on a 'need to know' basis
- it tells the story behind the standards – not just where we are but why
- it focuses on what the key 'need to learn' essential points are for exam room success
- it uses memory techniques
- it is written in a chatty, down to earth, understandable, style.

This book is a 'companion guide to the accounting standards', aiming principally to make a technical subject more digestible.

How to use this book

One of the problems with studying accounting standards is the size of the task. There are so many such standards that it can be difficult for a student to know where to begin. This book, uniquely, breaks the standards down, by difficulty of topic. (The standards are then colour coded on a 'need to know' basis.)

The 'orange standards'

The first eleven chapters are what we will refer to as 'the orange standards'. These are essential reading for a student who is just starting out – they cover the key basic areas that will be met in most exam situations.

The 'green standards'

As you progress through your studies you will meet more complex, less common transactions. These standards will not feature in every exam and we will refer to them as 'the green standards'.

The 'blue standards'

As well as being examined on individual company accounts, many (but not all) exam papers, ask for a consolidated set of accounts (referred to as 'group accounts'). If that is the case you will need 'the blue standards'.

The 'red standards'

Finally we come to 'the red standards'. These are the seriously advanced topics that you will need to get to grips with when you are say doing a final level professional accountancy exam.

Which topics do you need to know?

The first thing you need to know, therefore, is which topics are you expected to know for your exam. You need to ask your tutor for a list, or check your syllabus/guide to examinable documents to find out exactly what is relevant for you. If you are just starting your studies you may find many of the more difficult topics are not examined until later stages – so you can pick up the book again and study these topics when they become relevant.

About the chapters

Books on accounting standards normally start each chapter with the aims, key definitions etc. This book deliberately avoids such an approach. Each chapter starts with the background of what the issue is that gave rise to the need for a standard. In this way the scene is set for a better understanding of what the standard is about. Only then does the chapter introduce the aims and …**'SO…WHAT'S IT TRYING TO ACHIEVE?'** will become a familiar mantra.

Transactional example

To ensure the understanding of a given issue, each chapter includes a transactional example (excluding those couple of standards which are format rather than transactional based), thus allowing the explanation and application of the standard to the issue.

The pitfalls

We all actually learn a lot from making mistakes – getting something wrong is usually a sure way of making sure we get it right the next time. We can shortcut this process, however, by learning from the mistakes of others. There are some errors that are very common – student after student will trip up at the same point. Being forewarned of the issue helps you to learn from students who have gone before you.

The definitions

We can't avoid them forever, and once the understanding of the issue is 'anchored' with a transaction, the definitions from the standard are given. Note people do have variable learning styles and those of you who already have some comfort with the standard may like to turn first to the definitions box – reaffirm those and then read the chapter.

Key 'need to learn' bit

If you are facing a closed book exam, it will not be enough to be just comfortable with the subject matter and to feel you understand the issue – there are some key 'need to learn' bits for each standard. You will, therefore, have to commit some issues to memory. These are highlighted for you as you go through the topic.

The memory devices

Each chapter contains a suggested 'memory device'. It could be an acronym, mnemonic, 'cloud diagram' or 'image-story technique'. Remember however, many learners will benefit from constructing their own diagrams and creating their own mnemonics.

More about memory devices

The human brain has evolved to code and interpret very complex stimuli, we all do this every day. Limiting your learning to just reading words is not using your full potential. While language, i.e. words on a page, reflects one of the most important aspects of human evolution, it is only one of the many skills available to the human mind.

Most books, however, present the information to be remembered in only one way – as words. Memory devices seek to use a broader range of these resources. By coding language and using images, many people find the information much easier to recall. The book provides you with plenty of examples so you should easily find yourself preparing ones that are personal to you.

Key points when preparing your own devices:

- many people remember a diagram better than a list (this plays to the right hand side of the brain)
- colour enhances memory – invest in coloured pens
- smell is very evocative – it triggers memory. Have you tried using the scented pens that are available?
- try drawing your own 'cloud diagrams' when listening to a lecture
- when doing your own mnemonics, you can use risqué ones – generally the easiest to remember!

Throughout the book illustrations are provided of memory devices including mnemonics and cloud diagrams for remembering key points from accounting standards. Don't forget, however, learner–generated devices are always the most effective.

(I do appreciate some people have no problem with words on a page – a list does it for them – but hey – we are all different.)

Summary guide to the symbols

 Transactional Example

 Pitfalls

 Definitions

 Key 'Need to Learn' Bit

 Memory Device

Thank you to everybody who has supported me during this project, my family, friends, work colleagues, students, and publisher. Many many thanks to Safiya Rajpar for all her work.

All errors are my own and come with apologies.

A special thank you for all the work put in by my proof reader Dr David Holland CMath FIMA to whom I will be eternally grateful.

Starting out

"Knowledge is of two kinds. We know a subject ourselves or we know where we can find information on it."

Samuel Johnson (1709–1784)

Introduction

There are ten accounting standards which form the 'baseline' for anyone who is starting out studying financial accounting, and preparing their financial statements to the standards of the International Accounting Standards Board (IASB).

- IAS 1   Presentation of financial statements
- IAS 2   Inventory
- IAS 7   Statement of cash flows
- IAS 8   Accounting policies, changes in accounting estimates and errors
- IAS 10   Events after the reporting period*
- IAS 16   Property, plant and equipment
- IAS 18   Revenue
- IAS 37   Provisions, contingent liabilities and contingent assets
- IAS 38   Intangible assets
- IFRS 13 Fair value measurement

However, underpinning the accounting standards is the Framework document. This is arguably the most important examinable document for any student of accounting to be familiar with. This is covered in Chapter 1 – **Accounting standards – where are we and why?** Do not be tempted to miss this chapter, as the concepts and 'buzz words' you are introduced to or reminded of here, are key to success in many financial accounting exam questions. Do not be tempted to skip this one!

"You do not really understand something unless you can explain it to your grandmother."

Albert Einstein (1879-1955)

Note

Many books on accounting standards start by giving you the aims and definitions from the standard. This book deliberately does not structure the chapters in that style. Instead the issue is generally explained, with the sort of transactions that the standard relates to being introduced. We do get to the aims and definitions and, for those of you who already feel comfortable with the standard, you may like to turn first to the definitions box – re-affirm those and then read the chapter.

---

* In September 2007 the IASB amended the title of IAS 10 from Events after the balance sheet date to Events after the Reporting Period. The detail in the standard is unaltered.

1 Accounting standards – where are we and why?

Introduction

ONCE UPON A TIME a student of accounting only had to get to grips with the mechanics of double-entry bookkeeping and they could produce a set of accounts for any organisation. Definitions were simple – **'A balance sheet* is a summary of assets and liabilities'** we were told; **'assets are things we own and liabilities are things we owe'**. This was the staple diet of accounting lecture number 1 for those of us who trained before the late 1980s. Unfortunately we didn't get to 'live happily ever after' and we constantly have to learn new tricks and keep up with change. The modern accountancy student has a huge list of accounting standards to get to grips with as well as the mechanics of double-entry bookkeeping. Definition of an asset? – Well it's not as simple as **'something you own'** any more!

The fairy tales or creative accounting

Unfortunately the accountancy profession has shown itself to be very able in the practices of 'earnings management'/'off balance sheet finance'/'window dressing'. Whatever we call it, it involves deliberately structuring a series of transactions, and exploitation of loopholes in rules – creative accounting, thinking about the presentation of what the company wants to show rather than the needs of the reader of the financial statements. Two key 'hotspots' exist: manipulation of profit, and manipulation of liabilities. The first of these showing profit as a steady upward movement can give the impression of 'quality earnings'. This makes it easier for the company to present its results to the market. The second financial 'hotspot' is under-reporting of liabilities, i.e. off balance sheet* finance. This is why modern day accountancy students have so many accounting standards to learn – we really should blame ourselves (or other accountants anyway!!).

Needs of users

Accounting standards have always been about the needs of users. The International Accounting Standards Board (IASB) who produce the International Financial Reporting Standards (IFRSs) are actually not interested in what companies want their annual reports to show. Their job is to ensure that accounting standards help produce high quality, transparent and comparable information. In this way financial statements should help users make economic decisions.

---

* Please note in 2007 the IASB issued a revised IAS 1. The revised IAS 1 removed the traditional term 'balance sheet' and although the format was unchanged it is now called a 'statement of financial position'. In June 2011 the IASB further amended IAS 1, with the comprehensive income statement now being renamed 'a statement of profit or loss and other comprehensive income'.

Traditional approach to accounting standards – fire-fighting

Traditionally, standard setters in many countries waited for there to be a corporate collapse or other form of bad publicity before issuing an accounting standard to change accounting practice – waiting as it were, for the horse to bolt before closing the stable door. A classic example from the UK was the collapse of the package holiday business, Court Line Ltd. This company collapsed after receiving a clean audit report for a balance sheet* showing shareholders' funds of £18m. The shareholders quite correctly asked what was the value in these financial statements. As modern day accountants we would find this balance sheet* interesting and hopefully would have raised questions.

The Court Line Ltd balance sheet*

As Court Line was generating revenue by transporting people from the UK to the continent (for their package holidays) we would have expected to see the aircraft involved in their transport on the balance sheet*. However the aircraft were not on the balance sheet as Court Line had not bought them, but had entered into a lease agreement: therefore Court Line was not the legal owner. Under Generally Accepted Accounting Practice (GAAP) of the time, the aircraft, and more importantly the obligation to make payments to the leasing company, which stood at £40m, were not required to be on the balance sheet*. Court Line was following the legal form of the transaction, i.e. the leasing company was the owner of the aircraft, not Court Line.

Needs of users?

Neither the shareholders nor the creditors found it believable that accountants could consider that non-disclosure of a liability of £40m (which dwarfed the shareholders' funds figure of £18m) could be classed as giving a 'true and fair view'. Clearly there was a need for an accounting standard. International Accounting Standard 17 (IAS 17) would now require these aircraft and the associated obligation to be brought 'on balance sheet*'. The **'substance'** of the transaction was that the directors had bought aircraft for their exclusive use with the finance being provided by the leasing company – in commercial reality terms no different to buying the asset on credit – a finance deal. These assets would now be dealt with as 'finance leases', which are required to be capitalised, i.e. shown on the balance sheet* along with the associated debt.

Rules v principles

The problem with a 'fire-fighting' approach to producing accounting standards is that it tends to close one 'loophole' with some rules as to how a transaction must now be accounted for, but doesn't stop the underlying problem. For example having rules about finance leases did not stop off balance sheet* finance – it just stopped one particular scheme – so companies simply came up with other methods. Modern accounting standards, therefore, are based on principles rather than rules.

The Framework document

The Framework document was originally issued in 1989 and was revised and reissued in September 2010 as 'The Conceptual Framework for Financial Reporting'. Instead of producing standards in a fire-fighting way, the Framework provides assistance that the IASB will use in the development of accounting standards. It is based on the premise that financial statements are prepared for the purpose of providing information that is useful in making economic decisions.

So ... what's it trying to achieve?

The **Framework** does not have the force of a standard. Instead, its purposes include, firstly, to guide and assist the IASB as it develops new or revised standards and, secondly, to assist preparers of financial statements in applying standards and in dealing with topics that are not addressed by an accounting standard. If, therefore, there is a conflict between the **Framework** and a specific standard, the standard prevails over the **Framework**. The **Framework** is not an IFRS and hence does not define standards for any particular measurement or disclosure issue. Nothing in this **Framework** overrides any specific IFRS.

Aspects of the Framework document are vital for any accountancy student to learn. If you understand the key parts of the Framework document, it acts as a 'get out of jail free card' in many written questions on accounting standards. You will earn good marks by defaulting to the principles contained in the Framework document, especially when asked to 'explain why' in reference to any accounting standard.

Objective of general purpose financial reporting

You must learn the objective of financial statements, the qualitative characteristics of financial statements and the underlying assumptions. These are a **'need to learn'**.

At the user

The objective of general purpose financial reporting is to provide financial information about the reporting entity that is useful to existing and potential investors, lenders and other creditors in making decisions about providing resources to the entity. These decisions involve buying, selling or holding investments in shares or debt instruments, and providing or settling loans and other forms of credit.

Decisions made by users depend upon the returns that they expect to receive, for example dividend income, principal and interest payments or market price increases. Consequently users need information that helps them assess the prospects for future net cash inflows to an entity.

To assess the entity's prospects for future net cash inflows users need information about:

- the resources of the entity
- claims against the entity
- how efficiently and effectively the entity's management and governing board have discharged their responsibilities to use the entity's resources.

Many existing and potential investors, lenders and other creditors cannot require reporting entities to provide information directly to them and must rely upon general purpose financial reports for much of the financial information they need. Consequently they are the primary users to whom general purpose financial reports are directed.

> ## Note
>
> Please note the conceptual framework is clear that general purpose financial statements cannot provide all of the information that users need. Also the framework makes it clear that general purpose financial reports are not designed to show the value of a reporting entity.

Fundamental qualitative characteristics

The fundamental qualitative characteristics are:

- **relevance** and
- **faithful representation**.

 ### Relevance

Relevant financial information is capable of making a difference in the decisions made by users. Information may be capable of making a difference in a decision even if some users choose not to take advantage of it or are already aware of it from other sources.

Financial information is capable of making a difference in decisions if it has predictive value, confirmatory value or both.

Predictive value exists if financial information can be used as an input to processes employed by users to predict future outcomes.

Confirmatory value exists if it provides feedback about (confirms or changes) previous evaluations.

The predictive value and confirmatory value of financial information are interrelated. Information that has predictive value often also has confirmatory value.

Transactional example - relevance

Revenue information for the current year, which can be used as the basis for predicting revenues in future years, can also be compared with revenue predictions for the current year that were made in past years. The results of those comparisons can help a user to correct and improve the processes that were used to make those previous predictions.

Faithful representation

Financial reports represent economic phenomena in words and numbers. To be useful, financial information must not only represent relevant phenomena, but it must also faithfully represent the phenomena that it purports to represent. To be a perfectly faithful representation, a depiction would have three characteristics. It would be **complete, neutral** and **free from error**. Of course, perfection is seldom, if ever, achievable.

A complete depiction includes all information necessary for a user to understand the phenomenon being depicted, including all necessary descriptions and explanations.

Transactional example - faithful representation

A complete depiction of a group of assets would include, at a minimum, a description of the nature of the assets in the group, a numerical depiction of all of the assets in the group, and a description of what the numerical depiction represents (for example, original cost, adjusted cost or fair value). For some items, a complete depiction may also entail explanations of significant facts about the quality and nature of the items, factors and circumstances that might affect their quality and nature, and the process used to determine the numerical depiction.

Enhancing qualitative characteristics

Comparability, **verifiability**, **timeliness** and **understandability** are qualitative characteristics that enhance the usefulness of information that is relevant and faithfully represented. The enhancing qualitative characteristics may also help determine which of two ways should be used to depict a phenomenon if both are considered equally relevant and faithfully represented.

Underlying assumption

Going concern

Going concern is the underlying assumption adopted whenever we are preparing financial statements. You will have learnt about this from your first introduction to double-entry bookkeeping.

Note

Going concern - the assumption that an entity will continue in operation for the foreseeable future.

You may find a image-story memory techniques useful for remembering these.

Qualitative characteristics

An image-story technique works well for remembering these.

Once upon a time in the kingdom of financial statements lived the good King Relevance and his faithful Queen Representation.

The King and Queen had four daughters:

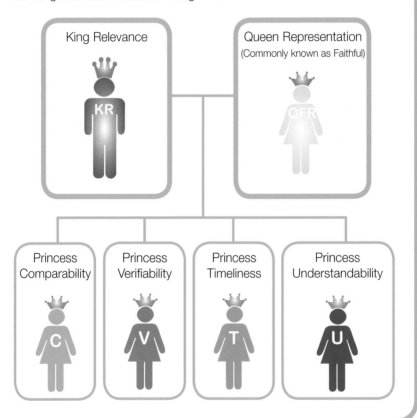

Sorry but you need to know ... DEFINITIONS

The elements of financial statements

The Framework also gives definitions for the elements of financial statements – clearly all accountancy students need to be able to define an asset and a liability when answering questions.

- **Assets** – an asset is defined as 'a resource controlled by the entity as a result of past events and from which future economic benefits are expected to flow to the entity'.

- **Liabilities** – a liability is defined as 'a present obligation of the entity arising from past events, the settlement of which is expected to result in an outflow from the entity of resources embodying economic benefits'.

- **Equity** – the residual interest in the assets of the entity after deducting all of its liabilities.

- **Income** – increases in economic benefit during the accounting period in the form of inflows or enhancements of assets or decreases of liabilities that result in increases in equity, other than those relating to contributions from equity participants.

- **Expenses** – decreases in economic benefits during the accounting period in the form of outflows or depletions in assets or incurrences of liabilities that result in decreases in equity, other than those relating to distributions to equity participants.

These definitions are **'ABSOLUTELY MUST LEARN'** for all accountancy students.

Transactional example

Jamie Inc was fined for the receipt of 'illegal' state subsidies of $600 million that were used to offset trade losses in previous years. Jamie Inc has to repay the government the $600 million plus interest of $320 million. Jamie Inc has decided to treat the repayment as an intangible asset which is being amortised over 20 years with a 20th being charged in the current year accounts. You need to discuss whether the accounting treatment is acceptable.

Even if you didn't know any accounting standards you could answer this question from the principles of the Framework document. As follows:

The Framework
The Framework describes the elements of financial statements as broad classes of financial effects of transactions and other events.

Definition of an asset
An asset is a 'resource controlled by the entity as a result of past events and from which future economic benefits are expected to flow'.

Payment of a fine
The payment of a fine does not meet this definition. Future economic benefits will not flow to the entity as a result of paying this fine. It is not a resource controlled by the company.

Inappropriate treatment
It is inappropriate to treat this transaction as an asset, as the payment of the fine is actually a cost to the company and needs to be treated as such.

Definition of an expense
Expenses are 'decreases in economic benefits during the accounting period in the form of outflows or depletions in assets or incurrences of liabilities that result in decreases in equity, other than those relating to distributions to equity participants'.

The fine should be charged against profit
Clearly the payment of this fine decreases economic benefit and incurs a liability for the company that will result in a decrease in equity (shareholders' funds) – it is an expense to be charged against current year profit.

Summary

By learning the definitions of the elements of financial statements you can apply the Framework to transactions – even if you don't know the specific standard you will be giving a very good answer.

 ## Cloud diagrams

As explained in the 'About this book' section (page iii), different students have different learning needs. When faced with a 'need to learn' area you have to decide what works best for you. For some learners the words on the page are adequate but for others there are better ways to aid recall.

Remember the human brain can code and interpret from a variety of stimuli, just reading the words is only one available way. Some, when faced with the task – 'OK so I need to remember the five elements of financial statements' – will benefit from drawing a diagram (see the following 'cloud diagram' as an example). This plays to the strengths of the right-hand side of the brain, which has been proven to recall colour and diagrams better than black and white writing.

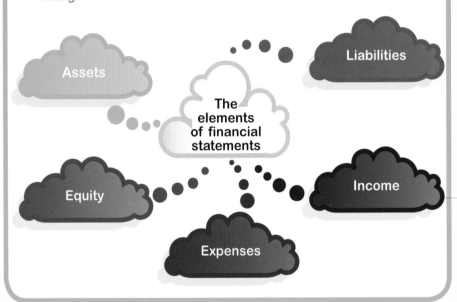

Conclusion

The Framework document will be central to the success of accounting students at all levels. It may appear painful to learn the definitions of the elements, but hey, you have chosen to study accountancy, so it hardly seems unreasonable. The sooner you learn the definitions, the easier it will be to get to grips with the standards as they are based on these definitions.

---

* Statement of profit or loss = Income statement

2 IAS 1 – Presentation of financial statements

Introduction

Economic models explained – with cows

Socialism
You have two cows, and you give one to your neighbour.

Communism
You have two cows. The State takes both and gives you some milk.

Fascism
You have two cows. The State takes both and sells you some milk.

Bureaucracy
You have two cows. The State takes both, shoots one, milks the other, and then throws the milk away...

Traditional capitalism
You have two cows. You sell one and buy a bull. Your herd multiplies, and the economy grows. You sell them and retire on the income.

Enron venture capitalism
You have 2 cows. You sell three of them to your publicly listed company, using letters of credit opened by your brother-in-law at the bank, then execute a debt/equity swap with an associated general offer so that you get all four cows back, with a tax exemption for five cows. The milk rights of the six cows are transferred via an intermediary to a Cayman Island company secretly owned by the majority shareholder who sells the rights to all seven cows back to your listed company. The annual report says the company owns eight cows, with an option on one more. Sell one cow to buy a new president of the United States, leaving you with nine cows. No balance sheet* provided with the release. The public buys your bull.

The Andersen model
You have 2 cows. You shred them.

Anon by e-mail

Enron

Enron was once the seventh largest public-listed entity in the USA. In 2002 it became the most famous bankruptcy of all time. The accounting malpractices that were uncovered culminated in the demise of Enron's audit firm, Andersen (one of the then 'Big Five' accounting firms), due to its alleged document shredding at Enron. It is important that we always consider the needs of the users when we provide financial information. In October 2001, the market valued Enron's shares at around US$89. Some of the Enron staff so believed in their own company (remember it was a top 'buy tip' throughout this time) that they invested their own pension funds heavily in Enron stock. By February 2002, the share price was under US$1 – investors had lost the lot. Enron prepared its accounts to US GAAP not to IFRS, but whenever we are talking about accounting standards it helps to understand the lessons from history. The fact is that presenting misleading financial statements has ruined lives.

When it comes to IFRS the starting point for any trainee accountant has to be with IAS 1 as this is the standard that gives us the content of the primary accounting statements. Accountancy exams are variable – some students are given formats, some do an 'open book' exam. For many, however, all they get to take into the exam hall is their brain and pen, which means you may have to learn a format.

So ... it's a 'meet the formats' standard

Well ... yes, although it is actually a 'minimum required content,' rather than a prescriptive 'here is the format' standard. From a student perspective, however, your exams will ask you to prepare financial statements. Therefore you will need to find out what you have signed up for – are you going to be given a format to use or do you need to learn one?

When you first learnt double-entry bookkeeping, you were probably preparing financial statements for 'internal use' only, i.e. revenue less a list of expenses equalling profit.

Your workings were probably done on the face of the accounts, i.e. non-current assets at cost less accumulated depreciation = Net Book Value (NBV).

Net Book Value (NBV) is also known as carrying value (CV).

Accounting (as opposed to bookkeeping) exams require us to take the detail off the face of the accounting statements, so we are showing summary rather than detailed figures.

Remember, the best way to get familiar with the formats is to access as many past paper questions as you can and **practise, practise, practise!!**

* Statement of profit or loss = Income statement

So ... what's it trying to achieve?

IAS 1 aims to prescribe the basis of presentation of financial statements, and to ensure comparability with previous periods and with the financial statements of other entities. The standard gives the minimum information required in financial statements.

Sorry but you need to know ... DEFINITIONS

Fair presentation – implies that the financial statements 'present fairly' or 'give a true and fair view' of the financial position, financial performance and cash flows of an entity.

Materiality – an item is deemed material if its omission or misstatement would influence the economic decisions of a user taken based on the financial statements. Materiality is based on the item's nature, size, and/or the surrounding circumstances.

Aggregation – each material class of similar items shall be presented separately in the financial statements. Material items that are dissimilar in nature should be separately disclosed.

Offsetting – assets and liabilities, income and expenses cannot be offset against each other unless required or permitted by a standard.

Comparative information – information relating to the previous period.

And the really important stuff ... accounting practice

IAS 1 is to be followed by all enterprises in preparing individual and group financial statements.

The content of a set of financial statements is:

- a statement of financial position as at the end of the period* (a balance sheet*)
- a statement of profit or loss and other comprehensive income
- a statement of changes in equity for the period
- a statement of cash flows for the period (this is covered by IAS 7)
- notes, comprising a summary of significant accounting policies and other explanatory information
- a statement of financial position as at the beginning of the earliest comparative period when an entity applies an accounting policy retrospectively or makes a retrospective restatement of items in its financial statements, or when it reclassifies items in its financial statements.

---

* Please note in 2007 the IASB issued a revised IAS 1. The revised IAS 1 removed the traditional term 'balance sheet' and although the format was unchanged it is now called a 'statement of financial position'. In June 2011 the IASB further amended IAS 1, with the comprehensive income statement now being renamed 'a statement of profit or loss and other comprehensive income'.

An entity may use titles for the statements other than those used in the standard and an entity shall present with equal prominence all of the financial statements in a complete set of financial statements.

The overall considerations in the presentation of accounts are:

- fair presentation and compliance with IFRS
- going concern (see Chapter 1)
- accruals
- consistency
- materiality and aggregation (see above)
- offsetting (see above)
- comparatives (see above).

The formats are not specified by IAS 1, however the standard gives the minimum information to be included. The proformas over the next pages are interpretations of that minimum information.

A choice also exists with regard to unusual (exceptional) items, which can be presented either on the face of the income statement*, or in the notes to the accounts.

A further choice exists with the 'statement of changes in equity'. The amount of dividends recognised as distributions to owners during the period can be presented either in the statement of changes in equity or in the notes.

Note

For a standard with a key aim of comparability we have just talked an awful lot about choice!!! Looking for a criticism? – yes, you've found it!!

Notes to the accounts must always be prepared, i.e.

- Accounting policies note.
- Disclose information required by any IAS/IFRS that is not on the face of the primary statements.
- Provide other relevant information.

Format of the financial statements

On the following pages are illustrative examples of the formats of financial statements. **(Note these full formats do not have a key next to them, so just scan and move on.)**

---

* Statement of profit or loss = Income statement

The statement of financial position* (balance sheet*) – full format

XYX Group- Statement of financial position* as at 31 December 20X7

	20X7	20X7	20X6	20X6
ASSETS				
Non-current assets				
Property, plant and equipment	X		X	
Goodwill	X		X	
Other intangible assets	X		X	
Investments in associates	X		X	
Investments in equity instruments	X		X	
		X		X
Current assets				
Inventories	X		X	
Trade and other receivables	X		X	
Other current assets	X		X	
Cash and cash equivalents	X		X	
		X		X
Total assets		X		X
EQUITY AND LIABILITIES				
Equity attributable to the holders of the parent				
Equity Share capital	X		X	
Other components of equity	X		X	
Retained earnings	X		X	
		X		X
Non-controlling interest		X		X
Non-current liabilities				
Long-term borrowings	X		X	
Deferred tax	X		X	
Long-term provisions	X		X	
		X		X
Current liabilities				
Trade and other payables	X		X	
Short-term borrowings	X		X	
Current portion of long-term borrowings	X		X	
Current tax payable	X		X	
Short-term provisions	X		X	
		X		X
Total equity and liabilities		X		X

The statement of financial position

* Please note in 2007 the IASB issued a revised IAS 1. The revised IAS 1 removed the traditional term 'balance sheet' and although the format was unchanged it is now called a 'statement of financial position'. In June 2011 the IASB further amended IAS1, with the comprehensive income statement now being renamed 'a statement of profit or loss and other comprehensive income'.

The statement of profit or loss and other comprehensive income*– full format (format 1)

Please note it is also acceptable to present this as two separate statements:

- separate statement of profit or loss
- separate statement beginning with profit or loss and displaying components of other comprehensive income.

*The statement of profit or loss and other comprehensive income**

XYX Group - Statement of profit or loss and other comprehensive income* for the year ended 31 December 20X7

(Illustrating the classification of expenses by function)

	20X7	20X6
Revenue	X	X
Cost of sales	(x)	(x)
Gross profit	X	X
Other income	X	X
Distribution costs	(x)	(x)
Administrative expenses	(x)	(x)
Other expenses	(x)	(x)
Finance cost	(x)	(x)
Share of profits of associates	X	X
Profit before tax	X	X
Income tax expense	(x)	(x)
Profit for the year continuing operations	X	X
Loss for the year from discontinued operations	(x)	(x)
PROFIT FOR THE YEAR	X	X
Other Comprehensive Income (OCI):		
Items that will not be classified to profit or loss:		
Gains on property revaluation	X	X
Remeasurements of defined benefit pension plans	X	(x)
Investments in fair value through other comprehensive income OCI equity instruments	X	(x)
Share of gain (loss) on property revaluation of associates	X	(x)
Income tax relating to items that will not be reclassified	(x)	(x)
Items that may be classified subsequently to profit or loss		
Exchange differences on translating foreign operations	X	(x)
Cash flow hedges	X	(x)
Income tax relating to items that may be reclassified	(x)	(x)
Other comprehensive income for the year, net of tax	X	X
TOTAL COMPREHENSIVE INCOME FOR THE YEAR	X	X

* Statement of profit or loss = Income statement

An error that some students make when they initially study IAS 1 is to try to learn the complete formats. In fact, many of the lines will only be relevant at the more advanced stages, e.g. when you prepare consolidated statements for groups of companies. Many students will not need to learn these formats in full. See below for what will be necessary.

The statement of financial position* (balance sheet) – the key bits

XYX Group- The statement of financial position* as at 31 December 20X7

	20X7	20X7	20X6	20X6
ASSETS				
Non-current assets				
Property, plant and equipment	X		X	
Other intangible assets	X		X	
		X		X
Current assets				
Inventories	X		X	
Trade and other receivables	X		X	
Cash and cash equivalents	X		X	
		X		X
Total assets		X		X
EQUITY AND LIABILITIES				
Equity attributable to the holders of the parent				
Equity share capital	X		X	
Other components of equity	X		X	
Retained earnings	X		X	
		X		X
Non-current liabilities				
Long-term borrowings	X		X	
Long-term provisions	X		X	
Deferred tax	X		X	
		X		X
Current liabilities				
Trade and other payables	X		X	
Short-term borrowings	X		X	
Current tax payable	X		X	
Short-term provisions	X		X	
		X		X
Total equity and liabilities		X		X

The statement of financial position*

The statement of profit or loss and other comprehensive income*- the key bits

The top half is the key bit, instead of learning the full format use a mnemonic such as:

Really cute guys distract accountants preventing infatuated fools passing the paper!

(Obviously a significant chunk of you would prefer to learn the 'REALLY CUTE GALS' version instead!)

To learn the initial key lines of the format for the top part of the statement of profit or loss*.

Cute guys version

Statement of profit or loss and other comprehensive income

XYX Group - Statement of profit or loss and other comprehensive income for the year ended 31 December 20X7

(Illustrating the classification of expenses by function)

	20X7	20X6
Revenue (Really)	X	X
Cost of sales **(Cute)**	(x)	(x)
Gross profit **(Guys)/(Gals)**	X	X
Distribution costs **(Distract)**	(x)	(x)
Administrative expenses **(Accountants)**	(x)	(x)
Profit from operations **(Preventing)**	X	X
Investment income **(Infatuated)**	X	X
Finance cost **(Fools)**	(x)	(x)
Profit before tax (Passing)	X	X
Tax expense **(The)**	(x)	(x)
Profit for the year (Paper)	X	X

The bottom half is even simpler when we first start preparing these accounts. Usually there is either no other items of comprehensive income or perhaps just the one - a revaluation gain.

Other Comprehensive income		
Gains on property revaluation	X	X
Total comprehensive income for the year	**X**	**X**

---

* Statement of profit or loss = Income statement

Another problem is time spent learning format 2. Note it doesn't have a key next to it.

The statement of profit or loss and other comprehensive income*

XYX Group - Statement of profit or loss and other comprehensive income* for the year ended 31 December 20X7

(Illustrating the classification of expenses by nature)

	20X7	20X6
Revenue	X	X
Other income	X	X
Changes in inventories of finished goods and work-in-progress	(x)	X
Work performed by the enterprise and capitalised	X	X
Raw material and consumables used	(x)	(x)
Employee benefits expense	(x)	(x)
Impairment of property, plant and equipment	(x)	(x)
Other expenses	(x)	(x)
Finance cost	(x)	(x)
Share of profit of associates	X	X
Profit before tax	X	X
Income tax expense	(x)	(x)
Profit for the period	X	X
Attributable to:		
Equity holders of the parent	X	X
Non-controlling interest	X	X
	X	X

Statement of profit or loss and other comprehensive income

Other Comprehensive income		
Gains on property revaluation	X	X
Total comprehensive income for the year	**x**	**x**

This format is not used very frequently and, therefore, whilst you will see it in textbooks the important format for the statement of profit or loss is the **REALLY CUTE GUYS one!!**

---

* Please note in 2007 the IASB issued a revised IAS 1. The revised IAS 1 removed the traditional term 'balance sheet' and although the format was unchanged it is now called a 'statement of financial position'. In June 2011 the IASB further amended IAS 1, with the comprehensive income statement now being renamed 'a statement of profit or loss and other comprehensive income'.

The statement of changes in equity – full format

 Again the format of the statement of changes in equity taken directly from IAS 1 looks pretty daunting … However, until you get pretty advanced most of this stuff is irrelevant. See below for full format. (Again, note no key!)

Statement of changes in equity

XYX Group – Statement of changes in equity for the year ended 31 December 20X7

	Share capital	Retained earnings	Translation of foreign operations	Fair value through OCI financial assets	Cash flow hedges	Revaluation reserve	Total	Non-controlling interest	Total equity
Balance at 1 January 20X6	X	X	(x)	X	X		X	X	X
Changes in accounting policy		X					X	X	X
Restated balance	X	X	(x)	X	X		X	X	X
Changes in equity for 20X6									
Dividends		(x)					(x)		(x)
Total comprehensive income for the year		X	X	(x)	X	X	X	X	X
Balance at 31 December 20X6	X	X	X	X	(x)	X	X	X	X
Changes in equity for 20X7									
Issue of share capital	X						X		X
Dividends		(x)					(x)		(x)
Total comprehensive income for the year		X	(x)	(x)	X	X	X	X	X
Transferred to retained earnings		X				X			
Balance at 31 December 20X7	X	X	X	X	(x)	X	X	X	X

Although this is the format you would see in IAS 1 and textbooks, it is covering everything and for most companies will be a lot simpler – it's just a column for each balance sheet* line of equity and reserves showing any changes that took place in the accounting period. SEE the example below for the common bits that need to be learnt!

Statement of changes in equity

XYX Group – Statement of changes in equity for the year ended 31 December 20X7

	Share capital	Retained earnings	Revaluation reserve	Total equity
Balance at 31 December 20X6	X	X	X	X
Dividends		(x)		(x)
Issue of share capital	X			X
Total comprehensive income for the year		X	X	X
Balance at 31 December 20X7 carried forward	X	X	X	X

* Please note in 2007 the IASB issued a revised IAS 1. The revised IAS 1 removed the traditional term 'balance sheet' and although the format was unchanged it is now called a 'statement of financial position'. In June 2011 the IASB further amended IAS 1, with the comprehensive income statement now being renamed 'a statement of profit or loss and other comprehensive income'.

From bookkeeper to accountant

So when we first learn double entry bookkeeping we learn our debits and credits and how to prepare a trial balance and we can put together basic financial statements for a sole trader or for internal use. The statements of profit or loss* will have looked like this:

Alexandra Ltd profit or loss account for the year ended 31 December 20X7

	$	$
Sales		x
Less		
Cost of goods sold:		
Opening inventory	x	
Plus Purchases	x	
Less Closing		
Inventory	(x)	(x)
Gross Profit		x
Less expenses:		
Wages	(x)	
Rent	(x)	
Electricity	(x)	
Motor expenses		(x)
Net Profit for the year		x

However, to move to preparing published accounts for companies you need to adopt the International Financial Reporting Standards (IFRS). Remember IAS - International Accounting Standards and IFRS are exactly the same thing, it is just that the name changed: some older ones are called IAS and newer ones called IFRS.

Preparing published accounts for a company is a step up from preparing the accounts of a sole trader or the accounts for internal use for a company. For a start the formats in IAS 1 – Presentation of financial statements will need to be used.

However, we start from the same position - we need to extract a trial balance and obtain key information to be the normal post trial balance adjustments such as inventory valuation, depreciation policies and accrual and prepayment information. In addition as a company an estimate will need to be made for corporation tax payable.

---

* Statement of profit or loss = Income statement

Transactional example

Alexandra Ltd

Further Information

(a) *Inventories were valued at $7,850,000 on 30 September 20X9.*

(b) *Depreciation is to be provided for the year to 30 September 20X9 as follows:*

Buildings 10% per annum straight line basis
Plant and Equipment 25% per annum reducing balance basis

Depreciation is to be apportioned as follows:

Cost of Sales 55%
Distribution costs 30%
Administrative expenses 15%

Land and buildings in the trial balance includes a value for land at $42,578. It is to be revalued at $61,000 and this revaluation is to be included in the financial statements for 30 September 20X9.

(c) A bad debt of $21,000 which is included in trade receivables is to be written off.

(d) Administrative expenses of $85,000 owing at 30 September 20X9 are to be provided for.

(e) The companies tax charge for the year has been estimated as $1,500,000.

Required

Prepare a statement of profit or loss* and a statement of changes in equity for Alexandra Ltd for the year ended 30 September 20X9 and also a statement of financial position** as at that date. They must comply with IAS 1 – Presentation of financial statements.

Get yourself organised: you will need to prepare a sheet for the statement of comprehensive income and a separate sheet for the statement of financial position.

SOPL

Alexandra Ltd

Statement of profit or loss for the year ended 30 September 20X9

SOFP

Alexandra Ltd

Statement of financial position as at 30 September 20X9

*Statement of profit or loss = Income statement

** Statement of financial position = Balance Sheet (see page 19)

You will also need a sheet for the statement of changes in equity to the accounts and a sheet for workings.

Some of the numbers you require for this answer will come straight out of the question. Some will require a working - Let's go through the answer line by line and indicate how the amount is calculated.

You must let the IAS 1 format dictate the order of working. We will use the most common – format 1 (the **REALLY CUTE GUYS** one!)

Let's start with the performance statement – the statement of comprehensive income.

> ## Note
>
> *There is no rule in IAS 1 about which operating expenses are classed as cost of sales, which as distribution costs and which as administrative expenses.*
>
> *This will be a matter of accounting policy for each company (see Chapter 5)*

Generally though direct costs of producing the sales revenue are treated as cost of sales so in addition to the usual

Opening Inventory

Add: Purchases

Less : Closing Inventory

= Cost of goods sold

Cost of sales would also include things like manufacturing wages and depreciation of the factory and plant and equipment.

Distribution costs are the costs associated with selling the goods – the wages of the salesforce, depreciation of the fleet of lorries and vans etc.

Administrative expenses are then the general expenses of the company – the wages of the finance team, depreciation of the administrative buildings, for example.

Once an accounting policy is decided it must be applied consistently but other than that it is not regulated what goes where.

So one of the first workings will be to allocate the operating expenses to those three headings – see below for Alexandra's treatment.

(W1) Expenses

	Cost of sales $000	Distribution costs $000	Administrative expenses $000
Opening inventories	5,460		
Purchases	67,206		
Distribution costs		8,000	
Salespeople commissions		2,920	
Administrative salaries			2,280
Manufacturing wages	2,000		
Administrative expenses			5,000
Closing inventories	(7,850)		
Depreciation – buildings (W1a)	2,750	1,500	750
Depreciation – plant (W1a)	2,707	1,477	738
Administrative expenses accrued			85
Bad debt written off			21
	72,273	13,897	8,874

(W1a) Deprecation is calculated as follows:

	$000	$000
Buildings 50,000 x 10%	5,000	
SPLIT:		
Cost of sales (5,000 x 55%)		2,750
Distribution costs (5,000 x 30%)		1,500
Administrative expenses (5,000 x 15%)		750
Plant and equipment (35,000 - 15,313 = 19,687 x 25%)	4,922	
SPLIT:		
Cost of sales (4,922 x 55%)		2,707
Distribution costs (4,922 x 30%)		1,477
Administrative expenses (4,922 x 15%)		738

The statement of profit or loss can then be formatted down to profit before tax. Revenue is taken directly from the trial balance as are finance costs. There is no investment income in this trial balance.

Statement of profit or loss

Alexandra Ltd – Statement of profit or loss for the year ended 30 September 20X9

	$000
Revenue (From trial balance)	103,500
Cost of sales (W1)	72,273
Gross profit	31,227
Distribution costs (W1)	(13,897)
Administrative expenses (W1)	(8,874)
Profit from operations	8,456
Investment income	nil
Finance costs	(540)
Profit before tax	**7,916**

You would then need a working for tax although this is a very simple company.

(W2) Tax on profit

	$000
Tax (at 30%) based on profits of the year	
(Known as current tax and given in supporting information)	1,500
(Over)/under provision for corporation tax in previous year	
(If we had got last year's estimate wrong there would be a balance remaining in the trial balance which we transfer to this working- here there isn't one)	0
Transfer to/(from) deferred tax	
(For position only – deferred tax is covered in the green section - there isn't any here)	0
	1,500

Statement of profit or loss

Alexandra Ltd – Statement of profit or loss* and other comprehensive income for the year ended 30 September 20X9

	$000
Revenue (From trial balance)	103,500
Cost of sales (W1)	72,273
Gross profit	31,227
Distribution costs (W1)	(13,897)
Administrative expenses (W1)	(8,874)
Profit from operations	8,456
Investment income	nil
Finance costs	(540)
Profit before tax	7,916
Tax (W2)	(1,500)
Profit for the period	**6,416**

Where a company has gains or losses in the year that are being taken directly to reserves these need to be reported in 'Other Comprehensive Income'. Alexandra is revaluing the land and buildings by $18,422 ($61,000-$42,578) . As this is taken directly to the revaluation reserve it will need reporting in 'Other Comprehensive Income'.

Alexandra Ltd – Statement of profit or loss* and other comprehensive income for the year ended 30 September 20X9

	$000
Revenue (From trial balance)	103,500
Cost of sales (W1)	72,273
Gross profit	31,227
Distribution costs (W1)	(13,897)
Administrative expenses (W1)	(8,874)
Profit from operations	8,456
Investment income	nil
Finance costs	(540)
Profit before tax	7,916
Tax (W2)	(1,500)
Profit for the period	**6,416**
Other Comprehensive Income (OCI):	
Items that will not be classified to profit or loss:	
Gain on property revaluation	18,422
Total comprehensive income for the year	**24,838**

* Statement of profit or loss = Income statement

With the statement of profit or loss complete, a statement of financial position can be prepared. One of the biggest workings will be the property, plant and equipment line and this will need to be done on your working paper:

(W3) Property, plant and equipment

	Land and buildings $000	Plant and machinery $000	Total $000
Cost at 1 October 20X8	92,578	35,000	127,578
Revaluation	18,422		18,422
Cost at 30 September 20X9	111,000	35,000	146,000
Depreciation at 1 October 20X8	25,000	15,313	40,313
Charge for year	5,000	4,922	9,922
Depreciation at 30 September 20X9	30,000	20,235	50,235
NBV at 1 October 20X8	67,578	19,687	87,265
NBV at 30 September 20X9	81,000	14,765	95,765

This can then be taken to the statement of financial position

Investments, inventories, and cash all come directly from the question.

Trade receivables are adjusted for the bad debt written off (16,395 - 21) = 16,374

The asset side (top half of the statement of financial position) can then be prepared:

Alexandra Ltd – Statement of financial position as at 30 September 20X9

Assets	$000
Non-current assets	
Property, plant and equipment (W3)	95,765
	95,765
Current assets	
Inventories (From question)	7,850
Trade and other receivables (From question as adjusted)	16,374
Cash and cash equivalents (From question)	2,685
	26,909
Total assets	**122,674**

For the equity section in the bottom half the equity share capital is directly from the trial balance. The revaluation reserve is increasing as a result of the revaluation gain on land and the biggest working is for retained earnings.

(W4) Retained earnings

The retained earnings figure comes from the retained earnings brought forward at 1/10/X8 of $8,495,000 and profit for the period of $6,416,000 from the income statement* less dividend paid of $2,820,000.

so..	$000
Retained earnings b/fwd	8,495
Profit for the period	6,416
Dividend paid	(2,820)
Retained earnings c/fwd	12,091

Alexandra Ltd – Statement of financial position as at 30 September 20X9

ASSETS	$000
Non-current assets	
Property, plant and equipment (W3)	95,765
	95,765
Current assets	
Inventories (From question)	7,850
Trade and other receivables (From question as adjusted)	16,374
Cash and cash equivalents (From question)	2,685
	26,909
Total assets	**122,674**
EQUITY AND LIABILITIES	
Equity	
Equity share capital (From trial balance)	60,000
Other components of equity (Revaluation reserve) (from additional info plus trial balance)	24,422
Retained earnings (W4)	12,091
	96,513

To complete the bottom half you need the liabilities – the biggest working is the trade and other payables – back to your working paper!

* Statement of profit or loss = Income statement

(W5) Current liabilities

(1) You will need a working for trade and other payables	
	$000
Trade payables (From trial balance)	5,861
Accruals (From trial balance)	715
Administrative expenses accrued	
(From additional information)	85
	——
	6,661

The non-current liability (a debenture loan) comes straight from the question. The statement of financial position* can now be completed.

---

* Statement of financial position = Balance Sheet (see page 19)

Alexandra Ltd – Statement of financial position as at 30 September 20X9

ASSETS	$000
Non-current assets	
Property, plant and equipment (W3)	95,765
	95,765
Current assets	
Inventories *(From question)*	7,850
Trade and other receivables *(From question as adjusted)*	16,374
Cash and cash equivalents *(From question)*	2,685
	26,909
Total assets	**122,674**
EQUITY AND LIABILITIES	
Equity	
Equity share capital *(From trial balance)*	60,000
Other components of equity *(revaluation reserve)* (from additional info plus trial balance)	24,422
Retained earnings (W4)	12,091
	96,513
Non-current liabilities	
Debenture Loans *(from trial balance)*	18,000
Current liabilities	
Trade and other payables (W5)	6,661
Current tax payable *(From question)*	1,500
Total equity and liabilities	**122,674**

Then all you have left to do is to complete the statement of changes in equity.

Alexandra Ltd - Statement of changes in equity for the year ended 30 September 20X9

	Share capital	Share premium	Revalua- tion	Other reserves	Retained earnings	Total
	£000	£000	£000	£000	£000	£000
At 31 October 20X8	60,000	0	6,000	0	8,495	74,495
Revaluation			18,422			18,422
Profit for the year					6,416	6,416
Dividends paid					(2,820)	(2,820)
At 30 September 20X9	60,000	0	24,422	0	12,091	96,513

Conclusion

IAS 1 is a key standard for all accountancy students. When you start out-use the simplified formats-then revisit this chapter as you progress through your studies to look at the full versions.

Revised IAS 1 - Presentation of financial statements

In 2007 the IASB issued a revised IAS 1. The revised IAS 1 removed the traditional term 'balance sheet' and although the format was unchanged it is now called a 'statement of financial position'. In June 2011 the IASB further amended IAS 1, with the comprehensive income statement now being renamed 'a statement of profit or loss and other comprehensive income'.

IAS 2 – Inventory

Introduction

> "We should all take inventory every morning when we wake up, take a pen and list your blessings."
>
> Anon

Inventory eh? Well it could be a stock of famous artwork - but just as easily something less interesting: a stock of metal pipes, cardboard boxes or plastic sink plugs! Whatever it consists of, it's only an itemised list of a company's goods that haven't been sold at the end of the reporting period. How difficult can that be to account for? Well actually this is an important issue for a number of reasons. Firstly, inventories will be shown as an asset on the company's statement of financial position*. The measurement of this is important as assets must not be carried at more than their recoverable amount (can we get our money back?) unless we wish to seriously mislead the user of accounts.

Secondly inventory has a direct impact on the measurement of profit – a key hotspot when it comes to creative accounting.

Are we saying inventory measurement can be used to create an accounting fairy tale?

Yes we are – the accruals/matching concept is considered 'bedrock' when we prepare financial statements, so if we recognise revenue we also need to recognise the cost of the goods we have sold. We do this by taking any opening inventory at the start of the period, adding it to the purchases in the period and deducting the closing inventory. This is then held on the statement of financial position* (as an asset to be sold in the future). Cost of goods sold is then part of cost of sales in the income statement (other direct costs are added to cost of goods sold to give us cost of sales).

---

* Statement of financial position = Balance Sheet (see page 19)

So ... what's it trying to achieve?

IAS 2 gives the accounting treatment for inventories. This includes the important issues in the recognition of costs and also gives guidance when assessing net realisable values.

 ## Transactional example

Suzanne Inc imports commemorative spoons from many countries, packages them and exports them to Australia.

At the end of its reporting period it has an itemised list of the spoons in stock. It has, however, incurred a range of expenses in obtaining these spoons.

In addition to the direct cost of their purchase, it has also paid carriage inwards, import duties and other handling costs related to imports and has to employ someone in the accounting department to deal with this paperwork.

Suzanne Inc needs to know which costs it can include as part of the cost of the inventory.

IAS 2 provides this guidance to companies like Suzanne Inc. The cost of inventories comprises all:

- costs of purchase
- 'other costs' incurred in bringing the inventories to their present location and condition
- costs of conversion.

The carriage inwards, import duties and other handling costs can certainly be included, but the salary of the person in the accounting department would not be allowed to be included in the cost of inventory.

 The common mistake made by students is to either exclude all costs mentioned or to include all costs mentioned, when the answer is usually a bit of both!! Beware particularly of carriage costs – carriage inwards should be included in valuing the inventories of a manufacturing company, but it would **NOT** be appropriate to include carriage outwards.

What about costs of conversion in a manufacturing company?

If we are looking at the inventory of a manufacturing company, costs of conversion could include variable and fixed manufacturing overheads incurred in converting raw material into finished goods, e.g.

- fixed costs – depreciation of factory building and factory plant
- variable costs – labour costs.

Remember, general administrative overheads that do not contribute to bringing inventories to their present location and condition are never included in valuing inventory. Also excluded are selling costs, storage costs (unless essential to the production process), abnormal amounts of wasted materials, labour, and other production costs.

Remember – SAGS

Excluded costs from inventory valuation

S Selling costs

A Abnormal amounts of wasted material, labour, and other production costs

G General administrative overheads

S Storage costs.

Sorry but you need to know ... DEFINITIONS

Inventories are assets:

- held for sale in the ordinary course of business; or
- in the process of production for such sale; or
- in the form of materials or supplies to be consumed in the production process or in the rendering of services.

 Net realisable value is the estimated selling price (ordinary course of business) less estimated completion and selling costs.

And the really important stuff … accounting practice

 Inventories should be valued at total of the lower of cost (all costs incurred in bringing to present location and condition) and net realisable value of separate items of stock, or of groups of similar items.

Inventories can be valued on the first in first out ('FIFO') basis, or using a weighted average method. Other methods would be rarely used.

Inventories should be sub-classified in the notes into main categories (e.g. raw materials, work-in-progress and finished goods).

 Watch the dates in questions – students often end up with opening inventory on the statement of financial position* rather than closing inventory!!

* Statement of financial position = Balance Sheet (see page 19)

Disclosures

For a student the key disclosures are:

- accounting policies adopted
- any inventories at fair value less costs to sell
- the write-down of inventories and the reversal of any write-down.

Conclusion

IAS 2 is a vital accounting standard. All questions from the very beginning will include opening and closing inventory – this is very much an 'orange standard', i.e. one you need to know right from the start of your studies.

IAS 7 – Statements of cash flow

Introduction

> "Revenue is vanity, profit is sanity and cash is reality."
>
> Anon

During your accountancy studies you will hear the phrase 'cash is reality or cash is king' an awful lot of times. It is certainly true that more companies go bust due to lack of cash rather than lack of profit. We have many of examples of corporate collapse where profit has been seriously manipulated over a long period of time. As mentioned in Chapter 2, the most famous is the US company Enron.

The Enron accounts – a real world fairy tale without a happy ending

Enron were an American company listed on Wall Street. Most Wall Street firms of analysts had Enron as a 'strong buy' right up to them filing for bankruptcy. The figure that the analysts were paying attention to was profit (often referred to by analysts as earnings). Earnings are notoriously easy for companies to manipulate. Enron reported pre-tax earnings for the last two quarters of 2000 at $650 million (accounts prepared to US GAAP). It is now considered that at least 80% were earnings from questionable transactions. It is general opinion that, if analysts had paid more attention to cash flow than earnings, these problems could have been identified as early as 1997.

In the September 1997 accounts Enron reported net operating income of $134 million.

However, when converted to operating cash flows we get the following:

Operating cash flow		$million
Operating income		134
Add back		
Depreciation (not a real cash expense)		110
Adjust for working capital changes	*(i.e. the accruals policy)*	
Inventory increase	*(piling up inventory worsens cash flow)*	(77)
Receivables increase	*(not collecting debts worsens cash flow)*	(969)
Payables/current liabilities increase	*(delaying payment to suppliers improves short-term cash flow but can lead to difficulties with suppliers)*	345
Other current assets decrease	*(selling current asset investments will improve cash flow)*	87
Operating cash flows		(370)

Negative operating cash flows should have rung warning bells. Operating activities are meant, yes, to generate profit, but when those profits are not cash backed there are questions to be asked. Enron continued to expand despite this position by borrowing. (Borrowed cash, of course, has to be repaid with interest).

In fact, out of the following 16 quarters, all but one reported positive earnings whilst cash flow was only positive three times. Clearly a statement of cash flow is important to put the statement of profit or loss* (earnings) in context.

So ... what's it trying to achieve?

IAS 7 is attempting to ensure that companies report their cash generation and absorption in a way which helps provide information to assist users who make economic decisions based on the accounts.

*Statement of profit or loss = Income statement

Transactional example

You are required to prepare a statement of cash flows for Bear Inc for the year ended 31 March 20X6. The statement of profit or loss* and statements of financial position** are given below.

Bear Inc – Statement of profit or loss* for the year ended 31 March 20X6

	$000
Continuing operations	
Revenue	14,734
Cost of sales	(8,104)
Gross profit	6,630
Profit on disposal of property, plant and equipment	217
Distribution costs	(2,641)
Administrative expenses	(1,993)
Profit from operations	2,213
Finance costs	(210)
Profit before tax	2,003
Tax	(501)
Profit for the period from continuing operations attributable to equity holders	1,502

Bear Inc – Statement of financial position** as at 31 March 20X6

	20X6 $000	20X5 $000
Assets		
Non-current assets		
Property, plant and equipment	22,708	16,797
Current assets		
Inventories	2,701	2,019
Trade and other receivables	2,456	1,009
Cash and cash equivalents	–	392
Total assets	27,865	20,217

* Statement of profit or loss = Income statement

** Statement of financial position = Balance Sheet (see page 19)

	20X6	20X5
	$000	$000
Equity and Liabilities		
Equity		
Share capital	6,000	4,000
Share premium account	4,000	1,000
Retained earnings	12,540	11,638
Non-current liabilities		
Bank loans	3,000	2,000
Current liabilities		
Trade and other payables	1,140	1,113
Tax liabilities	501	466
Bank overdraft	684	–
Total equity and liabilities	27,865	20,217

Note to the accounts:	
Retained earnings	$000
Balance at 1 April 20X5	11,638
Dividends paid	(600)
Profit for the year	1,502
Balance at 31 March 20X6	12,540

Further information:

- *The total depreciation charge for the year was $2,952,000.*
- *Property, plant and equipment costing $2,048,000 with accumulated depreciation of $1,011,000 was sold in the year.*
- *All sales and purchases were on credit. Other expenses were paid for in cash.*

A statement of cash flows?

IAS 7 believes all entities should prepare a statement of cash flows that analyses the actual cash flows of an entity (i.e. cash in less cash out). The starting point is to learn the format (see over for example from IAS 7). It takes the cash flows and divides them into three key sections:

- operating activities
- investing activities
- financing activities.

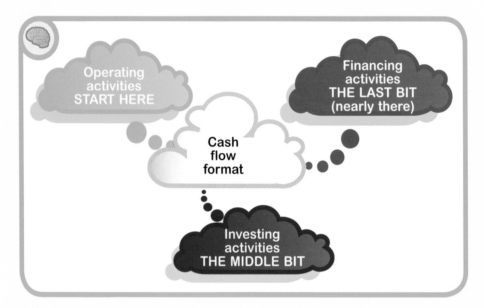

Often when students start this topic it seems very difficult. However, with a bit of practice using the questions from past papers, this can easily become your best topic. Still, it is a problem as to quite where to start, with the size of the format being pretty formidable. When you first begin, therefore, break it down into the three key sections and learn the format chunk by chunk – treat it as three topics not one.

First of all see if you can conquer cash flows from operating activities, using the accounts of Bear Inc. Let's start with the current year's statement of profit or loss*.

Pick up the company's profit from operations. This is the first number that goes into a statement of cash flow. As we illustrated with the Enron accounts, just because a company is generating profit does not mean that it is generating cash from operating activities. Accountants, as we know, put non-cash items into an statement of profit or loss – you will now need to read through the question to find out how much depreciation was expensed in the current year accounts – it is a **notional** expense and therefore to get back to cash flow you need to add it back. Once you've done that you are off!!

---

* Statement of profit or loss = Income statement

Note - which profit figure to use?

IAS 7 is not prescriptive about which profit figure should be adjusted. Many examiners start with profit from operations, which is what I am going to do here. It is worth checking with your past exam papers, which profit figure your examiner starts from, if your examiner starts with profit before tax you must use profit before tax. However as the cash flow is from operating activities you will see extra 'reconciling' items in your examiners answers.

Starting with profit from operations keeps it simple.

	$
Cash flows from operating activities	
Profit from operations	2,213
Adjustments for:	
Depreciation **(always an add back)**	2,952

Other adjustments may be necessary because we are trying to calculate cash flow from operating activities – which means the trading outcome of the company. The statement of profit or loss* however may include non-trading income such as profit on disposal of property, plant and equipment; so read the statement of profit or loss* again and, if this is the case, take it out.

Gain on disposal of property, plant and equipment **(always a deduction)**	(217)

Note

If it were a loss on disposal of property, plant and equipment it would be an add back.

Operating cash flows before working capital changes	4,948

Working capital items

Adjustments will be necessary due to movements in the working capital items since the statement of profit or loss will be prepared on the accruals basis. Revenues are sales made in the period whether or not you have received the cash. If the sales are recognised but the cash is not received, you will have put a receivable on your statement of financial position**. Look now at the two years', statements of financial position you have been provided with. You will always need to work out the movement on inventory/trade receivables and trade payables, since these could either have decreased or increased.

Inventories increase (2,701 - 2,019)	(682)
(holding increasing stocks of inventory worsens cash flow)	
Trade and other receivables increase (2,456 - 1,009)	(1,447)
(failure to collect debt promptly worsens cash flow)	
Trade payables increase (1,140 - 1,113)	27
(paying suppliers more slowly will improve cash flow)	
Cash generated from operations	2,846

* Statement of profit or loss = Income statement

** Statement of financial position = Balance Sheet (see page 19)

Note

If your movement worsens the company's cash flow you need brackets; and if it improves the company's cash flow you won't!!

Note

Worsens = ( )

Improves = no ( )

Put together – your first section looks like this:

Cash flows from operating activities	$
Profit from operations	2,213
Adjustments for:	
Depreciation	2,952
Gain on disposal of property, plant and equipment	(217)
Operating cash flows before working capital changes	4,948
Inventories increase (2,701 -2,019)	(682)
Trade and other receivables increase (2,456 -1,009)	(1,447)
Trade payables increase (1,140 -1,113)	27
Cash generated from operations	2,846

Statement of cash flow

Again you might find a mnemonic useful here, what about …

Plainly Dedicated Doctors Inspire Real People

Cash flows from operating activities

Profit from operations **(Plainly)**	x
Adjustments for:	
Depreciation **(Dedicated)**	x
Disposal of property, plant and equipment (gain)/loss **(Doctors)**	(x)/x
Operating profit before working capital changes	x
Inventories increase/decrease **(Inspire)**	(x)/x
Receivables increase/decrease **(Real)**	(x)/x
Payables decrease/increase **(People)**	(x)/x
Cash generated from operations	x

Interest paid and tax paid

The format then recognises that a company needs to be able to cover both its interest payments and its tax payments. These are definitely NOT optional items.

 Remember, however, that this is a statement of cash flow not a statement of profit or loss*. The amounts in the statement of profit or loss* for interest and tax will not necessarily be the same as the interest and tax paid out in cash terms. The accruals concept is being applied, with any outstanding amounts owing being shown on the statement of financial position** as accruals/ liabilities.

You must therefore make sure you look at the statement of financial position* to see if there are any liabilities for interest or tax at the start of the year and/ or at the end of the year. There MAY be one for interest but there is pretty well ALWAYS a tax liability or indeed two!! (including the deferred tax liability).

You will then need to use the following pro forma workings to calculate the actual cash paid out to slot into the cash flow statement.

(W1) Interest paid

(W1)	Interest paid	
		$000
Balance (liability) due on opening SOFP**		nil
Add: Interest charge (finance costs) for the year from the SOPL*		210
Less: Balance (liability) still due on closing SOFP**		(nil)
= Interest paid during year (figure for cash flow)		**210**

Alternatively you might prefer to use 'T' accounts for these workings – it is a personal preference, so decide which you prefer and stick with it.

(W1)	Interest paid		
	$000		$000
		Bal b/fwd	nil
= Interest paid		Interest charge on the	
during the year β	**210**	SOPL	210
Bal c/fwd	nil		
	210		210

---

* Statement of profit or loss = Income statement

** Statement of financial position = Balance Sheet (see page 19)

(W2) Taxation paid

(W2)	$000
Current tax liability due on opening SOFP**	466
Add: Deferred tax liability due on opening SOFP**	nil
Add: Tax charge for the year from the SOPL*	501
Less: Current tax liability still due on closing SOFP**	(501)
Less: Deferred tax liability still due on closing SOFP**	(nil)
= Tax paid during the year (figure for cash flow)	**466**

or …

(W2)	Taxation paid		
	$000		$000
		Balance b/fwd – current tax due on opening SOFP**	466
= Tax paid for the year β	**466**	Bal b/fwd – deferred tax liability on opening SOFP**	nil
Balance c/fwd – current tax liability on closing SOFP**	501	Tax charge from SOPL*	501
Balance c/fwd – deferred tax liability on closing SOFP**	nil		
	967		967

* Statement of profit or loss = Income statement

** Statement of financial position = Balance Sheet (see page 19)

The format then deducts these two figures from 'cash generated from operations' to give *Net cash from operating activities* (see below)

Bear Inc statement of cash flow for the year ended 31 March 20X6

	$000	$000
Cash flows from operating activities		
Profit from operations	2,213	
Adjustments for:		
Depreciation	2,952	
Gain on disposal of property, plant and equipment	(217)	
Operating cash flows before working capital changes	4,948	
Increase in inventories (2,701 - 2,019)	(682)	
Increase in trade receivables (2,456 -1.009)	(1,447)	
Increase in trade payables (1,140 -1,113)	27	
Cash generated from operations	2,846	
Interest paid (W1)	(210)	
Income taxes paid (W2)	(466)	
Net cash from operating activities		**2,170**

Cash flows from investing activities

Companies need to invest if they are to keep up with the competition. They may also be following a strategy of growth by acquiring other companies. This is the section which shows the reader what impact these policies have had on the cash flows of the company.

Acquisition of subsidiary net of cash acquired	(x)

(This can be ignored unless you are studying an advanced paper and being asked for a group cash flow)

The format of the investing activities section will commonly look like this:

Purchase of property, plant and equipment **(Purple)**	(x)
Proceeds from sale of equipment **(Pansies)**	X
Interest received **(Interested)**	X
Dividends received **(Dave)**	X
Net cash used in investing activities	(x)

Remember

Purple Pansies Interested Dave!

Remember it is always the cash you are interested in – how much did the company actually pay out to purchase property, plant and equipment and what were the proceeds from selling the old ones?

A common mistake made by students is to put the profit from the disposal of equipment in the cash flow rather than the cash proceeds. Remember the number in the income statement is a calculation of PROFIT – not the cash flow – which can always be worked out.

(W3) Proceeds from disposal of equipment

(W3)	$000
Proceeds from disposal of equipment	
NBV/CV of asset sold (what you expected to get) (2,048 – 1,011)	1,037
Add: Profit made on disposal (taken to SOPL*), i.e. you got more than expected	217
= Proceeds from sale (figure for cash flow statement)	**1,254**

or ...

(W3)	$000
NBV/CV of asset sold (what you expected to get)	x
Deduct: Loss made on disposal (taken to SOPL*), i.e. you received less than expected	(x)
= Proceeds from sale (figure for cash flow statement)	**xx**

You will also need to calculate the amount of cash spent on purchasing property, plant and equipment.

(W4) Non-current assets/Property, plant and equipment

(W4)	$000
Non-current assets/Property, plant and equipment (NBV)	
Bal b/fwd (from opening SOFP**)	16,797
Less: Depreciation	(2,952)
Less: NBV/CV of asset sold	(1,037)
Less: Bal c/fwd (from closing SOFP**)	(22,708)
= Additions in period (figure for cash flow statement)	**(9,900)**

or

Again you may prefer to use a 'T' account – either way we get the same answer.

(W4)
Non-current assets/Property, plant and equipment @ NBV/CV

	$000		$000
Bal b/fwd (NBV/CV) (from opening SOFP**)	16,797	Depreciation	2,952
		Disposals at NBV/CV	1,037
= Additions in the period	**9,900**		
		Bal c/fwd (NBV/CV) (from closing SOFP**)	22,708
	26,697		26,697

Note

Also take to this section any interest and dividends received.

Bear Inc doesn't have any interest or dividend received.

You now have two of the three sections.

Cash flows from operating activities	$000	$000
Profit from operations	2,213	
Adjustments for:		
Depreciation	2,952	
Gain on disposal of property, plant and equipment	(217)	
Operating profit before working capital changes	4,948	
Increase in inventories (2,701 - 2,019)	(682)	
Increase in trade receivables (2,456 - 1,009)	(1,447)	
Increase in trade payables (1,140 - 1,113)	27	
Cash generated from operations	2,846	
Interest paid (W1)	(210)	
Income taxes paid (W2)	(466)	
Net cash from operating activities		**2,170**
Cash flows from investing activities		
Acquisition of subsidiary net of cash acquired	nil	
Purchase of property, plant and equipment (W4)	(9,900)	
Proceeds from sale of equipment (W3)	1,254	
Interest received	nil	
Dividends received	nil	
Net cash used in investing activities		**(8,646)**

Cash flows from financing activities

Finally you need to look at the two position statements to see if the company has changed its financing arrangements in the current year. A company can only raise finance from one of two sources: debt (taking out loans) or equity (issuing shares). Any changes in shares or loans giving rise to either a cash inflow or cash outflow in the year are recorded in this section. Also record the actual cash dividend paid in the year (last year's final proposed plus any current year interim dividend).

	$ 000
Proceeds from issuance of share capital **(Purple)** (W5)	5,000
Proceeds from long-term borrowings **(Pansies) (3,000 – 2,000)**	1,000
Payment of finance lease liabilities **(Poison)**	(nil)
Dividends paid **(Dave)**	(600)
Net cash used in financing activities	**5,400**

Remember finally

Purple Pansies Poison Dave!

The proceeds from the issue of share capital can be calculated by looking at the share capital and the share premium accounts. Remember they are 'twin accounts' as far as the statement of cash flow goes. It is accounting convention that we post the nominal value of shares issued to the share capital account and post the premium on the issue to the share premium account. For Bear Inc. therefore, the share capital balance has increased by $2,000,000 and the share premium has increased by $3,000,000. You have therefore received total cash of $5,000,000 and this is the figure in the statement of cash flow.

(W5) Proceeds from issuance of share capital

Proceeds from issuance of share capital	$000
Share capital increase (6,000 – 4,000)	2,000
Share premium increase (4,000 – 1,000)	3,000
Figure for cash flow statement	**5,000**

The cash flow relating to loans can be calculated by looking at the movement on the loans line. Bank loans here have increased from $2,000,000 to $3,000,000. A cash injection of $1,000,000 has therefore arisen.

The dividend paid of $600,000 can be picked up from the movement in retained earnings in the notes to the accounts.

This should then reconcile to the movement on the cash and cash equivalents.

Remember, every exam question will vary slightly and there may be other non-standard cash flow items – however, these key elements will allow you to get a very high mark under exam conditions even if you miss something non-standard. Remember, the more past questions you practise the better you get at the standard things – AND – you start to meet and recognise non-standard stuff too.

Again, the key to numeric topics is – practise, practise, practise!!!

Note

If you are going to need to do a group statement of cash flows, you must read on to Chapter 30 in the blue section.

The whole thing will now look something like this:

Bear Inc statement of cash flows for the year ended 31 March 20X6

	$000	$000
Cash flows from operating activities		
Profit from operations	2,213	
Adjustments for:		
Depreciation	2,952	
Gain on disposal of property, plant and equipment	(217)	
Operating profit before working capital changes	4,948	
Increase in inventories (2,701 - 2,019)	(682)	
Increase in trade receivables (2,456 - 1,009)	(1,447)	
Increase in trade payables (1,140 - 1,113)	27	
Cash generated from operations	2,846	
Interest paid (W1)	(210)	
Income taxes paid (W2)	(466)	
Net cash from operating activities		**2,170**
Cash flows from investing activities		
Acquisition of subsidiary net of cash acquired (note a)	nil	
Purchase of property, plant and equipment (W4)	(9,900)	
Proceeds from sale of equipment (W3)	1,254	
Interest received	nil	
Dividends received	nil	
Net cash used in investing activities		**(8,646)**
Cash flows from financing activities		
Proceeds from issuance of share capital (W5)	5,000	
Proceeds from long-term borrowings	1,000	
Payment of finance lease liabilities	nil	
Dividends paid	(600)	
Net cash used in financing activities		**5,400**
Net increase/(decrease) in cash and cash equivalents		(1,076)
Cash and cash equivalents at the beginning of the period		392
(cash at start of year less bank overdraft at start of year)		
Cash and cash equivalents at the end of the period		(684)
(cash at end of year less bank overdraft at end of year)		

Notes to the cash flow statement

Dependent on your examiner you might get asked for the notes to the cash flow statement.

The notes that are normally required for the statement of cash flows are:

(1) Acquisition (disposal) of subsidiary (only examined in group cash flows for more advanced students)

This note analyses the net assets acquired and the cash flow on acquisition and disposal. An example (given in IAS7 appendix) is:

	$
Cash	40
Inventories	100
Accounts receivable	100
Property, plant and equipment	650
Trade payables	(100)
Long-term debt	(200)
Total purchase price	590
Less: Cash of subsidiary	(40)
Cash flow on acquisition net of cash acquired	550

(2) Major non-cash transactions

Any major non-cash transactions that require disclosure in order that the financial statements show a true and fair view should be given. Such things as inception of finance leases may meet this category.

(3) Cash and cash equivalents

A disclosure note must be given that analyses cash and cash equivalents and allows the amount to be reconciled into the statement of financial position*. This note should also disclose any significant amounts of cash and cash equivalents held by the enterprise that are not available for use by the group.

(4) Segmental cash flow information

IAS 7 encourages the presentation of operating, investing and financing cash flows by segment in a note. This disclosure is also encouraged (but not required) by IFRS 8.

Indirect method

In most circumstances companies should prepare statement of cash flows and notes in the formats as shown in Chapter 4. The method used to answer Bear Inc is known as 'The indirect method'.

However, there is some choice about the position of some of the items in the cash flow statement:

Interest paid	Operating or financing
Interest received	Operating or investing
Dividends received	Operating or investing
Dividends paid	Operating or financing

Direct method

Companies may, if they wish, use the indirect method which adds the following five lines at the top of the statement of cash flow to show the make-up of cash from operating activities:

	$
Cash received from customers	X
Cash paid to suppliers and employees	(x)
Cash generated from operations	X
Interest paid	(x)
Income taxes paid	(x)

Sorry but you need to know ... DEFINITIONS

Cash – cash on hand and demand deposits.

Cash equivalents – short-term, highly-liquid investments that are readily convertible to known amounts of cash and which are subject to an insignificant risk of changes in value.

Note

The guidance suggests that the investments will be within three months of maturity when acquired.

And the really important stuff ... accounting practice

IAS 7 believes all entities should prepare a statement of cash flow that analyses the actual cash flows of an entity (i.e. cash in less cash out). The starting point is to learn the format. It takes the cash flows and divides them into three key sections:

- operating activities
- investing activities
- financing activities.

Conclusion

Statements of cash flow are a primary accounting statement, i.e. they are as important as the statement of financial position** and the statement of profit or loss*. They are common exam questions. If you hate the topic when you first meet it, it is essential to familiarise yourself with it – with practice you will love this topic – honest!!

* Statement of profit or loss = Income statement

** Statement of financial position = Balance Sheet (see page 19)

IAS 8 – Accounting policies, changes in accounting estimates and errors

Introduction

> "Old accountants never die ... they simply lose their balance!"
>
> Traditional

The use of accounting policy is an important issue because accounting is not actually the science that it can be mistaken for. For example, in the telecoms industry, how should we account for the salary of a cable technician? It may initially seem very clear – if an employee's salary is not a direct cost, to be expensed in the statement of profit or loss*, then what is it? The telecoms industry would argue that it depends on what he is spending his time on – if he is repairing an old network he is an expense, but if he is working on a new one – which will accrue revenues in future periods – it could be argued to capitalise his salary (put it on the statement of financial position** as an asset) so it will be 'matched' via a depreciation expense to the future periods that will benefit from the revenue.

Rules v principles

All companies have to decide which accounting policies they are planning to adopt. There is a difference of opinion on how accounting standards should work. One view is that they should be rules-based – this is the US GAAP approach. IAS takes the principles-based approach.

It is a bit like when you were a teenager going out for the first time. Your parents could give you a list of rules – things you must not do, e.g. 'do not be home later than 1.00pm, do not get split up from your friends, do not have more than two drinks' etc. Or maybe your parents took a principles-based approach – 'Be good'!! – a catch all. This is the approach that IAS 8 is trying to take.

* Statement of profit or loss = Income statement

** Statement of financial position = Balance Sheet (see page 19)

So ... what's it trying to achieve?

IAS 8 prescribes the criteria for selecting and changing accounting policies, together with the accounting treatment and disclosure of changes in accounting .

 ## Transactional example

D W Swallow Inc noted in 20X6 that in 20X5 it had omitted to record a depreciation expense on an asset amounting to $60,000. Its accounts, before the correction of errors, looked like this:

	20X6	20X5
	$	$
Gross profit	*600,000*	*690,000*
Distribution costs	*(60,000)*	*(60,000)*
Administrative expenses	*(180,000)*	*(180,000)*
Depreciation	*(60,000)*	*nil*
Profit from operations	*300,000*	*450,000*
Income tax	*(60,000)*	*(90,000)*
Net profit	*240,000*	*360,000*

Swallow's retained earnings for the two years before the correction of errors are:

	20X6	20X5
	$	$
Retained earnings c/fwd	690,000	450,000
Retained earnings b/fwd	450,000	90,000

IAS 8 (revised) states that the correction of an error that relates to prior periods should be shown as an adjustment to the opening balance of retained earnings.

In the 20X6 accounts (ignoring all tax implications):

Dr Retained earnings b/fwd $60,000
Cr Accumulated depreciation $60,000

i.e. this will have no impact on the current year income statement* but is shown as a prior period adjustment in the statement of changes in equity:

* Statement of profit or loss = Income statement

	20X6
	$
Retained earnings b/fwd as reported previously	450,000
Prior period adjustment to correct error	(60,000)
Retained earnings, beginning, as restated	390,000
Net profit	240,000
Retained earnings c/fwd	630,000

Comparative information should be restated unless it is 'impracticable' to do so.

The statement of profit or loss* will be presented thus:

SOPL

	20X6	20X5 (restated)
	$	$
Gross profit	600,000	690,000
Distribution costs	(60,000)	(60,000)
Administrative expenses	(180,000)	(180,000)
Depreciation	(60,000)	(60,000)
Operating profit	300,000	390,000
Income tax	(60,000)	(90,000)
Net profit	240,000	300,000

The statement of changes in equity will also need comparators:

Statememt of changes in equity

	20X6	20X5 (restated)
	$	$
Retained earnings b/fwd as reported previously	450,000	90,000
Prior period adjustment to correct error	(60,000)	NIL
Retained earnings, beginning, as restated	390,000	90,000
Net profit	240,000	300,000
Retained earnings c/fwd	630,000	390,000

* Statement of profit or loss = Income statement

Sorry but you need to know ... DEFINITIONS

 Accounting policies are the specific principles, bases, conventions, rules and practices applied by an entity in preparing and presenting financial statements.

 Prior period errors are omissions from, and misstatements in, the entity's financial statements for one or more periods arising from a failure to use, or misuse of, reliable information. The errors must be ones that were reasonably identifiable when the financial statements were authorised for issue.

And the really important stuff ... accounting practice

Accounting policies selected should be in accordance with International Accounting Standards or interpretations. If no standard is applicable, policies should be selected in accordance with:

- relevance
- reliability
- faithful representation
- substance over form
- neutrality
- prudence
- completeness.

(i.e. be good!!)

Changes and corrections

Right from the start of your studies you will have seen examples where companies have maybe made errors or need to change accounting policies or estimates. You need to be able to handle this.

 Changes in accounting policy arise if required by a new standard, or because the new policy is more relevant and reliable. It is not a change in policy if a new policy is applied to a transaction different in substance to those undertaken previously, or a new policy is applied to a new type of transaction.

Changes in **accounting policy** should be applied **retrospectively** unless it is impracticable to do so. This would be very rare. Significant disclosures are required about the change in policy.

Retrospectively – change everything, pretend that the new policy had always been applied.

Changes in **accounting estimates** should be applied **prospectively.** A change in estimate is not a change of policy and occurs if new information becomes available that was not previously known. As a result they also cannot be treated as errors.

Prospectively – apply new policy, but do not restate the financial statements of a prior period.

Correction of **material prior period** errors should be accounted for **retrospectively** unless it is impracticable to do so. Significant disclosures are required if an error occurred.

 Students often get confused between identifying whether a change is a change in an accounting policy, or a change in an accounting estimate. If we are told that a company changes its method of valuation of inventory from weighted average method to 'first – in first out' (FIFO) method, this is a clear example of needing to account for this as a change in accounting policy with the accounting being performed retrospectively. This normally goes well for most students.

However, when we are told that a company changes the useful life of an asset from 10 years to 8 years, then often this is mistaken for a change in accounting policy. In fact the company's accounting policy has NOT changed – the policy was and still is to depreciate the asset over its useful economic life. What we have here is a change in accounting estimate which needs to be accounted for prospectively.

Remember, in accordance with the principle of consistency, an entity should apply the same accounting policy from one period to the next unless:

- the change is required by a standard or interpretation; or
- if the change will result in the financial statements providing reliable and more relevant information about the effects of transactions, other events or conditions on the entity's financial position, financial performance or cash flows.

Common examples of changes in accounting policy

- Changes in legislation.
- A new accounting standard.
- A change from measuring a class of assets at depreciated historical cost to a policy of regular revaluation.
- Changing from writing off to capitalising interest relating to the construction of non-current assets.
- Changing revenue recognition practices regarding the sale of goods and services.
- Changing inventory valuation from weighted average to FIFO.
- Changing the way in which an item is presented in the accounts, i.e. classifying depreciation expenses as cost of sales instead of administrative would also be a change of accounting policy.

Common examples of accounting estimates

- Bad debts.
- Inventory obsolescence.
- Provision for warranty obligations.
- Useful lives of property, plant and equipment.
- Fair values of financial assets and liabilities.

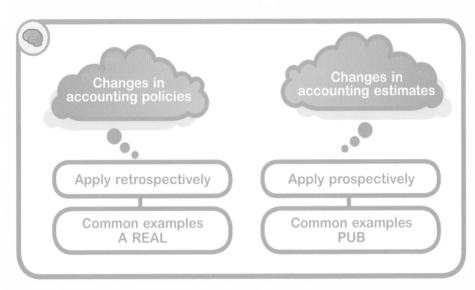

A REAL

A Asset measurement changed from depreciated historic cost to revaluation

R Revenue recognition policy is changed

E Expenses reclassified from cost of sales to administrative

A A new accounting standard forces change

L Legislation changes

PUB

P Provisions for warranty obligations

U Useful lives of property, plant and equipment

B Bad debts

Disclosures

When a company has made a material change to an accounting policy in preparing its current financial statements, the following disclosures are required by IAS 8:

- the reasons for the change
- the amount of the adjustment in the current period and in comparative information for prior periods.

Conclusion

IAS 8 is never going to be a 'deal-breaker' when it comes to answering exam questions. It is, however, fundamental to the real world. An understanding of the importance of a company's choice of accounting policies is also key to good performance in ratio analysis/interpretation of accounts questions.

IAS 10 – Events after the reporting period

Introduction

> "Do not seek to have events happen as you want them to, but instead want them to happen as they do happen, and your life will go well."
>
> Epictetus, Greek Philosopher (ad55–135)

Unfortunately events happen. As you chose to be an accountant rather than a philosopher like Epictetus, you will have to be able to account for such events, not just talk about it! As we know from the revised IAS 1, companies are required to prepare a statement of financial position* as at an agreed date. The end of the reporting period is the point at which the financial position of a company is determined and reported. Of course, we will not be able to actually prepare the statement of financial position* on the reporting period date as we will not have all the information available. Companies in fact have six months grace on filing their accounts.

Ahh ... stuff happens!

Yes, stuff happens. This means that decisions have to be made with regard to such stuff that we know about due to the time lag – but which actually occurred – or at least we found out about them after the reporting period. This guidance is what IAS 10 is all about.

> ## So ... what's it trying to achieve?
>
> IAS 10 explains the duties of companies and directors in looking for and adjusting for events after the reporting period.

---

* Statement of financial position = Balance Sheet (see page 19)

When events occur after the reporting period but before the date that the financial statements are say authorised for issue, we need to know what we should do about them when we prepare the accounts. The question is should we adjust the accounts, or simply give a disclosure in the notes to the accounts?

In order to make that decision, we need to know whether we have just been made aware of a condition that actually existed at the reporting period (in which case we will be required to adjust the accounts) or have we just been made aware of a condition that arose after the reporting period (in which case we will only be required to give disclosure).

 Transactional example

KPB Corp applies IAS 2 and includes its inventory at the end of the reporting period at the lower of cost and net realisable value. It prepares its accounts as at 31 December and as at 31 December 20X5 performed a stock take and itemised and valued its inventory at $20million.

In January 20X6 nothing at all was sold. On 5 February KPB Corp was made an offer by its competitor Mog Corp to take the whole of their inventory for a total price of $12 million. Owing to cash flow pressure, KPB agreed. You are responsible for preparing the accounts which are due to be authorised on 15 February. Do you adjust the inventory down to $12 million as an adjusting event or leave it in the accounts at $20 million and give a disclosure note?

This is a classic example of an **adjusting event** – the sale of inventory at a price substantially lower than its cost after the date of the reporting period confirms its net realisable value at the end of the reporting period.

 Transactional example

KPB Corp also acquired a new administration building during 20X5 at a cost of $40 million. At 31 December 20X5 the net book value of the building was $39 million. On 10 February 20X6 (again before the accounts were authorised on 15 February) the building was destroyed by fire due to the negligence of a director who was found drunk by the fire brigade having made a bonfire in a waste paper bin. The insurance company has indicated that this will invalidate any insurance claims.

This is a classic **non-adjusting event**, as at the end of the reporting period you had a building. It stays on the statement of financial position* and you disclose the details and financial effect of the event in the footnotes … unless the going concern concept is now undermined – see below.

 A common mistake with IAS 10 issues is to believe that when you are attempting a trial balance question all the supporting information must give rise to an adjustment. This is not true as sometimes the information provided relates to a non-adjusting event. It needs a disclosure in the notes – not an adjustment in the accounts.

Going concern considerations

IAS 10 requires that an entity should not prepare its financial statements on a going concern basis if management determines after the reporting period that it intends to liquidate the entity or cease trading. In which case the statement of financial position* would need to be presented on a non-going concern basis.

 Sorry but you need to know … DEFINITIONS

 Events after the reporting period are events, both favourable and unfavourable, that occur between the end of reporting period and when the financial statements are authorised for issue.

 Adjusting events are those events that provide evidence of conditions that existed at the end of the reporting period.

 Non-adjusting events are those that are indicative of conditions that arose after the reporting period.

And the really important stuff … accounting practice

The financial statements should be changed to include events after the reporting period if they are adjusting events.

The financial statements should disclose the event in the notes if they are material non-adjusting events after the reporting period.

Dividends declared after the reporting period (and therefore not an obligation at the reporting period) are treated as non-adjusting events.

The going concern basis should not be followed if management determines that, after the reporting period, the company intends to liquidate, or has no realistic alternative but to do so.

* Statement of financial position = Balance Sheet (see page 19)

Disclosures

The disclosures required from events disclosed in the notes are:

- the nature of the event
- an estimate of the financial effect, or a statement that it is not possible to estimate the financial effect.

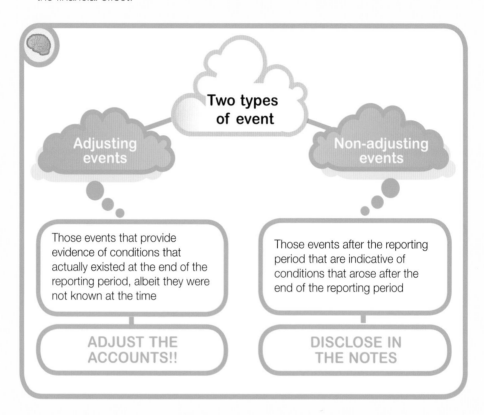

Conclusion

IAS 10 is a commonly examined standard. Once you are familiar with it, you should be pleased to see it featured in any accountancy exam!!

IAS 16 – Property, plant and equipment

Introduction

> "No man acquires property without acquiring with it a little arithmetic also."
>
> Ralph Waldo Emerson (1803-1882)

Accounting for property, plant and equipment is a very important issue. We have accepted that the accruals concept is 'bedrock' when it comes to preparing financial statements. Clearly if a company purchases a property or any equipment, this will involve a large chunk of cash. It would be wrong to show this as an expense immediately in the statement of profit or loss of the year they bought it. The equipment is going to be of use for a long period of time; hitting earnings only in the year of purchase will fail to give a correct picture. Earnings would look terrible in the year of purchase, but then particularly good for all the remaining years in which you generate income from the equipment with no expense being reflected.

And so it has passed into legend that the big chunk of cash spent on property, plant and equipment should not be immediately expensed but instead should be capitalised – put on the statement of financial position* initially – with depreciation being the accounting mechanism that, in effect, spreads the cost of a capitalised purchase over the useful economic life of the asset. The big chunk of cash appears on the statement of cash flow, the asset appears on the statement of financial position*, and a depreciation expense appears on the statement of profit or loss – simple, what's to worry about?

WorldCom – how the books got cooked

"I falsified financial statements of the company … for the purpose of meeting analyst expectations" – quote from Scott Sullivan, former Chief Financial Officer of WorldCom. This was said to the federal court when he testified against his former boss, the WorldCom Chief Executive Officer and President.

---

* Statement of financial position = Balance Sheet (see page 19)

One of the scams that WorldCom used was simply a ploy of taking some expenses that should have gone to the statement of profit or loss but instead putting them as property, plant and equipment on the statement of financial position*. Not surprisingly this meant that they were able to deliver earnings at the level expected by the market. WorldCom admitted having used this ploy to the tune of $3.8 billion!!! IAS 16 deals with the issue by being clear that an item of property, plant and equipment should be recognised as an asset *if and only if* it is probable that future economic benefits associated with the asset will flow to the entity and the cost of the item can be measured reliably.

So ... what's it trying to achieve?

IAS 16 prescribes the accounting treatments for property, plant and equipment where the principal issues are the recognition of assets, the determination of their carrying value and the depreciation and impairment charges recognised in relation to them.

Transactional example

Slaney Inc owns equipment with an original cost of $400,000. It was determined on acquisition that the equipment had a useful economic life of 10 years and the residual value was expected to be $40,000. The equipment is now 8 years old.

Each period that benefits from the equipment will be charged with an expense in the form of depreciation. The formula is:

Cost – Residual value
_____
Expected useful life

($400,000 – $40,000)/10 years = $36,000 each year.

Dr Statement of profit or loss – depreciation expense
Cr Accumulated depreciation

The carrying value of the asset in this year's SOFP* is:

	$
Original cost	$400,000
Less:	
Accumulated depreciation	
(8 x $36,000)	($288,000)
Net Book Value/Carrying Value	$112,000

A common error made by students is to muddle the accumulated depreciation account with the current year depreciation expense. The accumulated depreciation should NOT appear in the statement of profit or loss!! – it is the accumulated depreciation to date which is then shown netted against cost in the statement of financial position*. The statement of profit or loss should just show the current year (one year) effect of depreciation.

Sorry but you need to know ... DEFINITIONS

Property, plant and equipment are tangible assets that:

- are held for use in the production or supply of goods and services, for rental to others, or for administrative purposes; and
- are expected to be used during more than one period.

Carrying amount is the amount at which an asset is recognised after deducting any accumulated depreciation and accumulated impairment losses.

Depreciation is the systematic allocation of the depreciable amount (cost or valuation less residual value) of an asset over its useful economic life.

Residual value is the estimated amount that an entity would currently obtain from the disposal of the asset, after deducting the estimated costs of disposal, if the asset were already of the age and in the condition expected at the end of its useful economic life.

Fair value is the price that would be received to sell an asset or paid to transfer a liability in an orderly transaction between market participants at the measurement date (as per IFRS 13 amendments).

And the really important stuff ... accounting practice

Initial recognition and measurement of assets

The cost of an item of property, plant and equipment should be recognised as an asset if, and only if, it is probable future economic benefits will flow to the enterprise, and the cost can be measured reliably. (Remember the definition of an asset from the Framework.)

Assets should initially be measured at cost. Costs include the directly attributable costs incurred in bringing the asset into working condition for its intended use.

---

* Statement of financial position = Balance Sheet (see page 19)

Transactional example

Alfie, a sales tax registered trader, purchased a computer for use in his business. The invoice for the computer:

- *Computer*   *$ 890*
- *Additional memory*   *$ 95*
- *Delivery*   *$ 10*
- *Installation*   *$ 20*
- *Maintenance (1 year)*   *$ 25*
- *Sales tax*   *$ 182*

How much should Alfie capitalise as a non-current asset in relation to the purchase?

The cost of the computer is a basic $890. However, Alfie can capitalise the directly attributable costs – the additional memory, the delivery and installation costs. Alfie cannot capitalise the maintenance costs or the sales tax. The non-current asset in relation to the purchase would be $890 + 95 + 10 + 20 = $1,015.

Subsequent expenditure should be capitalised if the expenditure meets the criteria for initial recognition. For example, a replacement of a major part of an asset must be capitalised and the old part being replaced should be derecognised.

Subsequent measurement of assets

Companies can adopt a policy of revaluing assets if they wish. If they revalue assets the carrying amount should approximate to the fair value at the reporting period.

If companies choose to revalue assets they must:

- revalue the full class of asset
- revalue sufficiently often that the asset is retained at an up-to-date value on the statement of financial position*.

Note that gains on revaluation should be recognised in the revaluation reserve and losses on revaluation are treated consistently with impairments in value (IAS 36).

Transactional example

Andrew Inc, which makes up its accounts to 31 December each year, buys an asset on 1 January 20X1 for $10,000. The asset has an estimated useful economic life of ten years with no residual value. Therefore, straight-line depreciation will be $1,000pa and, on 31 December 20X2, the asset will be included in the statement of financial position* as follows:

	$
Non-current asset at cost	*10,000*
Accumulated depreciation	*(2,000)*
	8,000

On 1 January 20X3, Andrew revalues the asset to $16,000. The total useful economic life remains at ten years from 1 January 20X1.

Required

(a) Show the journal to record the revaluation.

(b) Show the journal to record the revised depreciation charge and reserves transfer.

(c) Andrew sells the asset on 1 January 20X4 for $15,000. Show how the disposal is recorded.

It is very important that we can account for all three aspects; the initial revaluation will be as follows:

(a) The revaluation will be recorded by.

1 January 20X3

	$	$
Dr Non-current assets cost/valuation	6,000	
Dr Accumulated depreciation	2,000	
Cr Revaluation reserve		8,000

(b) Equally key is that we can record the annual depreciation as at 31 December 20X3 and in subsequent years

	$	$
Dr Depreciation expense (SOPL)	2,000	
Cr Accumulated depreciation		2,000
Dr Revaluation reserve	1,000	
Cr Retained earnings		1,000

---

* Statement of financial position = Balance Sheet (see page 19)

Note: A common pitfall is to forget the reserve transfer. The revaluation reserve doesn't sit on the statement of financial position* in perpetuity; it gets written out over the useful economic life by a transfer to retained earnings. This way, when the asset is fully depreciated, the revaluation reserve should be written down to zero too.

(c) If we sell a revalued asset we need to be able to deal with that too. The profit on disposal in the statement profit or loss account for the year will be:

	$
Proceeds	15,000
Less: Net Book Value (16,000 – 2,000)	(14,000)
PROFIT ON DISPOSAL	1,000

The remaining balance on revaluation reserve is commonly transferred to retained earnings as a reserve transfer:

Transfer of realised profits	$	$
Dr Revaluation reserve (reducing it to zero)	7,000	
Cr Retained earnings		7,000

Depreciation of assets

The depreciable amount of a non-current asset (other than freehold land) should be allocated on a systematic basis over its useful economic life in a manner that reflects the consumption of economic benefits.

The residual value of assets should be reviewed each year end and based on year-end price levels.

A change in the method of depreciation is only allowed on the grounds of truth and fairness and does not constitute a change of accounting policy.

The depreciation rate should be reviewed at the end of each reporting period.

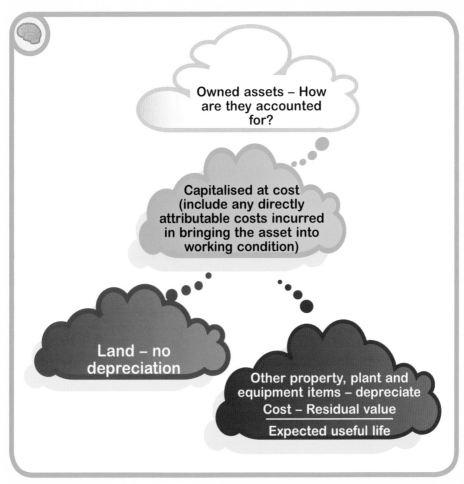

Disclosures

Very extensive disclosures exist for non-current assets.

Revaluations

If items of property, plant and equipment are stated at revalued amounts IFRS 13 disclosures will apply as well as IAS 16.

- The effective date of the revaluation.
- Whether an independent valuer was used.
- The historical cost equivalent values of non-current assets.
- The revaluation surplus and change for the period.

Note

IFRS 13 issued in May 2011 amended the definition of fair value:
Fair value is the price that would be received to sell an asset or paid to transfer a liability in an orderly transaction between market participants at the measurement date (i.e. an exit price).

Non-current assets and depreciation

- The depreciation methods used.
- The useful economic lives or the depreciation rates used.
- Where material, the effect of a change of depreciation rate or method during the period.
- The cost or revalued amount of the class of tangible non-current assets at the beginning and end of the period.
- The cumulative depreciation at the beginning and end of the reporting period.
- A reconciliation of the movements in non-current assets.
- Restrictions on title to assets.
- Expenditure on assets in the course of construction.
- Capital commitments.
- Impairment losses (if not separated on the face of the statement of profit or loss).

Conclusion

It is key that we have an accounting standard on property, plant and equipment, because without one we do have a very easy way for profit to be manipulated. IAS 16 provides such a standard.

8   IAS 18 – Revenue

Introduction

> "Corporate accounting does not do violence to the truth occasionally and trivially, but comprehensively, systematically, and universally, annually and perennially."
>
> R J Chambers (1917-1999)

These are harsh words indeed for accountants to read. However, revenue manipulation is one of the most common ways of creative accounting ... indeed, if a couple of US cases are anything to go by, some company employees consider faking sales figures a bit of fun. Staff at one software vendor filmed an in-house skit about how they inflated revenue. Employees of a swimwear manufacturer allegedly ran a sweepstake on how long they would have to keep the quarter open to meet sales targets. This was before they were forced into serious reinstatements after their improper accounting practices came to light.

Revenue recognition is an important underlying issue which will be vital at all stages of your studies. We need an accounting standard on revenue recognition because of the tendency for revenue manipulation. All accountancy students need to be completely clear when revenue can be recognised and that 'revenue' is not the same as 'gains'. Revenue arises from a company's ordinary trading activities. Gains will include one-offs such as profit on disposal of property or other non-current assets or on retranslating balances in foreign currencies – these gains are not revenue.

Revenue can take various forms, commonly the sale of goods or provision of a service but also could be other forms such as royalty fees, franchise fees, management fees, subscriptions and so on.

Plenty of hanky panky here!

The two scandals referred to above relate to the 1990s. However, it didn't end there. Many of the recent accounting scandals have allegedly been the result of companies recognising revenue based on inappropriate accounting policies. In 2002 a complaint was made by the Securities and Exchange Commission (SEC) in the US alleging that Xerox deceived the public between 1997 and 2000, by using several 'accounting manoeuvres', the most significant involving recording revenue in the period a lease contract was signed, instead of spreading it over the length of the contract. The SEC charged that the accounting irregularities increased fiscal year 1997 pre-tax earnings by $405 million, 1998 pre-tax earnings by $655 million, and 1999 pre-tax earnings by $511 million. Interestingly it happened that in each quarter of the year earnings were inflated just enough to exceed the expectations of the market. (The importance of standards in accounting for revenue has to be recognised by students at all levels).

So ... what's it trying to achieve?

IAS 18 identifies the criteria that need to be met in order to recognise revenue and also the method that should be used to measure the revenue. It addition it provides some practical examples and guidance to help in the application of the standard.

 ## Transactional example

AJF(sg) Inc has a year end of 31 March. It purchased goods costing $5,000 on 8 March 2006. It sells and delivers the items for $8,000 on 14 March. The contract however is one of 'sale or return', with the customer being allowed a 20-day period for approval. At 31 March the delivery has not been formally accepted by the buyer.

IAS 18 states that, if there is uncertainty about the possibility of return, revenue is recognised when the goods have been delivered and the period of time for rejection has expired.

Therefore in this case revenue of $8,000 will not be recognised in the year to 31 March as the conditions for its recognition are not met. The $5,000 spent on goods does qualify to be recognised as an asset as it gives the rights to future economic benefits. The $5,000 is therefore recognised as an asset – inventory.

A typical error made by students is just to take the revenue figure from the trial balance to the statement of profit or loss, without noticing that the supporting information is telling them that some sales included in revenue were made on a sale-or-return basis. Remember to exclude the transaction from both revenue and receivables and instead treat the cost of the goods as inventory.

 Sorry but you need to know ... DEFINITIONS

 Revenue is the gross inflow of economic benefits during the period arising in the course of the ordinary activities of an entity when those inflows result in increases in equity, other than increases relating to contributions from equity participants.

 Fair value is the price that would be received to sell an asset or paid to transfer a liability in an orderly transaction between market participants at the measurement date.

And the really important stuff ... accounting practice

Measurement

Revenue should be measured at the fair value of the consideration received or receivable.

If revenue is deferred it should be measured at present value.

In a barter transaction the revenue should be the fair value of the goods received and, only if unreliable, the fair value of the goods given up.

Recognition

Revenue is recognised for the sale of goods when a number of criteria are met:

(a) the entity has transferred to the buyer the significant risks and rewards of ownership of the goods

(b) the enterprise retains neither continuing managerial involvement to the degree normally associated with ownership nor effective control over the goods sold

(c) the amount of revenue can be measured reliably

(d) it is probable that the economic benefits associated with the transaction will flow to the enterprise; and

(e) the costs incurred or to be incurred in respect of the transaction can be measured reliably.

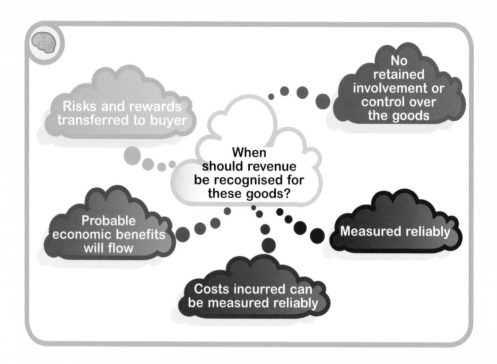

Revenue from services should be recognised over the period of service provided the following criteria are met:

(a) the amount of revenue can be measured reliably

(b) it is probable that the economic benefits associated with the transaction will flow to the enterprise

(c) the stage of completion of the transaction at the end of the reporting period can be measured reliably; and

(d) the costs incurred for the transaction and the costs to complete the transaction can be measured reliably.

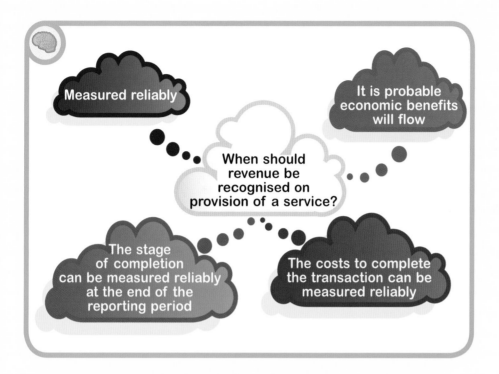

Revenue from interest, dividends and royalties should be recognised as follows:

Interest	Time proportion basis reflecting the effective interest method on the asset
Royalties	Accruals basis
Dividends	Right to receive payment is established

Conclusion

It really is vital that the point of recognition of revenue is properly determined. There are multiple possibilities even for a simple transaction such as the sale of an item (sale of goods). Is it revenue when the customer places an order? Is it revenue when you ship the goods to the customer? Is it revenue when the customer receives the goods? Is it revenue when the customer pays? The decision made about when and how revenues are recognised will have a direct impact on the statement of profit or loss and is therefore a major 'hotspot' in determining a company's 'earnings'. Students will need to understand and recognise the importance of this issue right from the early days of preparation of financial statements.

IAS 37 – Provisions, contingent liabilities and contingent assets

Introduction

> "How many accountants does it take to change a light bulb? ... What kind of answer did you have in mind?"
>
> Traditional

An old joke maybe but with a serious undertone. Traditionally there were no rules with regard to accounting for provisions and contingencies. However accountants were taught that, under the prudence concept, revenue and profits are not anticipated but provision is made for all known liabilities and expected losses. This concept on the face of it seems difficult to argue against. However, accountants managed to use this concept as one of the most powerful weapons in the manipulation of profit.

Ideally companies like to present a pattern of 'earnings' showing that in this period the company actually did a little bit better than in the previous period. This gives the impression of 'quality earnings', i.e. that management is doing a great job and deserves a nice bonus. Companies are therefore reluctant to show they have had an exceptionally good period because traditionally the market will then expect them to deliver the same (plus a bit more!!) in the next.

Instead of reporting such profits it became quite normal for companies to start to foresee 'future costs'. Under the guise of 'prudence,' they were able to 'slush' these excess profits on the statement of financial position* using a general provision. These non-specific provisions, often referred to as 'big bath' provisions, are now outlawed by IAS 37.

Once these 'big bath' provisions had been created on the statement of financial position*, companies would use them to create endless periods of 'good news'. Instead of starting the statement of profit or loss at the top with revenue and deducting costs to calculate profit, it was possible to decide from the bottom, what you wanted profit to be. By releasing some of the provision it was easy to directly manipulate profit.

Unfudgeability??

Maybe what the accounting profession needs is the concept of 'unfudgeability'!!! – a reminder that accounts are meant to fairly report profit as it is, rather than a 'fudged' figure. Well, we haven't got a concept of 'unfudgeability' but we have now got an accounting standard covering provision accounting.

So ... what's it trying to achieve?

IAS 37 aims to ensure that appropriate measurement and recognition criteria are applied to provisions, contingent liabilities and contingent assets, and that sufficient disclosure is made in the financial statements to enable users to understand the provisions made.

 ## Transactional example

Hill Corp is a very diverse group. It prepares its accounts to 31 March 20X6. You are responsible for preparing the accounts to 31 March 20X6. Certain events have occurred which need to be considered as possibly giving rise to the need for a provision or a disclosure in the notes.

On 12 February 20X6 the board of Hill Corp decided to close down a large factory in Aylesbury. The board is planning to transfer the production to other factories. A detailed formal plan has been drawn up and it is expected that the closure will occur on 31 August 20X6. Letters were sent out to customers, suppliers and workers soon after 12th February. The employees and any other interested parties have been invited to meetings to discuss the features of the formal plan. The overall costs of this closure are foreseen as $79 million.

In order for Hill to provide for these costs, all of the following conditions must be met:

(a) it has a present obligation (either legal or constructive) arising as a result of past events

(b) it is probable that a transfer of economic benefits will be required to settle the obligation; and

(c) the obligation can be measured reliably.

Here Hill can provide for the $79 million because, although it does not have a legal obligation to close down this factory, it will have raised a 'constructive obligation'. A constructive obligation arises when a valid expectation is raised in third parties, i.e. the formal plan has been communicated to interested parties. We do have a probable transfer of economic benefit (it is 'more likely than not' that Hill will pay the closure costs) and an estimate of $79 million is made. Provision for these costs should be made on the statement of financial position.

Transactional example

One of Hill Corp's most profitable products is the 'Sophie Beauty' range. However, it has recently come to light that a new brand of face cream was produced with an inappropriately high lead content. Although recalled, one customer has started legal proceedings against the company claiming the product is responsible for a recent skin complaint. The company's lawyers have advised that the chances of this action succeeding are possible with damages being awarded of around $30,000.

This time Hill cannot provide for the $30,000. Again, when we look at the conditions, we can see that we have only a possible, rather than a probable, transfer of economic benefits. This, however, would require disclosure in the notes to the accounts as a possible contingent liability.

 It is a common problem with trial balance type questions for students to believe that all additional information gives rise to an adjustment in the accounts. This is not actually the case – some like this give rise only to a disclosure.

Sorry but you need to know ... DEFINITIONS

A **provision** is a liability of uncertain timing or amount.

A **liability** is a present obligation of an entity to transfer economic benefits as a result of past transactions or events.

A **legal obligation** is an obligation that could:

- be contractual or
- arise due to a legislation or
- result from other operation of law.

A **constructive obligation** is an obligation that results from an entity's actions where:

- by an established pattern of past practice, published policies, or a sufficiently specific current statement, the entity has indicated to other (third) parties that it will accept certain responsibilities; and
- as a result, the entity has created a valid expectation in the minds of those parties that it will discharge those responsibilities.

A **contingent liability** is a possible obligation that arises from past events whose outcome is based on uncertain future events or, an obligation that is not recognised because it is not probable, or cannot be measured reliably.

A **contingent asset** is a possible asset that arises from past events and whose existence will only be confirmed by uncertain future events not wholly within the control of the enterprise.

And the really important stuff ... accounting practice

Provisions should be recognised when:

(a) an entity has a present obligation (either legal or constructive) arising as a result of past events

(b) it is probable that a transfer of economic benefits will be required to settle the obligation; and

(c) the obligation can be measured reliably.

When deciding if a provision should be recognised, an entity should determine whether the future expenditure can be avoided. If the future expenditure can be avoided no provision should be made.

If material to the amount of the provision, provisions should be discounted.

Contingent liabilities should not be recognised in the financial statements, however disclosure should be made unless the possibility of the transfer of economic benefits is remote.

Contingent assets should not be recognised, and disclosure is only allowed if the possible profit is considered probable. Virtually certain profits could be recognised in the financial statements.

The requirements in relation to contingent assets and liabilities are summarised in the following table.

Degree of probability	Liability of uncertain timing or amount	Asset of uncertain timing or amount
Virtually certain (therefore not contingent)	Make provision	Recognise (receivable)
Probable	Make provision	Disclose by note (contingent asset)
Possible	Disclose by note (contingent liability)	No disclosure
Remote	No disclosure	No disclosure

Note

When there is the possibility of the recovery from a third party of all or part of a contingent liability, this must be treated as a separate matter, and a contingent asset is only recognised if its receipt is virtually certain, as shown in the table.

Disclosure

Key disclosures include:

- the movements in all classes of provision over the period
- additional provisions made in the period, including increase to existing provisions
- the nature of the provision and any uncertainties and assumptions used in recognising and measuring it
- for contingent liabilities, the nature of the liability, the uncertainties surrounding it and the possible financial effect.

Conclusion

Traditionally it wasn't thought necessary to have a standard on provisions. The reason why you have to learn this one is because of what accountants have done in terms of manipulation of financial statements!

10 IAS 38 – Intangible assets

Introduction

> "Intangible asset? – Well it's an asset you can't kick isn't it?"
>
> Anon

All successful companies will have assets that we traditionally class as intangible, i.e. without physical substance. The most common one is goodwill – the difference between the value of a business as a whole and the aggregate of the fair value of its separable net assets. When you agree a price for a business you are prepared to pay more than the value of the assets because you are acquiring other stuff:

- an established list of customers
- an experienced workforce
- strategic location
- reputation
- good labour relations, etc.

These items and others can contribute to, or influence, the value of goodwill.

Err ... but purchased goodwill is not covered by IAS 38!! Why are we discussing it?

 Exactly – one of the most common mistakes students make when asked about intangibles is to talk about purchased goodwill in their answer. Well yes, purchased goodwill is an intangible asset and yes, the title of IAS 38 is 'intangible assets', but the issue of purchased goodwill is actually covered by IFRS 3 – doh!! Please do not pick it to discuss when you are asked about IAS 38.

So ... what sort of transactions could you discuss?

You could talk about internally generated goodwill – in essence it's the same as purchased goodwill, the difference between the two being simply that the goodwill is not actually valued, as nobody has bought the company from you. The accounting rule is simple – the standard does not allow you to include internally generated goodwill as an asset on the statement of financial position* – period.

Other transactions you could discuss when answering IAS 38 questions would include expenditure incurred on stuff like patents, brands, advertising, training, software, licences, etc. – assets you have purchased without physical substance (things you can't kick!).

So ... what's it trying to achieve?

IAS 38 prescribes the treatment of intangible assets that are not dealt with specifically by other standards. Intangibles can only be recognised if certain criteria are met.

 ### Transactional example

Lockwood Inc, a multinational company, has recently introduced a new razor to its toiletry range. It has decided to hire the services of the famous motorcyclist, turned rock star, Christopher Swallow, to head up its advertising campaign. It is paying $3,000,000 and believes the benefit from this promotion will last for three years. It is planning to spread his fee over the next three years, recognising the rest as an intangible asset.

It will **not** be possible to treat these costs as an asset. The standard is clear – the costs of introducing new products or services such as advertising cannot be included. The costs will have to be expensed immediately.

Sorry but you need to know ... DEFINITIONS

An **intangible** asset is an identifiable non-monetary asset without physical substance. Assets are identifiable because they are separable, or because they are identifiable through legal or contractual rights.

Research is original and planned investigation undertaken with the prospect of gaining new scientific knowledge and understanding.

Development is the application of research findings or other knowledge to a plan or design for the production of new or substantially improved materials, devices, products, processes, systems or services prior to the commencement of commercial production or use.

And the really important stuff ... accounting practice

Intangibles should be recognised if, and only if, the following criteria are met:

* it is probable that future economic benefits will flow to the enterprise; and
* the cost of the asset can be measured reliably.

It is important to recognise the difference between internally generated intangibles and purchased intangibles.

Internally generated intangible assets

Problems arise with these because of the need as above to identify a probable future economic benefit and to reliably determine its cost. For this reason the standard does not allow internally generated goodwill to go on the statement of financial position* as an asset.

The same issue arises if you are being asked about other internally generated intangibles such as internally generated brands, mastheads, publishing titles, customer lists and similar items – you cannot put them on the statement of financial position* as an intangible asset.

All internally generated intangibles must be treated as either research or development costs. Costs for assets in the research phase must be charged to the statement of profit or loss, whilst those in the development phase must be capitalised if certain criteria are met.

* Statement of financial position = Balance Sheet (see page 19)

The criteria for capitalising internally generated intangibles are:

(a) technically feasible (totally)

(b) intention to complete and use or sell the asset (important)

(c) ability to use or sell the asset (always)

(d) existence of a market or demonstration of usefulness of intangible (employ)

(e) availability of technical, financial or other resources to complete the asset (attractive)

(f) measure the cost reliably (men).

Totally important – always employ attractive men!!

Purchased intangible assets

For purchased intangibles the probability criterion is always met and therefore they are recognised on the statement of financial position*, albeit subject to an impairment review.

For intangibles acquired in a business combination there is an assumption that the probability criterion is met, and there is always information to measure the cost separately from goodwill. This means the following sorts of intangibles (plus others) must be recognised separately from goodwill:

- customer lists
- in-progress research and development (R&D)
- employment contracts below market rate
- order or production backlogs.

Intangible assets should be amortised over their useful economic lives. If no amortisation is charged because the life is indefinite, the asset must be subject to an annual impairment review.

Intangibles can be revalued only if an active market exists for the asset (very rare).

---

* Statement of financial position = Balance Sheet (see page 19)

Disclosures

The following are key disclosures for intangibles:

- useful lives and amortisation rates
- amortisation methods
- the line items of the statement of profit or loss where amortisation is included
- reconciliation of the movement in intangibles over the year
- commitments for the purchase of intangibles.

Conclusion

It is necessary to have an accounting standard on intangibles. Without one we had situations such as the 1988 accounts of Rank Hovis McDougall, a UK company. They decided back in 1988 to bring more than 50 of their internally developed brand names such as 'Hovis' (the bread) onto the statement of financial position*. The company came up with the figure of £678 million and, hey presto, increased net asset value per share from 83p to 272p. Although other UK companies had purchased brand names and capitalised them on the statement of financial position*, this was the start of a new trend – capitalising internally generated brands. There was no accounting standard at the time to prevent such a practice. IAS 38 now provides such a standard.

---

* Statement of financial position = Balance Sheet (see page 19)

IFRS 13 – Fair value measurement

Introduction

> "Price is what you pay. Value is what you get."
>
> Warren Buffett

Some IFRSs require or permit entities to measure or disclose the fair value of assets, liabilities or their own equity instruments. IFRSs were developed over many years and the requirements for measuring fair value and for disclosing information about fair value measurements were spread across many different standards and in many cases were vague about how to measure fair value and also unclear as to the disclosure objective.

So it's a 'how to measure fair value standard?'

Yes –some IFRSs contained limited guidance about how to measure fair value, whereas others contained extensive guidance and that guidance was not always consistent across those IFRSs that refer to fair value. Inconsistencies in the requirements for measuring fair value and for disclosing information about fair value measurements have contributed to diversity in practice and have reduced the comparability of information reported in financial statements. IFRS 13 remedies that situation.

> ## So ... what's it trying to achieve?
>
> IFRS 13 defines fair value; sets out in a single IFRS a framework for measuring fair value; and requires disclosures about fair value measurements.

The IASB therefore wanted to enhance disclosures for fair values so that users could better assess the valuation techniques and inputs used to measure it. There are no new requirements in IFRS 13 about when fair value accounting is required - the IASB is relying on guidance on fair value measurements in existing standards. IFRS 13 also moves IFRS closer to US GAAP on how to measure fair value, differences remain about when fair value measurements are required and the recognition of gains and losses on initial recognition.

 Sorry but you need to know ... DEFINITIONS

 Fair Value

IFRS 13 defines fair value as the price that would be received to sell an asset or paid to transfer a liability in an orderly transaction between market participants at the measurement date (i.e. an exit price).

 Exit Price

The price that would be received to sell an asset or paid to transfer a liability.

The exit price

Fair value has a different meaning depending on the usage and context. As you can see from above the IASB definition is now based on an exit price. Under IFRS 13 the basic principles of fair value remain similar to original IFRS, but if an entity did not use those principles before IFRS 13, it could result in quite significant changes.

E.g.   Revaluing Property, Plant and Equipment

Prior to IFRS 13 an entity would not have to consider the highest and best use of the asset when revaluing an asset. Now under IFRS 13 the resulting fair value could be considerably higher than the entity would have used before.

Also it will no longer be a relevant argument to the valuation process for an entity to insist that prices are too low relative to its own valuation of the asset and that it would be unwilling to sell at such low prices. The prices to be used are those in an 'orderly transaction' – one that assumes exposure to the market for a period before the date of measurement to allow for normal marketing activities and to ensure that it is not a forced transaction'.

If the transaction is not 'orderly' there will not have been enough time to create competition and potential buyers may reduce the price that they are willing to pay. Similarly, if a seller is forced to accept a price in a short period of time, then the price may not be representative.

It does not mean, however, that just because a market has few transactions that it is not 'orderly'. If there has been sufficient time with information available about the asset and competitive price tension exists then the market may return a fair value for the asset.

Unit of account

The unit of account to be employed for measuring fair value is not actually specified by IFRS 13, users will need to consider the underlying specific accounting standard. The characteristics of an asset or liability must be distinguished from a characteristic arising from the holding of an asset or liability by an entity.

Transactional example

Freya Inc purchased an investment in a large block of shares. As a result of pressure on cash flow Freya now needs to sell the entire holding. Because it is a large number of shares coming onto the market to find a buyer Freya needs to discount the shares below the market price.

Required

Discuss whether this discount should be taken into account when fair valuing the asset.

This discount though is a characteristic of holding the asset rather than the asset itself and therefore should NOT be taken into account when fair-valuing the asset.

Which market?

Fair value measurement assumes that the transaction to sell the asset or transfer the liability takes place in the principal market for the asset or liability or, in the absence of a principal market, in the most advantageous market for the asset or liability.

So what does 'principal' and 'most advantageous' market mean?

The principal market is the one with the greatest volume and level of activity for the asset or liability that can be accessed by the entity. The most advantageous market is the one that maximises the amount that would be received for an asset or paid to extinguish the liability after transport and transaction costs. These markets will usually be the same.

Be careful with transaction costs

Although transaction costs are taken into account when identifying the most advantageous market, the fair value is **NOT** after adjustment for transaction costs because these costs are a characteristic of the transaction, not the asset or liability. If location is a factor, then the market price is adjusted for the costs incurred to transport the asset to that market.

Market participants **MUST** be independent of each other and knowledgeable, able and willing to enter into transactions.

Inputs and their hierarchy

The assumptions that market participants would use when pricing the asset or liability, including assumptions about risk, such as the following:

(a) the risk inherent in a particular valuation technique used to measure fair value (such as a pricing model); and

(b) the risk inherent in the inputs to the valuation technique.

Inputs may be observable or unobservable.

Level 1 inputs

Quoted prices (unadjusted) in active markets for identical assets or liabilities that the entity can access at the measurement date.

As with IFRS before IFRS 13, if there is a quoted price in an active market, an entity uses that price without adjustment when measuring fair value.

Level 2 inputs

Inputs other than quoted prices included within level 1 that are observable for the asset or liability, either directly or indirectly.

Examples here include interest rates and yield curves.

Adjustments may be needed to level 2 inputs, and if these are significant, the fair value may need to be classified as level 3.

Level 3 inputs

Unobservable inputs for the asset or liability.

The entity should maximize the use of relevant observable inputs and minimize the use of unobservable ones. The general principle of using an exit price remains and IFRS 13 does not preclude an entity from using its own data.

An example here would be a cash flow forecasts or profit and loss.

Market approach

A valuation technique that uses prices and other relevant information generated by market transactions involving identical or comparable (i.e. similar) assets, liabilities or a group of assets and liabilities, such as a business.

Market-corroborated inputs

Inputs that are derived principally from or corroborated by observable market data by correlation or other means.

 Transactional example

Examples of level 1 inputs

If you are valuing a financial asset that is traded on a stock exchange such as the London Stock exchange , then you have an observable market with prices readily available and generally representative of fair value.

If you have some used equipment, there is often an observable input – a dealer market exists i.e. the price a dealer in the asset is prepared to pay.

Examples of level 2 inputs

If you are valuing a more complex instrument such as a derivative (See IAS 39) you would have inputs from the financial markets such as the London Interbank offered Rate (LIBOR) swap rate. This would be a level 2 input for valuing an interest rate swap for example.

Example of level 3 inputs

Valuing a decommissioning liability that was taken on as part of a business combination. The valuation is based on the company's own estimates of future cash flows taken at present value.

And the really important stuff...accounting practice

The IFRS explains that a fair value measurement requires an entity to determine all of the following:

(a) the particular asset or liability being measured;

(b) for a non-financial asset, the highest and best use of the asset and whether the asset is used in combination with other assets or on a stand-alone basis;

(c) the principal market in which an orderly transaction would take place for the asset or liability; and

(d) the appropriate valuation technique(s) to use when measuring fair value. The valuation technique(s) used should maximise the use of relevant observable inputs and minimise unobservable inputs. Those inputs should be consistent with the inputs a market participant would use when pricing the asset or liability.

Fair value is a market-based measurement, not an entity-specific measurement. For some assets and liabilities, observable market transactions or market information might be available. For other assets and liabilities, observable market transactions and market information might not be available. However, the objective of a fair value measurement in both cases is the same–to estimate the price at which an orderly transaction to sell the asset or to transfer the liability would take place between market participants at the measurement date under current market conditions (i.e. an exit price at the measurement date from the perspective of a market participant that holds the asset or owes the liability).

When a price for an identical asset or liability is not observable, an entity measures fair value using another valuation technique that maximises the use of relevant observable inputs and minimises the use of unobservable inputs. Because fair value is a market-based measurement, it is measured using the assumptions that market participants would use when pricing the asset or liability, including assumptions about risk. As a result, an entity's intention to hold an asset or to settle or otherwise fulfil a liability is not relevant when measuring fair value.

The definition of fair value focuses on assets and liabilities because they are a primary subject of accounting measurement. In addition, this IFRS shall be applied to an entity's equity instruments measured at fair value.

Market participants

An entity shall measure the fair value of an asset or a liability using the assumptions that market participants would use when pricing the asset or liability, assuming that market participants act in their economic best interest.

In developing those assumptions, an entity need not identify specific market participants. Rather, the entity shall identify characteristics that distinguish market participants generally, considering factors specific to all the following:

(a) the asset or liability;

(b) the principal (or most advantageous) market for the asset or liability; and

(c) market participants with whom the entity would enter into a transaction in that market.

The price

Fair value is the price that would be received to sell an asset or paid to transfer a liability in an orderly transaction in the principal (or most advantageous) market at the measurement date under current market conditions (i.e. an exit price) regardless of whether that price is directly observable or estimated using another valuation technique.

Application to non-financial assets

Highest and best use for non-financial assets.

A fair value measurement of a non-financial asset takes into account a market participant's ability to generate economic benefits by using the asset in its highest and best use or by selling it to another market participant that would use the asset in its highest and best use.

Valuation techniques

IFRS 13 sets out a valuation approach that refers to a broad range of techniques. These techniques are threefold: the market, income and cost approaches.

Market approach

The market approach uses prices and other relevant information generated by market transactions involving identical or comparable (i.e. similar) assets, liabilities or a group of assets and liabilities, such as a business.

For example, valuation techniques consistent with the market approach often use market multiples derived from a set of comparables. Multiples might be in ranges with a different multiple for each comparable. The selection of the appropriate multiple within the range requires judgement, considering qualitative and quantitative factors specific to the measurement.

Valuation techniques consistent with the market approach include matrix pricing. Matrix pricing is a mathematical technique used principally to value some types of financial instruments, such as debt securities, without relying exclusively on quoted prices for the specific securities, but rather relying on the securities' relationship to other benchmark quoted securities.

Cost approach

The cost approach reflects the amount that would be required currently to replace the service capacity of an asset (often referred to as current replacement cost).

From the perspective of a market participant seller, the price that would be received for the asset is based on the cost to a market participant buyer to acquire or construct a substitute asset of comparable utility, adjusted for obsolescence. That is because a market participant buyer would not pay more for an asset than the amount for which it could replace the service capacity of that asset. Obsolescence encompasses physical deterioration, functional (technological) obsolescence and economic (external) obsolescence and is broader than depreciation for financial reporting purposes (an allocation of historical cost) or tax purposes (using specified service lives). In many cases the current replacement cost method is used to measure the fair value of tangible assets that are used in combination with other assets or with other assets and liabilities.

Income approach

The income approach converts future amounts (e.g. cash flows or income and expenses) to a single current (i.e. discounted) amount. When the income approach is used, the fair value measurement reflects current market expectations about those future amounts.

Those valuation techniques include, for example, the following:

(a) present value techniques

(b) option pricing models, such as the Black-Scholes-Merton formula or a binomial model (i.e. a lattice model), that incorporate present value techniques and reflect both the time value and the intrinsic value of an option; and

(c) the multi-period excess earnings method, which is used to measure the fair value of some intangible assets.

Disclosures

An entity shall disclose information that helps users of its financial statements assess both of the following:

(a) for assets and liabilities that are measured at fair value on a recurring or non-recurring basis in the statement of financial position after initial recognition, the valuation techniques and inputs used to develop those measurements.

(b) or recurring fair value measurements using significant unobservable inputs (Level 3), the effect of the measurements on profit or loss or other comprehensive income for the period.

Conclusion

As the business world has become more complex we have seen the profession moving away from the simple days of historic cost accounting onto fair value accounting in an attempt to improve the relevance of financial reporting. It was inevitable that at some point better guidance would be needed in this area and IFRS 13 is giving it. It will take some time before its success or otherwise can be judged.

2

More advanced

"The only thing more expensive than education is ignorance."

Benjamin Franklin (1706-1790)

Introduction

You mean there's more? – for the more advanced student – yes!! As you get further into your accountancy studies, you find that companies get involved in more complex transactions. Instead of just buying assets they may lease them, instead of building a client a garden wall, they build the new national football stadium. There are twelve 'green' standards that deal with these more advanced but still relatively common transactions:

- IAS 11 Construction contracts
- IAS 12 Income taxes
- IAS 17 Leases
- IAS 20 Accounting for government grants and disclosure of government assistance
- IAS 23 Borrowing costs
- IAS 33 Earnings per share
- IAS 36 Impairment of assets
- IAS 40 Investment property
- IFRS 5 Non-current assets held for sale and discontinued operations
- IAS 32 Financial instruments: presentation
- IFRS 9 Financial instruments
- IFRS 7 Financial instruments: disclosures

"Not everything that can be counted counts and not everything that counts can be counted."

Albert Einstein (1879–1955)

Note

Many books on accounting standards start by giving you the aims and definitions from the standard. This book deliberately does not structure the chapters in that style. Instead the issue is generally explained, with the sort of transactions that the standard relates to being introduced. We do get to the aims and definitions and for those of you who already feel comfortable with the standard, you may like to turn first to the definitions box – re-affirm those and then read the chapter.

(12) IAS 11 – Construction contracts

Introduction

> "The whole difference between construction and creation is this: that a thing constructed can only be loved after it is constructed; but a thing created is loved before it exists."
>
> Charles Dickens (1812-1870)

Accounting for a large construction contract can be problematic. Accounting convention requires that companies prepare accounts on an annual basis. Every year a company has to prepare financial statements that summarise the activity that has taken place. These summaries – the accounting statements – are meant to be useful to the reader of the accounts, who may use them as a basis for an investment decision.

Well that's OK for some companies!!

If the company is one that fits into a normal 'one year's pretty much like another' style of business, then accounts prepared annually should be fairly useful both for establishing a trend of performance, and as a basis for comparison with similar companies. But, and it's a big 'but…', there are many companies whose activities just do not slice up nicely into 12-month chunks. What about companies that undertake large construction contracts?

What's the problem?

If a company is undertaking a large project – say to build a new national football stadium – initially all it will have is costs. The project could take three or four years to complete. Do we think it's helpful to report only costs for years 1, 2 and 3, and only when the project is complete and the first match is played to finally report the company as having made a massive profit? This would not be helpful to the readers of the accounts – all costs in one period and revenues in another. It certainly does not apply to our accruals concept.

The solution?

Companies that are undertaking construction contracts need an accounting standard that deals with their specific circumstances and issues. Sometimes a 'one size fits all' approach is just not going to work, and this is one of those occasions – specific guidance for a specific issue.

So ... what's it trying to achieve?

IAS 11 is trying to provide that guidance by prescribing the accounting treatment for revenue and costs associated with construction contracts. The primary issue is the allocation of revenue and costs into relevant accounting periods.

Transactional example

Michael Inc is part way through a contract to build a new football stadium for Earlswood Town FC at a contracted price of $600 million.

All costs incurred to date are recorded and as Michael Inc invoices Earlswood Town FC for stage payments the progress payments received are also recorded. These are the only records as far as the accounting system is concerned.

The balances are as follows:

Total costs incurred to date $390 million
Total progress payment received $360 million

Michael is preparing accounts for the year ended 31 March 20X7 and has estimated that, at the statement of financial position* date, outstanding costs to complete the project will be $90 million. Michael's surveyor has estimated that the sales value of the work completed as at March 20X7 was $440 million.

Michael's accounting policy is to recognise revenue and profits using the work certified to date method – i.e. sales value earned to date compared to the contract price.

How will Michael show this contract in its accounts for the year to 31 March 20X7?

First of all Michael will need to know whether the contract is estimated to make a profit or a loss as expected profits are treated differently to losses. You will need to provide extracts from the accounts and a working paper.

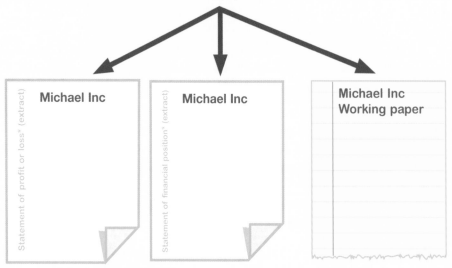

Start with the workings as follows:

(W1) Estimate of the outcome

	$m
Contract price	600
Costs to date	(390)
Estimated costs to complete	(90)
Estimated total profit	**120**

Then it needs to estimate the degree of completion, based on its stated policy:

(W2) Estimated stage of completion

	$m
Work certified complete to date/	440/
Contract price	600

As the 440/600 doesn't give us a round percentage but 73.3333%, we are best to use the fraction as the degree of completion in our workings the project is 440/600 complete.

Therefore profit can be recognised of 120 x 440/600 = $88 million in current year accounts. We will transfer the work certified as complete to revenue. Also we transfer our proportion of total costs (390 + 90) = total costs of $480 x 440/600 = 352 to cost of sales.

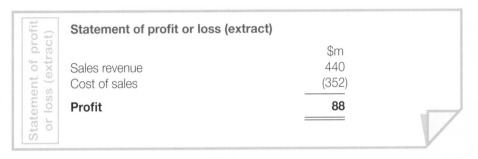

Statement of profit or loss (extract)	
	$m
Sales revenue	440
Cost of sales	(352)
Profit	**88**

We then compare the cash paid out in the form of costs incurred with the amount transferred to cost of sales.

(W3) Cash paid out v cost of sales

	$m
Cash paid out (cost incurred)	390
Cost of sales	(352)
Work in progress (for the statement of financial position*)	38

We then compare the sales revenue recognised to the cash received in the form of progress payments.

(W4) Cash received in v sales revenue

	$m
Sales revenue	440
Cash received	(360)
Receivable (for the statement of financial position*)	80

* Statement of financial position = Balance Sheet (see page 19)

So the statement of financial position* extract will show:

Statement of financial position* as at 31 March 20X7 (extract)

$m

Current assets

Amounts due re contract work (38 + 80)   118

In the statement of financial position* the following balance is recognised

Costs incurred to date	390
Profit recognised to date/loss recognised to date	88
Less: Progress billings	(360)
Receivable recoverable on contract, or	
Payable payable on contract	118

A common mistake is to do the same for a foreseen loss, i.e. only account for proportion. Remember, losses on contracts must be recognised in full as soon as they are foreseen (prudence concept).

Sorry but you need to know ... DEFINITIONS

A **construction contract** is a contract specifically negotiated for the construction of an asset or a combination of assets that are closely interrelated or interdependent in terms of their design, technology and function or their ultimate purpose or use.

And the really important stuff ... accounting practice

Contract revenue is measured at the fair value of the consideration received or receivable. Revenue and costs on contracts should be recognised over the period of the contract. Profit should also be recognised over the period of the contract as long as the outcome of the contract can be measured reliably.

Losses on contracts must be recognised in full, as an expense, as soon as they are foreseen.

---

* Statement of financial position = Balance Sheet (see page 19)

Transactional example - losses

Isaacs is a construction company that prepares its financial statements to 31 March each year. During the year ended 31 March 20X6 the company commenced a contract which it expects to take more than one year to complete. The position on the contract as at 31 March 20X6 is as follows:

	$000
Agreed contract price	*1,200*
Estimated total cost of contract at commencement	*900*
Estimated total cost at 31 March 20X6	*1,250*
Agreed value of work completed at 31 March 20X6	*840*
Progress billings invoiced and received at 31 March 20X6	*880*
Contract costs incurred to 31 March 20X6	*720*

The agreed value of the work completed at 31 March 20X6 is considered to be equal to the revenue earned in the year ended 31 March 20X6. The percentage of completion is calculated as the agreed value of work completed to the agreed contract price.

What should appear in the statement of profit or loss* and statement of financial position** of Isaacs as at 31 March 20X6?

We would need to set up a working paper and estimate the outcome:

(W1) Estimate of the outcome

	$000
Agreed contract price	1,200
Estimated total contract cost at 31 March 20X6	(1,250)
Expected loss	(50)

Note

Because we are expecting a loss instead of bringing in a percentage, we bring in the full loss (remember the Framework document and the need to present 'reliable' information). Losses are therefore easier to account for.

---

* Statement of profit or loss = Income statement

** Statement of financial position = Balance Sheet (see page 19)

Statement of profit or loss* (extract)

	$000
Revenue *(value of work completed)*	840
Cost of sales *(balancing figure)*	**(890)**
Loss on contract (W1)	(50)

You have actually spent $720,000 and are also providing for future costs of $170,000 to give you the loss of ($50,000).

For the statement of financial position**:

(W2) Cash paid out v cost of sales

	$000
Cash paid out	720
Cost of sales	890
Provision for future costs	(170)

(W3) Cash received in v sales revenue

	$000
Cash received in (progress billing)	880
Sales revenue (work completed)	(840)
Amount due to customer	(40)

Statement of financial position** (extract)

Current liabilities

	$000
Amounts due to customers on construction contract (170 + 40)	210

Estimated stage of completion

Different accounting policies can be used to estimate the percentage completion. The policy used will vary from company to company and therefore exam question to exam question. You will also find variability between a single company with more than one contract.

---

*Statement of profit or loss = Income statement

** Statement of financial position = Balance Sheet (see page 19)

If the work certified method is used the percentage completion can be calculated by:

$$\text{Work certified method} = \frac{\text{Work certified to date}}{\text{Contract price}}$$

If the cost method is used the percentage completion can be calculated by:

$$\text{Cost method} = \frac{\text{Cost to date}}{\text{Total contract costs}}$$

The statement of profit or loss will include:

Revenue	% completion × Contract price
Profit	% completion × Expected profit (or 100% of loss)
Cost of sales	Balancing figure

An image story

Work certified method

An image-story technique works well for remembering these.

Invent a project you have quoted a price to build. Imagine it ¾ complete. Now think of the money you are due to get under the contract – that is one way of measuring the degree of completion. The work certified method conjures positive imagery – a building nears completion/loads of money to be earned.

Cost method

The cost method creates more negative imagery – cash going out of your bank whilst you undertake the project.

And under the line even more cash yet to be paid out – a sad face.

If a number of contracts are negotiated together and performed concurrently as a single contract they should be accounted for as a single contract. If an individual contract covers a number of independent assets, each asset should be treated as a single contract.

Fixed cost contract

With respect to a fixed price contract, the outcome can be estimated reliably when all of the following conditions are satisfied:

- total contract revenue can be measured reliably
- it is probable that the economic benefit of the contract will flow to the entity
- both the costs to complete the contract and the stage of completion can be reliably measured
- the costs attributable to the contract can be clearly identified and measured reliably.

Cost-plus contract

With respect to a cost-plus contract, the outcome can be estimated reliably when all of the following conditions are satisfied:

- it is probable that the economic benefit of the contract will flow to the entity
- the costs attributable to the contract, whether specifically reimbursable or not, can be clearly identified and measured.

Conclusion

IAS 11 is actually a nice easy mark-earning topic if you learn it. Look at your examiner's past questions on construction contracts. Practise a few, learn the approach and hey presto – a favourite topic.

* Statement of profit or loss = Income statement

13 IAS 12 – Income taxes

Introduction

> **"In this world nothing can be said to be certain, except death and taxes."**
>
> Benjamin Franklin (1706-1790)

An old quote maybe, but as true today as it was then. Different countries will have different tax rules, and the tax requested may get called by different names such as 'corporation tax' or 'income tax', but at the end of the day if a company makes profit, it will certainly have to pay tax on that profit.

Well, you may ask, companies pay lots of expenses – rent, electricity, telephone. Why is tax so different that it needs an accounting standard? It is true that accounting for the tax of companies could be so easy (maybe it is in a parallel universe!). Imagine a world where the tax rules simply said 'take your calculation of profit from the income statement* and multiply it by say 30%' – hey presto, we have a tax expense and the company has a liability to the tax authorities. That however is not our world (and it keeps accountants in work!!).

Why can life never be that simple?

Well it couldn't be could it! For most countries (unfortunately) the way profit is calculated for accounting purposes is not the same as the way profit is calculated for tax purposes. In addition to preparing the statement of profit or loss down to profit before tax, companies will then need to do a working of their taxable profit. It is this 'taxable profit' that forms the basis of the tax computation commonly known as 'the tax comp'. As accounting profit is different to taxable profit, accounting for tax becomes a subject of two parts: current tax and deferred tax.

---

*Statement of profit or loss = Income statement

Current tax

Current tax is not a problem. Once tax is estimated based on taxable profit (i.e. the tax comp is done) it becomes a current tax liability. It will be debited to the statement of profit or loss* and credited to current liabilities in the statement of financial position.

Tax rates used to calculate current tax should be those that have been enacted by the statement of financial position** date. This will include those 'substantially enacted' by the statement of financial position** date.

Deferred tax

This then is the problem child – recognising and dealing with the fact that, because the accounting profit is not the same as taxable profit, there may be future tax consequences based on current period transactions. This is what we call 'deferred tax'.

So ... what's it trying to achieve?

IAS 12 aims to provide guidance on accounting for the current and future tax consequences of the future recovery or settlement of assets and liabilities, and transactions and other events that have occurred in the same period.

Temporary differences

In order to make any sense of IAS 12 we need to look at what happens when we prepare accounts, using the simple approach – only accounting for current tax and ignoring future (deferred) tax consequences.

A company could possibly report an accounting profit of say $200,000 and yet be required to pay no current tax. This is because of temporary differences, which distort the timing of when tax is paid.

The normal effect of temporary differences is to delay when tax is paid (i.e. defer) and, as a result there will be a need to provide for a deferred tax liability to ensure that the tax effects of transactions are reported in the same period when they are recognised. This is simply an application of the matching/accruals concept to tax.

*Statement of profit or loss = Income statement

** Statement of financial position = Balance Sheet (see page 19)

It is possible for temporary differences to accelerate the timing of when tax is paid, in which case, although not as commonly, this will reduce the amount of the deferred tax liability or maybe create a deferred tax asset. It is impossible to understand deferred tax until we understand timing differences. This concept is best understood with the following example.

Transactional example

Let us assume that Tyrrell makes up financial statements to 31 December each year. On 1 January 20X1 the company purchased a piece of equipment for $40,000 that had an anticipated useful economic life of four years but qualified for immediate tax relief of 100% of the cost of the asset. For the year ending 31 December 20X1 the draft accounts of the company showed a profit before tax of $100,000. The directors anticipate that this level of profit will be maintained for the foreseeable future. Tyrrell pays tax at a rate of 30%.

Apart from the differences caused by the purchase of the non-current asset in 20X1 there are no other differences between accounting profit and taxable profit of the tax base and net book value of net assets.

This example illustrates the key issue – the common major difference between accounting profit and taxable profit relates to the difference in treatment of non-current assets. We, as accountants, will spread the cost of the asset over four years' statements of profit or loss. This is an application of the matching concept – the equipment has a useful economic life of four years and we will depreciate the asset over that period. Most tax jurisdictions, however, do not accept the depreciation expense as part of the calculation of taxable profit. Instead the tax authorities allow companies a tax allowance when they purchase non-current assets.

The tax comp will usually involve taking accounting profit and adding back the depreciation expense. We can then deduct the tax allowance to get taxable profit. This forms the basis of the tax calculation. If we account for current tax based on this calculation but ignore the deferred tax, we will seriously misstate the accounts, particularly in the year we purchase a non-current asset.

Example

Based on the example of Tyrrell above assume you are the accountant preparing the income statement* for the year ended 31 December 20X1, and that you have no knowledge or understanding of deferred tax.

*Statement of profit or loss = Income statement

Tyrrell – Statement of profit or loss (extract) for the year ended 31 December 20X1 (ignoring deferred tax)

	20X1
	$000
Profit before tax	100
Current tax at 30% (see tax comp at W1)	(21)
Profit after tax	79

To estimate the current year's tax you would need to have on file a tax computation (as below). This would involve taking current year accounting profit and first of all adding back depreciation. You would then deduct the tax allowance to get taxable profit. This is multiplied by the tax rate (here 30%) to get the current tax liability*:

Dr Statement of profit or loss* – tax expense

Cr Statement of financial position** – current tax liability

Workings

(W1) Tax computation

	20X1
	$000
Accounting profit	100
Add back depreciation	
(40/4 years)	10
Less: Capital allowances	(40)
Taxable profits	70
Current tax at 30%	21

The 'can you sleep at night?' test

By ignoring deferred tax you are presenting the accounts of Tyrrell as showing profit after tax of $79,000 (100,000 – 21,000). You prepared them – the test is – 'can you sleep at night?'.

*Statement of profit or loss = Income statement

** Statement of financial position = Balance Sheet (see page 19)

Paul Browne now wishes to buy this company and he speaks to the owner who is confident this trading outcome of $100,000 profit before tax can be delivered for the three following years using this one piece of equipment. Paul is delighted, he is not an accountant but buys the company believing next year's accounts will show profit after tax of $79,000 – just like the 20X1 accounts.

The director was true to his word, trading profit of $100,000 was indeed delivered – you again do the accounts.

Tyrrell – Statement of profit or loss* (extract) for the year ended 31 December 20X2 with comparators (still ignoring deferred tax)

	20X1	20X2
	$000	$000
Profit before tax	100	100
Current tax at 30% (W1)	(21)	(33)
Profit after tax	79	67

Oh dear! – Paul, the new owner is now grumpy!

You now have to break the news that this year the tax estimate for current tax is not the $21,000 as it was last year but an unpleasant $33,000!! – see the tax comp working below, Paul not surprisingly is not happy with you!

(W1) Tax computation

	20X1	20X2
	$000	$000
Accounting profit	100	100
Add back depreciation	10	10
Less: Capital allowances	(40)	–
Taxable profits	70	110
Current tax at 30%	21	33

*Statement of profit or loss = Income statement

In the year equipment was bought, a temporary difference artificially reduced the tax bill. This was not a permanent reduction in tax but simply a postponement – a deferral. In fact, if you look at the X1/X2/X3 and X4 accounts, you will find that if Tyrrell does make a constant trading profit of $100,000 a year for the four years, i.e. $400,000 total, it will pay $400,000 x 30% tax = $120,000.

	Year ended 31 December				Total
	20X1	20X2	20X3	20X4	
	$000	$000	$000	$000	$000
Accounting profit	100	100	100	100	400
Add back depreciation	10	10	10	10	40
Less: Capital allowances	(40)	–	–	–	(40)
Taxable profits	70	110	110	110	400
Current tax at 30%	21	33	33	33	120

The differences between the accounting profit and the taxable profit that occur from one year to another, cancel out over the four years as a whole.

If we ignore deferred tax we get the following statements of profit or loss for each period and for the four years as a whole:

	Year ended 31 December				Total
	20X1	20X2	20X3	20X4	
	$000	$000	$000	$000	$000
Profit before tax	100	100	100	100	400
Current tax at 30%	(21)	(33)	(33)	(33)	(120)
Profit after tax	79	67	67	67	280

Ignoring deferred tax produces a performance profile that appears to suggest a declining performance between 20X1 and 20X2. In fact the decline in profits is caused by the timing of the current tax charge on them. Yes, in the year the asset was bought the tax bill was pushed down to $21,000 but in the next three years it has gone up to $33,000. This is not a surprise; we know that these temporary differences arise, we know they cause a temporary deferment of tax and we should have accounted for the deferred tax if the accounts are to present fairly.

The original statement of profit or loss* we prepared did not present fairly because we have ignored the deferred tax. We have misled Paul Browne, he is right to be cross … and, no, we shouldn't have slept that night.

What should we have done to sleep soundly? Well, recognised the deferred tax of course

If we have a temporary difference we should have had a Working 2 on our file. It is not enough just to calculate the current tax, we have also to calculate the amount of tax we have deferred and to make a provision on the statement of financial position**. To get the provision on the statement of financial position* we charge the income statement*.

So what does this Working 2 look like?

We calculate a deferred tax provision based on a 'temporary difference'. We have a 'temporary difference' if the figure on the statement of financial position** – the Net book Value/Carrying Value (NBV/CV) – is different to its 'tax base', i.e. its tax written down value (WDV) – the amount that can be set against future tax bills.

This is the key working for all deferred tax questions – learn it

(W2) Deferred tax provision required for statement of financial position**

	20X1 $000
Cost – Depreciation (NBV) (40 – 10) (Carrying value)	30
Tax value (WDV) (40 – 40) (Tax base)	Nil
Temporary difference at year end	30
Closing deferred tax liability [30%]	9

---

* Statement of profit or loss = Income statement

** Statement of financial position = Balance Sheet (see page 19)

If you want a memory device for remembering this working an image-story method might work for you.

Imagine a CD on top of a TV with a teddy (TD) under the TV.

Decode it

C – D (Cost less Depreciation)

TV (Tax Value)

TD (Temporary Difference)

Where we have a temporary difference, i.e. when the cost less depreciation (the Net Book Value /carrying value of the asset) is different to the cost less tax allowances taken (tax base or tax written down value), we have a deferred tax issue. Here the temporary difference is $30, and we multiply it by the current rate of tax. This tells us the amount to provide on the statement of financial position* – $30 x 30% = $9 provision for deferred tax is required.

To achieve this we:

Dr Statement of profit or loss** – tax charge
    – transfer to deferred tax

    Cr Statement of financial position*
      – provision for deferred tax

If we had done this our statement of profit or loss** in the year we purchased the equipment would have looked like this:

Statement of profit or loss	**Tyrrell – Statement of profit or loss for the year ended 31st December 20X1 (after accounting for deferred tax)**	
		20X1
		$000
	Profit before tax	100
	Current tax (W1)	(21)
	Deferred tax (W2)	(9)
	Profit after tax	70

So, we have effectively accounted for all tax on current year transactions, whether current or deferred. This is what we mean by 'provide in full for all temporary differences', or 'use full provision method for deferred tax'. The accruals concept is being applied to tax and the tax charge is shown as 30% of accounting profit – we can once again sleep at night!!

Every accounting period would require us to revisit and recalculate any temporary differences. We calculate the required provision on the statement of financial position* and use the statement of profit or loss** entry to either increase or reduce the balance. We can illustrate this with Tyrrell's 20X2 accounts.

* Statement of profit or loss = Income statement

** Statement of financial position = Balance Sheet (see page 19)

We need to recalculate the temporary difference, noting the asset will now have been depreciated by two years and not one. This will reduce the temporary difference to 20:

(W2) Tax deferred

	20X2 $000
Cost – depreciation (40 – 10 – 10) (carrying value)	20
Tax value (40 – 40) (tax base)	Nil
Temporary difference at year end	20
Closing deferred tax liability [30%]	6
Opening deferred tax liability	(9)
So charge/(credit) to income	(3)

As the temporary difference has reduced then so does our calculation of the deferred tax provision. We already have a provision of $9,000, and we now need to reduce it to $6,000. The entries required would be:

Dr Statement of financial position** $3,000 (9,000 – 6,000)

– Provision for deferred tax

Cr Statement of profit or loss* $3,000

– Transfer from deferred tax

For the 20X2 accounts the income statement would look like this:

Tyrrell – Statement of profit or loss* for the year ended 31 December 20X2 (including deferred tax)

	20X1 $000	20X2 $000
Profit before tax	100	100
Current tax	(21)	(33)
Deferred tax	(9)	3
Profit after tax	70	70

Statement of profit or loss*

* Statement of profit or loss = Income statement

** Statement of financial position = Balance Sheet (see page 19)

No shocks here for Paul Browne!!

At 31 December 20X4 the temporary difference is gone and no deferred tax provision is required – see the four-year effect below:

(W2) Tax deferred

	Year ended 31 December			
	20X1	20X2	20X3	20X4
	$000	$000	$000	$000
Cost – Depreciation (carrying value)	30	20	10	Nil
Tax value	Nil	Nil	Nil	Nil
Temporary difference at year end	30	20	10	Nil
Closing deferred tax liability [30%]	9	6	3	Nil
Opening deferred tax liability	Nil	(9)	(6)	(3)
So charge/(credit) to income	9	(3)	(3)	(3)

The statement of profit or loss* (extracts) for the four year period including deferred tax are shown below:

	Year ended 31 December				Total
	20X1	20X2	20X3	20X4	
	$000	$000	$000	$000	$000
Profit before tax	100	100	100	100	400
Current tax	(21)	(33)	(33)	(33)	(120)
Deferred tax	(9)	3	3	3	Nil
Profit after tax	70	70	70	70	280

By accounting for deferred tax we are showing profits of $30,000 each year for the four trading periods. Total tax remains as $120,000, but the way it is being presented reflects the accounting concept of accruals.

* Statement of profit or loss = Income statement

Deferred tax assets

Most companies have deferred tax liabilities not deferred tax assets. This is because they experience temporary differences like we have just seen in Tyrrell. This means that they have an asset on the statement of financial position* whose tax base (amount that can be charged against future tax) is lower than the Net Book Value / carrying value of the asset. Therefore they have postponed tax and need a deferred tax liability on the statement of financial position*.

It is possible that the company will have a deferred tax asset, however. The most common example of a temporary difference which gives a potential asset is a company with unused tax losses. This is not shown anywhere on the company's statement of financial position* – it has a nil carrying value, but it does have a 'tax base' – it may be utilised to offset a future tax bill. But we don't just automatically put a deferred tax asset on a statement of financial position*. We would have to be convinced that the asset will be recoverable. This would mean it was probable that the company will return to profit and only then will it be able to take the benefit.

Sorry but you need to know ... DEFINITIONS

Current tax is the amount of income taxes payable (recoverable) in respect of the taxable profit (tax loss) for a period.

Temporary differences are differences between the carrying amount of an asset or liability in the statement of financial position* and its tax base. Temporary differences may be either taxable (giving rise to deferred tax liabilities) or deductible (giving rise to deferred tax assets).

The **tax base** of an asset or liability is the amount attributed to that asset or liability for tax purposes.

And the really important stuff ... accounting practice

Recognition

Current tax should be recognised as a current asset or liability.

Deferred tax is provided in full on all temporary differences (a statement of financial position* calculation approach), except for any relating to non-deductible goodwill and assets purchased that are ineligible for capital allowances.

Deferred tax assets can be created (mainly for tax losses) as long as it is probable that the asset will be recovered.

Measurement

Deferred tax must not be discounted to present value.

The tax rate used should be the one when the differences reverse, however based on legislation enacted or substantially enacted by the statement of financial position* date.

Presentation

Deferred tax is always presented as a non-current item on the statement of financial position*.

If the item giving rise to the deferred tax is in reserves (for example, a revaluation of an asset), then the deferred tax should be recognised in reserves.

The tax line in the income statement is shown as one number including both the estimate for current tax and the transfer to or from deferred tax. The detail is then disclosed in the notes.

Disclosure

There are extensive disclosure requirements for tax including a reconciliation of the accounting profit to the total tax charge.

Conclusion

There are many different circumstances that could give rise to deferred tax, and as you progress with your studies it will become an increasingly important topic. What is important is that you are clear on your understanding of what a temporary difference is. If you understand this, you can apply it to any situation, with a bit of practice.

* Statement of financial position = Balance Sheet (see page 19)

IAS 17 – Leases

Introduction

> **"The basic drives of man are few: to get enough food, to find shelter and to keep debt off the balance sheet*."**
>
> Anon

Back in Chapter 1 we talked about the concept of substance over form. Accounting statements are not about reflecting the legal form of a transaction but only about reflecting the commercial reality – economic substance. One of the 'hotspots' in financial statements is the attempt that companies sometimes make to understate the company's liabilities. Before we had an accounting standard, we had companies deliberately using leases as a means of 'off balance sheet* finance'. Instead of purchasing assets using loan finance, they leased them. Before IAS 17 existed because they were not the legal owner of the asset, neither the asset nor the obligation to make repayments under the lease terms were on the statement of financial position*

So do we have to learn IAS 17 because of accountants coming up with ways of manipulating the level of liabilities?

Absolutely! Because of this creative accounting, some lease contracts do now give rise to an asset and an associated liability on a company's statement of financial position* even though it is not the legal owner of the asset.

So ... what's it trying to achieve?

IAS 17 gives guidance on the accounting treatments for operating and finance leases for both lessors and lessees.

IFRS 13 measurement of fair value does not apply to IAS 17 transactions.

---

* Statement of financial position = Balance Sheet (see page 19)

All lease contracts under IAS 17 have to be classified. If they are classified as a finance lease, the assets are brought on the statement of financial position*. If they are classified as an operating lease, they are kept off the statement of financial position* – two radically different treatments.

Transactional example

Noonan Inc has an accounting year end of 31 December.

Noonan acquired the use of a piece of machinery for the next five years by entering into a lease contract on 1 January 20X1. To buy the machine outright would have cost Noonan $10,000.

Under the terms of the lease contract, however, Noonan has agreed to pay $2,500 in advance (i.e. on 1 January each year). The rate of interest implicit in the lease is 12.6%. The equipment has a useful economic life of five years. Noonan is required to insure the plant and cannot return it to the lessor without severe penalties.

The sort of question you may be asked would include deciding whether the above lease should be classified as an operating or a finance lease. The key to the classification is who bears substantially all the risks and rewards associated with ownership of an asset – the lessee (the user of the asset) or the lessor (the legal owner of the asset).

If the risks and rewards of ownership of the machine are with Noonan (the lessee), this would be classified as a finance lease. If the risks and rewards associated with ownership are with the lessor it will be classified as an operating lease.

Primary indicators of a finance lease

- **The lessee/the user (Noonan) has the use of the asset for the substantial majority of its economic life.**
- **The present value of guaranteed minimum lease payments is substantially all of the fair value of the asset at the start of the lease.**

The lease in the above example would classify as a finance lease.

The contract is for five years and the equipment would normally be expected to last three years – this indicates a finance lease.

---

* Statement of financial position = Balance Sheet (see page 19)

If Noonan had bought the asset outright it would have cost $10,000 – the fair value. We need to compare that to the present value of the minimum lease payments (this just means taking the cash flows to which we are committed and applying a discount factor to take account of the time value of money).

We will need a working paper therefore:

Workings

(W1) Cash flow commitment at present value

Lease payments	Date	Amount	@ PV	Present value
1.	1.1.20X1	$2,500	–	$2,500
2.	1.1.20X2	$2,500	x 1/1.126	$2,220
3.	1.1.20X3	$2,500	x $1/1.126^2$	$1,972
4.	1.1.20X4	$2,500	x $1/1.126^3$	$1,751
5.	1.1 20X5	$2,500	x $1/1.126^4$	$1,555
				$9,998

As the present value of the lease payments is substantially all of the fair value (cash price), again this indicates a finance lease.

$$\frac{\$9,998}{\$10,000} = \text{virtually } 100\%$$

The substance of the transaction is that, although Noonan is not the legal owner of the asset, it has – in commercial reality terms – acquired the asset, using a finance deal.

You may also be asked to show the impact of this transaction in the statement of financial position** and statement of profit or loss* for the year ended 31 December 20X1.

Initial recognition – what we do first

Finance leased assets are capitalised (brought on the statement of financial position**) at their fair value, or the present value of the guaranteed minimum lease payments if lower than fair value, and a lease creditor is set up for the same amount.

The ledger entry would be:

Dr Non-current assets $9,998

    Cr Obligations under a finance lease $9,998

---

* Statement of profit or loss = Income statement

** Statement of financial position = Balance Sheet (see page 19)

The non-current asset should be depreciated over the shorter of the useful economic life of the asset and the lease term. This means that thereafter the entries for the leased asset and its associated depreciation will be exactly the same as for a purchased asset.

The annual depreciation charge is $9,998/5 years = $1999.6 per annum.

What about when we pay the leasing company?

The initial payment in advance on the 1 January 20X1 is entirely a repayment of capital – it's like a deposit and means we have only effectively borrowed $7,498 ($9,998 – $2,500).

Dr Obligation under a finance lease $2,500

    Cr Cash $2,500

The balance on the obligations under a finance lease is now showing the initial $9,998 – $2,500 = $7,498. This is a loan from the leasing company on which you are going to pay 12.6% interest.

What about at the year end?

Well at the year end this interest will need to be accrued, $7,498 x 12.6% = $945. This will need to be expensed via the statement of profit or loss.

Dr Statement of profit or loss*: interest expense under a finance lease

    Cr Statement of financial position**: obligations under a finance lease – interest accrual.

You may be asked to extract from the accounts as follows:

Statement of financial position* (extract)	$
Non-current assets	
Property, plant and equipment (9,998 – 1,999.6)	7,998.4
Liabilities	
Obligations under a finance lease	
– principal outstanding	7,498 **(W2)**
– accrued interest	945 **(W2)**

*Statement of profit or loss = Income statement

** Statement of financial position = Balance Sheet (see page 19)

Statement of profit or loss* (extract)	$
Operating expense	
Depreciation	1,999.6
Finance cost	
Interest	945 (W2)

Note

To be strictly accurate you really need to show the principal outstanding liability split between current and non-current. The use of the leasing table will be the best way to do this.

(W2) Leasing table

In advance payments

Balance b/fwd	Cash paid	Capital outstanding	Interest at 12.6%	Balance c/fwd
$	$	$	$	$
9,998	(2,500)	7,498	945	8,443
8,443	(2,500)	5,943 *(this is still outstanding in 12 months time and is therefore a non-current liability)*		

To be strictly accurate therefore the statement of financial position* should show:

Statement of financial position** (extract)	$
Non-current assets	
Property, plant and equipment	
(9,998 – 1,999.6)	7,998.4
Non-current liabilities	
Obligations under a finance lease	
– principal only	5,943 (W2)
Current liabilities	
Obligations under a finance lease	
– principal outstanding (7,498 – 5,943)	1,555
– accrued interest	945 (W2)

Note

The total liability is $8,443 – made up of the $5,943 + $1,555 + $945

*Statement of profit or loss = Income statement

** Statement of financial position = Balance Sheet (see page 19)

Other potential requirements

Some questions ask for an extract, others could ask you to show the impact over the whole life of the lease. Again the leasing table will give you the numbers you need to answer this sort of question:

In advance payments

Balance b/fwd	Cash paid	Capital outstanding	Interest at 12.6%	Balance c/fwd
$9,998	(2,500)	$7,498	945	$8,443
$8,443	(2,500)	$5,943	749	$6,692
$6,692	(2,500)	$4,192	528	$4,720
$4,720	(2,500)	$2,220	280	$2,500
$2,500	(2,500)	nil	nil	nil

Statement of financial position* (extracts)

Year	1	2	3	4	5

The asset part is pretty straightforward

Non current assets	$	$	$	$	$
Leased plant					
Cost	9,998	9,998	9,998	9,998	9,998
Accumulated dep'n	(1,999.6)	(3,999.2)	(5,998.8)	(7,998.4)	(9,998)
Net Book Value	7,998.4	5,998.8	3,999.2	1,999.6	nil

* Statement of financial position = Balance Sheet (see page 19)

Use the leasing table for the liabilities

Statement of financial position*

Statement of financial position (extract)**

Non-current liabilities

Obligations under finance lease

	1	2	3	4	5
	$	$	$	$	$
– principal	5,943	4,192	2,220	nil	nil

Current liabilities

– interest	945	749	528	280	nil
– principal	1,555	1,751	1,972	2,220	nil
		(5,943-4,192)	(4,192-2,220)	(2,220-nil)	

Statement of profit or loss* (extracts)

Year	1	2	3	4	5
Operating expense	$	$	$	$	$
Depreciation	1,999.6	1,999.6	1,999.6	1,999.6	1,999.6
Finance costs					
Interest	945	749	528	280	nil

Sorry but you need to know ... DEFINITIONS

A **lease** is an arrangement whereby a lessor conveys to the lessee in return for a series of payments the right to use an asset for an agreed period of time.

A **finance lease** is a lease that substantially transfers all the risks and rewards incidental to ownership of an asset to the lessee.

An **operating lease** is a lease other than a finance lease.

---

* Statement of profit or loss = Income statement

** Statement of financial position = Balance Sheet (see page 19)

And the really important stuff ... accounting practice

 Leases must first be classified between operating and finance leases. Examples of the factors that indicate whether the risks and rewards, incidental to ownership of the leased asset lie with the lessor or lessee are:

(a) the lessee has the use of the asset for the substantial majority of its economic life

(b) the lease transfers legal title at the end of the lease term

(c) at the inception of the lease the present value of the minimum lease payments amounts to at least substantially all of the fair value of the leased asset

(d) due to criteria (a) above (which can never be met) land leases are operating leases unless legal title passes at the end of the lease term. Leases of land and buildings must be treated as two leases.

Lessee accounting

Finance leases

Finance leased assets are capitalised (brought on the statement of financial position*) at their fair value, or the present value of the guaranteed minimum lease payments if lower than fair value, and a lease obligation is set up for the same amount.

The non-current asset should be depreciated over the shorter of the useful economic life of the asset and the lease term.

Interest is allocated to the lease obligation and charged to the statement of profit or loss using either the interest rate implicit in the lease, or occasionally the sum-of-digits method. As the rental payments are made the lease obligation falls.

In numerical questions we use a leasing table to sort the numbers for us. You will need to first of all ascertain whether the lease payments are made in advance or in arrears. This is vital as it will change the calculations.

 It is a common mistake for students to not notice an in-advance payment and to treat it as a payment in arrears.

Leasing tables

 ### In arrears payments

Period	Balance b/fwd	Finance cost	Cash paid	Balance c/fwd
	X	X	(X)	X

 ### In advance payments

Period	Balance b/fwd	Cash paid	Capital outstanding	Finance cost	Balance c/fwd
	X	(X)	X	X	X

Operating leases

The rentals are charged to the statement of profit or loss* on a straight-line basis over the lease term (unless another systematic basis is more appropriate).

Lessor accounting

Finance leases

The lessor will record a receivable at the amount of the net investment in the lease (total future income less future finance costs).

---

* Statement of profit or loss = Income statement

The gross earnings under the lease should be allocated to give a constant rate of return using the net investment method.

Operating leases

The asset should be recorded in the statement of financial position** according to the nature of the asset.

Rental income should be recognised in the statement of profit or loss* on a straight-line basis over the lease term (unless another systematic basis is more appropriate).

Sale and leaseback as a finance lease

If the sale and leaseback results in a finance leaseback, any profit or loss on the sale is deferred and amortised over the shorter of the lease term and the useful economic life of the asset.

Transactional example

William owned a building on which it raised finance. William sold the building for $5 million to a finance company on 1 June 2011 when the carrying amount was $3.5 million. The same building was leased back from the finance company for a period of 20 years, which was felt to be equivalent to the majority of the asset's economic life.

The lease rentals for the period are $441,000 payable annually in arrears. The interest rate implicit in the lease is 7%. The present value of the minimum lease payments is the same as the sale proceeds.

William wishes to know how to account for the above transaction for the year ended 31 May 2012.

William has entered into a sale and lease back as a finance lease as the risks and rewards of ownership have not passed to the lessee.

The transaction is accounted for as follows.

The building is derecognised at its carrying amount with any disposal gain in this instance $1.5 million ($5m-$3.5m) being deferred over the new lease term.

Sale of building		
	$000	$000
Dr Cash	5,000	
Cr Building		3,500
Cr Deferred Income		1,500

* Statement of profit or loss = Income statement

** Statement of financial position = Balance Sheet (see page 19)

The building is then reinstated at its fair value with a finance lease obligation being established.

Reinstatement of building	$000	$000
Dr Building (finance lease)	5,000	
Cr Finance lease obligation		5,000

The building is then depreciated over the shorter of the lease term and useful economic life, so 20 years. $5,000,000/20 years = $250,000

Depreciation of asset	$000	$000
Dr Depreciation expense	250	
Cr Building (finance lease)		250

Finance lease accounting results in a liability being created, finance charge accruing at the implicit rate within the lease, in this case 7%, and the payment reducing the lease liability in arriving at the year end balance. A leasing table can be used in the normal way:

Leasing table

Date	Balance b/fwd	Finance cost 7%	Cash (rental)	Balance c/fwd
	$m	$m	$m	$m
1 June 2011	5,000	350	(441)	4909

...or as a double entry

Rentals paid	$000	$000
Dr Finance costs	350	
Dr Finance lease obligations	91	
Cr Cash		441

And finally the deferred income will be release to profit each year $1,500,000 / 20 years = $75,000

Deferred income release	$000	$000
Dr Deferred income	75	
Cr Profit or loss		75

Sale and leaseback as a operating lease

If the leaseback is an operating lease:

- if the sale is at fair value, the profit/loss should be recognised immediately
- if the sale is below fair value, any loss can be deferred and recognised over the lease term (as long as the loss is compensated by rentals at less than market value)
- if the sale is above fair value, the excess profit (above a sale at fair value) should be deferred and amortised over the lease term.

Disclosures

Some main disclosures for lessees are:

- the gross amounts for assets held under finance leases and the accumulated depreciation on those assets
- the obligations under finance leases analysed between amounts due within one year, within two to five years, and over five years
- for operating leases the total of future minimum lease payment under non-cancellable operating lease analysed between leases finishing within one year, from two to five years, and over five years.

Conclusion

IAS 17 is actually very controversial and therefore the topic of leasing is a very current issue. It is not the treatment of finance leases that is causing concern, but the treatment of operating leases which continue to be a form of off balance sheet* finance. It is likely that IAS 17 will be replaced by a standard that requires all non-cancellable leases to be brought on the statement of financial position*. For now, however, the need to classify remains.

* Statement of profit or loss = Income statement

IAS 20 – Accounting for government grants and disclosure of government assistance

Introduction

> "Never spend your money before you have it."
>
> Thomas Jefferson (1743-1826)

Without an accounting standard on government grants, we saw some very inconsistent treatments. Remember that often a company receiving a government grant is receiving it to help pay for an item of capital – plant or machinery maybe. Well, if we receive a government grant for such an item, we have a cash injection to account for (let us say $5,000,000).

We definitely:

Dr Cash $5,000,000.

But what to do with the credit!

 Without a standard we saw companies crediting the whole amount to the statement of profit or loss in the year they received the grant.

– Cr Statement of profit or loss* $5,000,000

---

*Statement of profit or loss = Income statement

Suddenly this company has made massive profits – some would argue this is seriously misleading to a reader who may believe the same will be shown in next year's accounts. If this item of plant and machinery has a useful economic life of say, five years, the accruals concept would clearly require that we spread the benefit over the five periods. A credit of $5,000,000 is unacceptable but $1,000,000 each year for the next five years? Yes, that we can live with.

IAS 20 therefore is not rocket science; it is applying basic principles to a specific area of transactions.

So ... what's it trying to achieve?

IAS 20 is explaining the accounting treatment for government assistance received by companies, and the disclosure required for the government assistance.

 ## Transactional example

Alexandra Inc acquired an item of plant at a gross cost of $800,000 on 1 January 20X6. The plant has an estimated life of ten years with a residual value equal to 15% of its gross cost. Alexandra uses straight-line depreciation and prepares accounts as at 31 December. The company received a government grant of 30% of the plant's cost price at the time of the plant's purchase. Alexandra Inc is unsure of how to account for the government grant.

As the grant relates to a capital item it would be inappropriate to take the whole $800,000 x 30% = $240,000 to the statement of profit or loss*. Instead Alexandra Inc has two options.

Option 1

Treat the cash receipt as a deferred credit, i.e.

Dr Cash $240,000

   Cr Deferred income $240,000

This will then be released to the statement of profit or loss* over the ten-year life of the plant, i.e. each statement of profit or loss for the next ten years will receive a credit of $240,000/10 = $24,000 and the deferred income account is written down:

Dr Deferred income $24,000

   Cr Statement of profit or loss* $24,000

---

* Statement of profit or loss = Income statement

Option 2

The grant would be deducted from the asset account. i.e.

Dr Cash $240,000

   Cr Asset account $240,000

> ## Note
>
> *The effect on the operating results is the same with either option, since with option 1 the grant is being directly taken to ten years' statements of profit or loss, but with option two, the same effect is achieved indirectly via a reduced depreciation charge for the next ten years.*

Sorry but you need to know ... DEFINITIONS

Government refers to government, governmental agencies and similar bodies whether local, national or international.

Government assistance is action by government designed to provide an economic benefit specific to an entity or range of entities qualifying under certain criteria.

Government grants are assistance by government given to the entity in return for past or future compliance with certain conditions relating to the operating activities of the entity.

And the really important stuff ... accounting practice

Government grants, including non-monetary grants at fair value, shall not be recognised until there is reasonable assurance that:

(a) the entity will comply with the conditions attaching to them; and

(b) the grants will be received.

Government grants should be recognised in the statement of profit or loss to match them against the expenditure to which they contribute.

Non-current asset grants – over the useful economic life of the asset.

For past costs incurred – immediately in the profit and loss account.

For current/future costs – in the period that the costs are recognised.

For non-current asset grants the standard would allow the grant to be deducted from the cost of the asset, or treated as deferred income (a liability) in the statement of financial position* and released to the statement of profit or loss over the useful economic life.

A government grant that becomes repayable shall be accounted for as a change in accounting estimate (IAS 8).

Grants towards future expenditure will be treated as deferred income when they are received and credited to the statement of profit* or loss to match against the expenditure.

 Grants can only be recognised when the conditions for their receipt have been complied with.

 Provision must be made for the repayment of grants if this is likely to happen.

Disclosure

The following should be disclosed:

- the accounting policy for grants, including the methods of presentation adopted in the financial statements
- the nature and extent of government grants recognised in the financial statements
- unfulfilled conditions and other contingencies attached to government assistance that have been recognised.

Conclusion

A full question on government grants is unlikely, but it can crop up as part of a bigger question. It is however an excellent example, if asked, of a conflict between the Framework (Chapter 1) and a standard. The IASB Framework defines liabilities as 'obligations to transfer economic benefit'. The IAS 20 treatment of allowing a government grant to be treated as a deferred credit does not meet this definition. IAS 20 is a simple application of the matching concept. Remember, if there is a conflict between the 'Framework' and a standard – then the standard prevails.

---

* Statement of profit or loss = Income statement

(16) IAS 23 – Borrowing costs

Introduction

> **"Neither a borrower nor a lender be; for loan oft loses both itself and friend; And borrowing dulls the edge of husbandry (economy)."**
>
> **William Shakespeare (1564-1616), Hamlet Act I Scene iii**

Well borrowing does have a cost – if not the loss of a friend, at a minimum we are talking about 'interest payable'. You will have prepared many statements of profit or loss' which have included the line, 'interest payable', without feeling the need to consult IAS 23. The standard treatment for interest payable has always been and continues to be … it's a 'period expense', no harder than dealing with rent payable or telephone costs. Period expenses are charged to the statements of profit or loss … well almost always!

What's the deal then? Why do we have an accounting standard?

There is a problem with the standard treatment if for example, a company chooses to, construct its new headquarters rather than buy them ready built. If you buy a building, the price you pay will include not just the costs of the bricks, mortar and labour. The seller will have built in a cost of capital (an interest cost) to the selling price. This will end up on your statement of financial position* as part of the cost of the asset.

It would seem reasonable, therefore, that if you choose to build the asset yourself, you should be able to include the cost of your own capital, i.e. the interest you are paying, in the asset account.

---

* Statement of financial position = Balance Sheet (see page 19)

So ... what's it trying to achieve?

IAS 23 prescribes the accounting treatment for borrowing costs. Generally it requires recognition as an expense, however if the borrowing cost relates to an asset that takes a substantial period of time to get ready for use or sale, the borrowing costs should be capitalised.

Transactional example

George Inc has raised a long-term loan from a bank for the purpose of constructing a major city centre complex, incorporating an art gallery, restaurants and a variety of shops. The construction is planned to take two years from the date the project is launched.

This sort of transaction would usually involve IAS 23, as the asset will take a substantial period of time to get ready for its intended use. As the borrowing costs that relate to the asset are readily identifiable they should be capitalised.

A common misunderstanding is to believe that, if an asset is expensive to purchase, it is appropriate to capitalise the borrowing costs. If the asset does not take a substantial period of time to get ready for its intended use, it would not qualify for capitalisation.

Sorry but you need to know ... DEFINITIONS

Borrowing costs are interest and other costs incurred by an enterprise in connection with the borrowing of funds. They include:

(a) interest expense calculated using the effective interest method as described in IFRS 9

(b) finance charges on finance leases recognised in accordance with IAS 17 Leases.

(c) exchange differences on foreign currency borrowings.

A **qualifying asset** is an asset that necessarily takes a substantial period of time to get ready for its intended use or sale.

And the really important stuff … accounting practice

The benchmark treatment is that borrowing costs should be recognised as an expense in the period they are incurred.

Borrowing costs directly attributable to the acquisition, construction or production of a qualifying asset are capitalised.

If general borrowings are used to finance the construction of the asset, a weighted average borrowing rate should be used to calculate the finance cost to capitalise.

Borrowing costs can only be capitalised for the period of construction, and must cease when all activities necessary to get the asset to its intended use have been completed. Capitalisation must also cease during periods when construction is suspended.

Disclosures

Key disclosures include:

- the accounting policy adopted
- the amount of borrowing costs capitalised during the period
- the capitalisation rate used to determine the amount of finance costs during the period.

Conclusion

IAS 23 is intended to improve consistency of treatment of borrowing costs and to bring some 'fairness' to the treatment of interest relating to the cost of self-constructing an asset.

IAS 33 – Earnings per share

Introduction

> **"I never knew an early rising, hard-working, prudent man, careful of his earnings and strictly honest who complained of bad luck."**
>
> **Henry Ward Beecher (1813-1887)**

We have to have a standard on earnings per share (EPS) because it is the most important accounting ratio. It forms part of the price/earnings ratio (P/E ratio) and, rightly or wrongly, the stock market places great emphasis on a company's P/E ratio and therefore a standard form of measurement of EPS is required.

The basic EPS calculation is simply $\dfrac{\text{Earnings}}{\text{Shares}}$

This should be presented as cents per share to one decimal place.

We have to have a standard that governs both calculation and disclosure, because companies will follow the calculation rules but will then sometimes do their 'own' calculations of EPS and present them with equal prominence.

It's just a ratio then?

Yes it is just a ratio – earnings means:

The amounts attributable to ordinary equity holders of the parent entity i.e.

- Profit or loss from continuing operations attributable to the parent entity; and
- Profit or loss attributable to the parent entity

These profit or loss figures should be adjusted for the after-tax amounts of preference dividends, differences arising on the settlement of preference shares, and other similar effects of preference shares classified as equity.

The figure 'earnings per share' (EPS) is used to assess the ongoing financial performance of a company from year to year, and to compute the major stock market indicator of performance, the price/earnings ratio (P/E ratio). The calculation for the P/E ratio is:

$$P/E = \frac{\text{Market value of share}}{\text{EPS}}$$

So ... what's it trying to achieve?

The aim of IAS 33 is to improve the comparison of the performance of different periods and between entities in the same period by prescribing the way EPS is to be calculated and how it is to be disclosed.

Transactional example

Here is some information relating to a listed company, Gerard Inc.

Gerard Inc

Draft Statement of profit or loss* for the year ended 31 December 20X4

	$000
Profit before tax	4,508
Taxation	(2,300)
Profit after tax	2,208

On 1 January 20X4 the issued share capital of Gerard was 9,200,000 6% preference shares of $1 each and 8,280,000 ordinary shares of $1 each.

Calculate the earnings per share (EPS) in respect of the year ended 31 December 20X4 on the basis that there was no change in the issued share capital of the company during the year ended 31 December 20X4.

Basic earnings per share *is calculated by dividing the profit or loss attributable to ordinary equity holders of the parent (the numerator) by the weighted average number of ordinary shares outstanding (the denominator) during the period.*

Basic EPS for Gerard Inc

The amount of earnings generated by the ordinary shares (i.e. exclude the preference dividend) is divided by the number of ordinary shares:

$$\frac{\$2,208,000}{8,280,000} = 26.7c$$

IAS 33 requires public companies to disclose the EPS figure on the face of the statement of profit or loss, so Gerard would disclose 26.7c as its EPS figure (called the basic EPS).

---

*Statement of profit or loss = Income statement

What if the company issues shares in the year?

Well, if the number of shares has changed during the period, a weighted average number of shares has to be used under the line.

 Transactional example

In the example of Gerard, suppose that the company had issued 3,312,000 shares at full market value on 30 June 20X4.

 This is the basic weighted average table – you must learn this.

Date	Actual number of shares	Fraction of year	Total
1 January 20X4	8,280,000	$\frac{6}{12}$	4,140,000
30 June 20X4	11,592,000 (W1)	$\frac{6}{12}$	5,796,000
Number of shares in EPS calculation			9,936,000

(W1) New number of shares

Original number	8,280,000
New issue	3,312,000
New number	11,592,000

The earnings per share for 20X4 would now be calculated as:

$$\frac{\$2,208,000}{9,936,000} = 22.2c$$

What if it was a bonus (cash free) issue?

Assume that the bonus shares have always been in issue (and therefore alter the comparative EPS amount).

 Transactional example

Suppose now that Gerard Inc made no issue of shares at full price but instead made a bonus issue on 1 October 20X4 of one ordinary share for every four shares in issue at 30 September 20X4.

A bonus issue causes no impact on earnings; but the new extra shares will cause a dilution to EPS. This will need to be reflected. EPS calculated whilst ignoring the bonus issue will need to be restated taking into account the dilutory impact.

Ignoring the bonus issue

$$\frac{2,208,000}{8,280,000} = 26.7c$$

Restated for the dilutive effect

26.7c x $\dfrac{8,280,000 \text{ (number of shares before the bonus issue)}}{10,350,000 \text{ (number of shares after the bonus issue (W1))}}$ = 21.4c

(W1) 8,280,000 × ¼ = 2,070,000 extra shares

Original number of shares 8,280,000

New number of shares 10,350,000

Ahh – but it could be a rights issue – what then?

Assume that the shares issued are a mix of bonus and full price shares. For the bonus element assume that they have always been in issue and therefore adjust the comparative.

Transactional example

Suppose now that Gerard's only share issue in 20X4 was a rights issue of $1 ordinary shares on 1 October 20X4 in the proportion of one for every five shares held at a price of $1.20. The market price for the shares on the last day of quotation cum rights was $1.80 per share.

When a rights issue takes place shares are issued at less than full market price. We treat this as a combination of a bonus issue and an issue at full market price. We will therefore need to calculate the rights issue bonus fraction by using share prices:

Rights issue bonus fraction = $\dfrac{\text{Actual cum rights price}}{\text{Theoretical ex rights price}}$

Actual cum rights price = Price of share with rights attached immediately before rights issue.

Theoretical ex rights price = Expected share price immediately after rights issue (weighted average of actual cum rights price and exercise price of rights issue shares)

In the present case, we have a rights issue made in the proportion of one for every five shares held, (i.e. for every five shares previously owned you now own six).

Rights issue bonus fraction

	$	$
5 shares at	1.80	9.00
1 share at	1.20	1.20
6 shares		10.20

$$\frac{\$10.20}{6} = \$1.7$$

Therefore rights issue bonus fraction $= \dfrac{\$1.80}{\$1.70}$

Use a table for full computation of the number of shares, as follows:

Date	Actual number of shares	Fraction of year	Rights issue bonus fraction	Total
1 January 20X4	8,280,000	$\dfrac{9}{12}$	$\dfrac{1.80}{1.70}$	6,575,294
1 October 20X4	9,936,000 (W1)	$\dfrac{3}{12}$		2,484,000
Number of shares in EPS calculation				9,059,294

This is the basic weighted average table with an additional column – you must learn this too!

A common mistake made by students is to apply the rights issue bonus fraction a second time in the second line of the table. This is wrong – apply it once at the point the rights issue takes place as that is when the dilution occurs.

$$\text{EPS} = \frac{\$2,208,000}{9,059,294} = 24.4c$$

(W1) New number of shares

8,280,000 × 1 ÷ 5	=	1,656,000 extra shares
New number of shares	=	8,280,000 + 1,656,000 = 9,936,000

Diluted earnings per share (DEPS)

This is calculated where potential ordinary shares have been outstanding during the period which would cause EPS to fall if exercised (dilutive instruments). It is calculated in addition to basic EPS.

Equity share capital may change in future owing to circumstances which exist now. Diluted EPS (DEPS) attempts to alert shareholders to the potential impact on EPS.

Potential changes may arise for any of the following reasons:

- shares not yet ranking for dividend
- convertible debt or preference shares in issue
- options granted to subscribe for new shares.

To deal with this, adjust basic earnings and number of shares assuming convertibles, options, etc had converted to equity shares on the first day of the accounting period, or on the date of issue of convertibles, options, etc if later.

Diluted earnings per share is calculated as follows:

$$\frac{\text{Earnings} + \text{Notional extra earnings}}{\text{Number of shares} + \text{Notional extra shares}}$$

The earnings should be adjusted by adding back any costs that will not be incurred once the dilutive instruments have been exercised. This will include, for example, interest on convertible debt.

The number of shares will be adjusted to take account of the exercise of the dilutive instrument. This means that adjustment is made:

For convertible instruments   By adding the maximum number of shares to be issued in the future.

For options or warrants   By adding the number of effectively 'free' shares to be issued when the options are exercised.

Some companies have more than one dilutive instrument in issue, such as both convertibles and share options. In this case diluted EPS is calculated by adding each dilutive instrument in turn, with the most dilutive first. If any instrument causes the diluted EPS figure to increase, this instrument, and any subsequent instruments, are ignored. The standard calls these antidilutive potential shares.

Transactional example

Continuing with the example of Gerard we can calculate diluted EPS on the basis that the company made no new issue of shares during the year ended 31 December 20X4, but on that date it had in issue $2,300,000 10% convertible loan stock 20X6 to 20X9. Assume a corporation tax rate of 50%.

This loan stock will be convertible into ordinary $1 shares as follows.

20X6   90 $1 shares for $100 nominal value loan stock

20X7   85 $1 shares for $100 nominal value loan stock

20X8   80 $1 shares for $100 nominal value loan stock

20X9   75 $1 shares for $100 nominal value loan stock

The earnings should be adjusted by adding back any costs that will not be incurred once the dilutive instruments have been exercised. This will include, for example, interest on convertible debt.

The number of shares will be adjusted to take account of the exercise of the dilutive instrument. This means that adjustment is made:

For convertible instruments By adding the maximum number of shares to be issued in the future.

If this loan stock was converted to shares, the impact on earnings would be as follows:

	$	$
Basic earnings		2,208,000
Add: Notional interest saved ($2,300,000 × 10%)	230,000	
Less: Tax relief $230,000 × 50%	(115,000)	
		115,000
Revised earnings		2,323,000
Number of shares if loan converted		
Basic number of shares		8,280,000
Notional extra shares under the most dilution possible		
$2,300,000 \times \dfrac{90}{100}$		2,070,000
Revised number of shares		10,350,000

$$DEPS = \frac{\$2,323,000}{10,350,000} = 22.4c$$

But it could be options outstanding?

Yes, it could, and in that case we need to add the number of effectively 'free' shares to be issued when the options are exercised.

 Transactional example

Now assume that Gerard made no issue of shares during the year ended 31 December 20X4, but on that date there were outstanding options to purchase 920,000 ordinary $1 shares at $1.70 per share. The average fair value for the year of ordinary shares was $1.80.

Options or warrants

	$
Earnings	2,208,000
Number of shares	
Basic	8,280,000
Options (W1)	51,111
	8,331,111

The DEPS is therefore $\dfrac{\$2,208,000}{8,331,111} = 26.5c$

(W1) Number of shares at option price

Options $= 920,000 \times \$1.70$

$= \$1,564,000$

At fair value: $\dfrac{\$1,564,000}{\$1.80} = 868,889$

Number issued free = 920,000 − 868,889 = 51,111

Where there are several categories of dilutive potential ordinary shares, the IAS requires that they should be taken into account in the calculation of DEPS in their order of dilution (i.e. greatest dilution first). This ensures that the worst possible DEPS figure emerges.

Sorry but you need to know ... DEFINITIONS

An **ordinary share** is an equity instrument that is subordinate to all other classes of equity instrument.

A **potential ordinary share** is a financial instrument or contract that may entitle its holder to ordinary shares.

Examples of potential ordinary shares are:

- convertible instruments
- options.

Disclosure

The disclosures are required are:

- basic and diluted EPS are presented on the face of the profit and loss*
- the numerators for each calculation should be disclosed and reconciled to the net profit or loss for the period
- the denominators should be disclosed and reconciled to each other
- a description of ordinary share transactions or potential ordinary share transaction
- any alternative measures of EPS (other than basic or diluted) must only be disclosed in the notes to the financial statements.

Conclusion

IAS 33 requires that public companies disclose both the basic EPS and the DEPS (where relevant) on the face of the income statement with equal prominence.

You must be able to calculate the basic EPS when the share capital in issue changes during the period, and also the diluted EPS when there are dilutive potential ordinary shares in issue.

* Statement of profit or loss = Income statement

18 IAS 36 – Impairment of assets

Introduction

> "Old accountants never die ... they simply lose their assets."
>
> **Traditional**

It would be incorrect if the statements of financial position* were put together and assets were carried at a figure which could not be recovered, i.e. retrieved, by the shareholders. It has always been the case that accountants believe that assets must not be carried on the statement of financial position* at more than their recoverable amount – this is nothing new.

Recoverable amount ... hmmm ... what exactly does it mean?

Well a company can recover the amount it has invested in its assets in one of two ways:

- it can opt to sell the asset to someone else, generating a net selling price i.e. fair value less costs of disposal; or
- it can trade with the asset, making stuff, selling stuff, providing some form of service and generating cash flow. If we predict cash will be generated from the asset, the asset has what we call a 'value in use'.

If the asset is on the statement of financial position* and carried at a figure bigger than the amount that we can recover from it, it is clearly 'impaired,' i.e. we need to write off some of the value. An impairment loss is therefore like an extra depreciation expense. An impairment loss is the amount by which the carrying amount of an asset or a cash generating unit exceeds its recoverable amount.

---

* Statement of financial position = Balance Sheet (see page 19)

So ... what's it trying to achieve?

IAS 36 prescribes the procedures that should be followed by a company to ensure that its assets are not held at more than their recoverable amount. The standard gives the rules to write down assets for impairment and also the circumstances when impairment can and should be reversed.

 ## Transactional example

Mary Inc is a manufacturer of cardboard boxes. However a change in the market means that the inventory produced by the machine that makes small gift boxes is being sold below its cost. Due to this impairment circumstance an impairment test needs to be carried out.

The following information is relevant:

The carrying value of the productive machinery at depreciated historical cost is $290,000 and its net selling price is estimated at $120,000. The anticipated net cash inflows from the machines are now $100,000 per annum for the next three years. A market discount rate is 10% per annum.

An impairment test does need to be carried out due to the impairment circumstance – the change in the market. The machine's carrying value will need to be compared to its recoverable amount. An impairment test needs to be set up.

Impairment test

Carrying amount	$290,000
Recoverable amount (W1)	$248,685
IMPAIRMENT LOSS	$41,315

You will need a supporting working paper to calculate recoverable amount – remember:

Recoverable amount

- they can opt to sell the asset to someone else, generating a net selling price; or
- they can trade with the asset, making stuff, selling stuff, providing some form of service and generating cash flow. If we predict cash will be generated from the asset, the asset has what we call a 'value in use'.
- If it is not possible to estimate the recoverable amount of the individual asset, an entity shall determine the recoverable amount of the cash-generating unit to which the asset belongs.

> ## Note
>
> **Recoverable amount is the greater of these two.** *A common error made by students is to use the smaller – Doh!!*

Recoverable Amount

(W1) Recoverable amount is the greater of:

Fair Value less costs to sell	Value in use			$
(Net selling price)				
$120,000	Year 1	$100,000 × 1/1.1	=	90,909
	Year 2	$100,000 × 1/1.1^2	=	82,645
	Year 3	$100,000 × 1/1.1^3	=	75,131
				————
	Value in use		=	248,685

Value in use is greater than fair value less costs to sell so, this becomes the **recoverable amount.**

This is then like additional depreciation. The carrying value needs reducing from $290,000 down to $248,685. An impairment loss of $41,315 has arisen.

Dr Statement of profit or loss* $41,315

   Cr Machinery account $41,315

Sorry but you need to know ... DEFINITIONS

An **impairment loss** is the amount by which the carrying value of an asset exceeds its recoverable amount.

 Recoverable amount of an asset or cash-generating unit is the higher of its fair value less cost of disposal and its value in use. **(Learn this!)** Cost of disposal are incremental costs directly attributable to the disposal of an asset or cash generating unit, excluding finance costs and income tax expenses.

Fair value is the price that would be received to sell an asset or paid to transfer a liability in an orderly transaction between market participants at the measurement date.

Value in use is the present value of estimated future cash flows expected to be derived from an asset or a cash generating unit.

CGU A cash-generating unit is the smallest identifiable group of assets that generates cash inflow that are largely independent of the cash inflows from other asset or group of assets.

---

* Statement of profit or loss = Income statement

Recognising the impairment loss

An impairment loss shall be recognised immediately in profit or loss, unless the asset is carried at a revalued amount. Any impairment loss of a revalued asset shall be treated as a revaluation decrease.

 Transactional example

Key holds a non-current asset, which was purchased for $10 million on 1 December 20X6 with an expected useful life of 10 years. On 1 December 20X8, it was revalued to $8.8 million. At 30 November 20X9, the asset was reviewed for impairment and written down to its recoverable amount of $5.5 million.

With a revalued asset the impairment test is working in the same way as for an asset carried on the depreciated historic cost basis

Impairment test

Carrying amount (W1)	$7,700,000
Recoverable amount	$5,500,000
IMPAIRMENT LOSS	$2,200,000

This time, however, recoverable amount is being given by the question and the student has instead to work out the carrying value (by applying IAS 16)

(W1) Carrying amount	**$m**
Cost at 1 December 20X6	10
Depreciation to 30 November 20X7 (10/10)	(1)
Carrying value /NBV as at 30 November 20X7	9
Depreciation to 30 November 20X8 (10/10)	(1)
Carrying value /NBV as at 30 November 20X8	8
Revaluation reserve created 1 December 20X8 (8.8m - = 8m)	0.8
Carrying value/NBV as at 1 December 20X8	8.8
Depreciation of revalued amount	(1.1)
(remember you start again depreciating the revalued amount over its remaining UEL) (8.8/8 years)	
Carrying value/ NBV as at 30 November 20X9	**7.7**

So the impairment loss is $2,200,000 million but because this is a revalued asset the treatment of the impairment loss is different.

An impairment loss on a revalued asset is recognised in other comprehensive income to the extent that the impairment loss does not exceed the amount in the revaluation surplus for the same asset. Such an impairment loss on a revalued asset reduces the revaluation surplus for that asset.

So with regard to Key, in order to know how to treat the $2,200,000 impairment loss we need to again be solid on IAS 16, and be able to identify the balance on the revaluation reserve, in regards to this asset.

Revaluation reserve			
	$m		**$m**
Reserve transfer	0.1	Asset revalued on	0.8
(0.8/8years)		1 December 20X8 (W1)	
Bal c/fwd	0.7		
	0.8		0.8

See Chapter 7 – IAS 16, if you need a reminder of that reserve transfer

The impairment loss needs splitting therefore between OCI and Profit		
	$m	**$m**
DR Revaluation reserve (and report in OCI)	0.7	
DR Statement of profit or loss (2.2-0.7)	1.5	
CR Non-current asset account		2.2

Cash generating units (CGUs) and goodwill

If there is any indication that an asset may be impaired, recoverable amount shall be estimated for the individual asset. If it is not possible to estimate the recoverable amount of the individual asset, an entity shall determine the recoverable amount of the cash generating unit to which the asset belongs.

For example, a mining entity owns a private railway to support its mining activities. The private railway could be sold only for scrap value and it does not generate cash inflows that are largely independent of the cash inflows from the other assets of the mine.

The recoverable amount of the private railway cannot be determined and is probably different from its scrap value. The railway will need to be grouped with the mines other assets and tested as a cash-generating unit.

Transactional example

Path owned a 100% subsidiary, Taylor, that is treated as a cash generating unit. On 31 March 20X2, there was an industrial accident (a gas explosion) that caused damage to some of Taylor's plant. The assets of Taylor immediately before the accident were:

	$000
Goodwill	1,800
Patent	1,200
Factory building	4,000
Plant	3,500
Receivables and cash	1,500
	12,000

As a result of the accident, the recoverable amount of Taylor is $6.7 million

The explosion destroyed (to the point of no further use) an item of plant that had a carrying amount of $500,000.

Taylor has an open offer from a competitor of $1 million for its patent. The receivables and cash are already stated at their fair values less costs to sell (net realisable values).

A cash-generating unit to which goodwill has been allocated shall be tested for impairment annually, and whenever there is an indication that the unit may be impaired, by comparing the carrying amount of the unit, including the goodwill, with the recoverable amount of the unit.

The impairment loss shall be allocated to reduce the carrying amount of the assets of the unit in the following order:

(a) first, to reduce the carrying amount of any goodwill allocated to the CGU

(b) then, to other assets in the CGU pro rata on the basis of the carrying amount of each asset.

Note

Never reduce an asset under the amount by which it could be recovered. These accounts will be 'protected' from the impairment pro rata exercise.

So for Taylor, the receivables and cash are already stated at net realisable value. This is therefore a 'protected account' as the receivables are collectable and cash – well $20 should be worth $20- don't consider allocating impairment losses against cash (or bank for that matter!).

An impairment loss working for a CGU is basically the same as for an individual asset, except you need a table as you have a group of assets.

The starting point is to compare the carrying values in total to the recoverable amount in total – see below.

Impairment loss table for CGU

	Carrying amount	Recoverable amount	Impairment loss
	$000	$000	$000
Goodwill	1,800		
Patent	1,200		
Factory building	4,000		
Plant	3,500		
Receivables and cash	1,500		
	12,000	6,700 *(told in question)*	

The impairment loss should be charged to the income statement*, but a decision has to made which assets are written down based on the IAS 36 rules

The plant with a carrying value of $500,000 should be written off as it has been damaged to the point of no further use. (It no longer meets the definition of an asset.)

The protected account of receivables and cash will not be written down at all.

Impairment loss table (skeleton) continued

	Carrying amount	Recoverable amount	Impairment loss
	$000	$000	$000
Goodwill	1,800		
Patent	1,200		
Factory building	4,000		
Plant	3,500	3,000	500
Receivables and cash	1,500	1,500	nil
	12,000	6,700 *(told in question)*	

We have a remaining impairment loss of $4,800,000 (5,300 - 500) to be allocated on the IAS 36 rules – first to goodwill which reduces it to nil. The patent can only have $200,000 written off, because any more reduction would drop it below its recoverable amount.

---

* Statement of profit or loss = Income statement

Impairment loss table (skeleton) continued

	Carrying amount	Recoverable amount	Impairment loss
	$000	$000	$000
Goodwill	1,800	nil	1,800
Patent	1,200	1,000	200
Factory building	4,000		
Plant	3,500	3,000	500
Receivables and cash	1,500	1,500	nil
	12,000	6,700 *(told in question)*	5,300

This leaves an impairment loss of $2,800,000 (5,300,000 - 500,000 – 1,800,000 - 200,000) to be allocated on the pro rata basis.

The accounts available are the factory building and the remaining plant balance. These give you your 'base' position.

Pro rata

	Carrying amount	Impairment loss on pro rata basis	Recoverable amount
	$000	$000	$000
Factory building	4,000	(1,600)	2,400
Plant (3,500- 500)	3,000	(1,200)	1,800
Base for pro rata	7,000		

Pro rata

2,800 x 4,000/7,000 = 1,600 allocated to Factory building account

2,800 x 3,000/7,000 = 1,200 allocated to Plant account

So your full answer looks like this:

Impairment loss table (CGU)

	Carrying amount	Recoverable amount	Impairment loss
	$000	$000	$000
Goodwill	1,800	nil	1,800
Patent	1,200	1,000	200
Factory building	4,000	2,400	1,600
Plant - damaged	500	nil	500
Plant – remaining balance (3,500-500)	3,000	1,800	1,200
Receivables and cash	1,500	1,500	nil
	12,000	6,700 *(told in question)*	5,300

Corporate assets

Corporate assets include group or divisional assets such as a headquarters of the entity. The distinctive characteristics of corporate assets are that they do not generate cash inflows independently of other assets or groups of assets.

The recoverable amount of an individual corporate asset cannot be determined unless management has decided to dispose of the asset. As a consequence, if there is an indication that a corporate asset may be impaired, its recoverable amount is determined for the cash-generating unit or group of cash generating units to which the corporate asset belongs.

In testing a cash-generating unit for impairment, an entity shall identify all the corporate assets that relate to the cash-generating unit under review. If a portion of the carrying value of a corporate asset can be allocated on a reasonable and consistent basis to that unit, the entity should include that portion when comparing to recoverable amount.

Reversing an impairment loss

Note

It is never acceptable to reverse an impairment loss on goodwill

For assets other than goodwill, the entity shall assess at the end of each reporting period whether there is any indication that an impairment loss recognised in prior periods may no longer exist or may have decreased.

If there is a positive change in the estimates used to determine the asset's recoverable amount, the asset can be increased to its recoverable amount.

This is termed a reversal of an impairment loss and is recognised immediately in profit or loss (except for a revalued asset which is treated as a revaluation increase and recognised in OCI). However if an impairment loss on a revalued asset was partially recognised in profit or loss, a reversal of that impairment loss is also recognised in profit or loss.

Note

When you reverse an impairment loss be sure you do not increase the asset above the carrying value that would have been determined (i.e. cost less depreciation) had no impairment loss been recognised in prior years.

Transactional example

Cambridge Inc had purchased non-current assets in a development area, which are carried at cost less depreciation. These assets cost $3 million on 1 June 20X0 and are depreciated on the straight-line basis over their useful life of five years. An impairment review was carried out at 31 May 20X1 and the projected cash flows relating to these assets were as follows:

	Cash flow	@ PV	Present Value
	$000		$000
31 May 20X2	280	1/1.05	267
31 May 20X3	450	1/1.052	408
31 May 20X4	500	1/1.053	431
31 May 20X5	550	1/1.054	452
Total			1,558

Impairment test at 31 May 20X1

Carrying value (3,000,000- 600,000 depn)	$2,400,000
Recoverable amount	$1,558,000
IMPAIRMENT LOSS	$842,000

However at 30th November 20X1 the directors used the same cash flow projections and noticed the resultant value in use was above the carrying value of the assets. They wish to reverse the impairment loss recognised at 31 May 20X1.

The directors will not be able to reverse this impairment loss because there is no positive change in the estimated cash flows used to determine recoverable amount. The figure is increasing simply because of the time value of money.

Disclosures

Extensive disclosures are required for impaired assets including:

- the amounts of impairment losses recognised
- segmental information
- how the recoverable amounts have been calculated
- information on the reversal of impairment losses
- a description of the cash-generating unit, the amount if impairment loss recognised or reversed by class of asset.

Conclusion

IAS 36 is an important standard. It is frequently examined and often carries lots of marks. Learn the basics and apply to past questions set by your examiner.

IAS 40 – Investment property

Introduction

> **"An investment in knowledge pays the best interest."**
>
> Benjamin Franklin (1706–1790)

Well, although the idea in the quote is lovely, many companies like many individuals decide instead to invest in property. We, as accountants, do have to recognise that the IAS 16 basis of accounting for property may not be appropriate when the property is not being used to operate/trade from, but is instead held for its investment potential. The requirement for depreciation seems a bit silly in this case.

Not all properties are the same then?

Exactly – we have to have an alternative treatment for some properties, if the accounts are to present fairly. IAS 40 gives companies that opportunity.

So ... what's it trying to achieve?

IAS 40 prescribes the accounting treatment for investment property and the related disclosure requirements.

A company may only use IAS 40 to account for a property when the definition of an investment property is met. Otherwise another accounting standard must be applied – maybe IAS 16 or indeed IAS 2, if the asset is in fact 'inventory' (see transactional example).

Transactional example

Munchkin Inc has the following properties and it is not sure which accounting standard is applicable.

- *Factory held by Munchkin Inc for use in production of its goods.*
- *Land held by Munchkin Inc, unused at present, no plans to sell.*
- *An empty building owned by Munchkin Inc and to be leased out using an operating lease.*

A factory held by a company for use in production should not be accounted for under IAS 40, because it is owner-occupied. It is a non-current asset – property per IAS 16.

The land however would qualify as an investment property under IAS 40, as indeed would the empty building leased out under an operating lease.

 A common mistake is to treat an owner-occupied building as an investment property because of its capital appreciation potential.

Sorry but you need to know ... DEFINITIONS

Investment property is property (land or a building – or part of a building – or both) held (by the owner or by the lessee under a finance lease) to earn rentals or for capital appreciation or both, rather than for:

(a) use in the production or supply of goods and services or for administrative purposes; or

(b) sale in the ordinary course of business.

Properties held under operating leases may be investment properties if, and only if, the property would otherwise meet the definition of an investment property and the lessee uses the fair value model.

Owner-occupied property is property held (by the owner or by the lessee under a finance lease) for use in the production or supply of goods and services or for administrative purposes.

And the really important stuff ... accounting practice

Investment properties should be recognised as assets when, and only when:

(a) it is probable that the future economic benefits will flow to the enterprise; and

(b) the cost can be measured reliably.

Investment properties should initially be measured at cost. Fair value is the price that would be received to sell an asset or paid to transfer a liability in an orderly transaction between market participants at the measurement date.

 Subsequent measurement of investment properties should follow the **preferred fair value model** or the alternative cost model.

Fair value model	Cost model
• The investment properties are revalued to fair value at each statement of financial position* date. The fair value shall reflect market conditions at the end of the reporting period.	• The investment properties are held using the benchmark method in IAS 16 (cost) unless asset is classified as held for sale (IFRS 5)
• Gains or losses on revaluation are recognised directly in the statement of profit or loss** for the period in which it arises.	• The properties are depreciated like any other asset
• The properties are not depreciated	• An entity that chooses the cost model discloses the fair value of its investment property.

Transfers into and out of investment property should only be made when supported by a change of use of the property.

What is an investment property?

An investment property is a property held to earn rentals or for capital appreciation – held for its investment potential

A property that is owner-occupied should not be treated under IAS 40 as IAS16 applies

---

* Statement of financial position = Balance Sheet (see page 19)

** Statement of profit or loss = Income statement

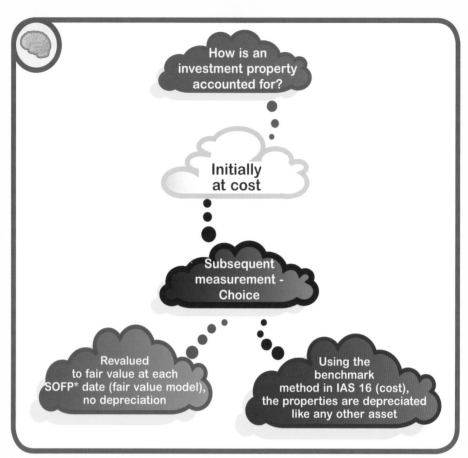

Disclosures

Key disclosures include:

- whether the fair value or cost model has been followed
- if following the fair value model whether any assets held under operating leases have been classified as investment properties
- the methods and significant assumptions in determining fair values
- the extent of valuations performed by an independent professionally qualified valuer
- the amounts recognised in profit or loss* for:
  - rental income
  - direct operating expenses.
- reconciliations of the movement in the investment property on the statement of financial position** (for both property held under the fair value and the cost models).

There are other specific disclosures for properties held under both the fair value or cost models.

Conclusion

Again this is a standard that is not an 'exam dealbreaker'. It is likely to be part of a bigger exam question rather than a full blown question.

---

*Statement of profit or loss = Income statement

** Statement of financial position = Balance Sheet (see page 19)

IFRS 5 – Non-current assets held for sale and discontinued operations

Introduction

> "Ah! this is the one we use when companies decide to stop doing the stuff they used to do ... isn't it?"
>
> Anon accounting student

Well to be fair that quote just about sums it up – companies stop doing stuff they used to do. For most sets of accounts that you prepare you will use IAS 16 to account for property, plant and equipment. If, however, you are looking at a question where you are told the company has committed to stop doing stuff, 'discontinues an activity' or plans to sell a building, for example then you may also have to consider whether IFRS 5 will apply. The questions you would need to ask include:

- is the building available for immediate sale?
- is it being actively marketed at a price that makes the sale highly probable?

If the answer to both is yes, then an alternative treatment of the asset may be available under IFRS 5.

So some owned assets are accounted for under IAS 16, some under IAS 40, and now you're telling us some are under IFRS 5 ... big sigh!!

Sorry you are right: most owned assets are accounted for under IAS 16, fewer are treated as 'investment properties' under IAS 40 and fewer still, but still relevant, are those 'held for sale' under IFRS 5.

Under IAS 16 the building will be depreciated over its remaining useful economic life (UEL) in the usual way. If, however, IFRS 5 applies and it gets classed as 'held for sale', the building will not need to be depreciated.

So ... what's it trying to achieve?

IFRS 5 was the first exposure draft issued by the IASB in its convergence project with US GAAP. As such its requirements are driven by US GAAP. Its aim is to give guidance on the presentation of non-current assets held for sale and to give rules on discontinued operations.

Transactional example

The board of Alfie Inc approved a plan to sell its head office site, both land and buildings. A new head office has been acquired and the staff have moved across. The old site, including renovated vacant buildings are being offered for sale via a local real estate dealer. The board is not sure how to deal with the old head office in the accounts.

Under IFRS 5, a non current asset should be classified as 'held for sale' if its carrying amounts will be recovered principally through a sale transaction rather than its continuing use. The criteria which have to be met are:

M	Management committed to a plan
A	Actively trying to find a buyer and marketing assets
A	Assets available for immediate sale
S	Sale is highly probable, and
S	Sale expected to complete within one year of classification.

Remember the acronym – **MAASS** or maybe you prefer mnemonics:

Management accountant available – seriously sexy!!

Non-current assets held for sale should not be depreciated. The assets should be measured at the lower of carrying amount and fair value, less costs to sell on and depreciation on such assets to cease.

Be careful with these transactions. Just having gone to an estate agent/real estator doesn't make it held for sale – it will have to be priced so it is realistically expected to sell in order to meet the criteria. This is a controversial standard as it is believed it can be used for manipulation – with regard to non-depreciation of assets.

Sorry but you need to know ... DEFINITIONS

A **component of an entity** is operations and cash flows that can be clearly distinguished, operationally and for financial reporting purposes, from the rest of the entity.

A **disposal group** is a group of assets to be disposed of, by sale or otherwise, together as a group in a single transaction, and liabilities directly associated with those assets that will be transferred in the transaction. The group includes goodwill acquired in a business combination if the group is a cash-generating unit to which goodwill has been allocated in accordance with IAS 36.

And the really important stuff ... accounting practice

Non-current assets held for sale

Non-current assets held for sale, and assets and liabilities to be disposed of together in a single transaction (a disposal group) should be separately presented on the statement of financial position*. The assets and liabilities in a disposal group should not be offset however.

The IFRS gives the same criteria for distinguishing assets held for sale or a disposal group as in SFAS 144 (i.e. the US equivalent accounting standard):

- management committed and actively marketing assets
- assets available for immediate sale
- very unlikely to withdraw from the plan and
- sale expected to complete within one year of classification.

The assets should be measured at the lower of carrying amount and fair value less costs to sell.

* Statement of financial position = Balance Sheet (see page 19)

Discontinued operations

 A discontinued operation is a component of an entity:

- that either has been disposed of or is classified as held for sale
- is part of a single co-ordinated plan to dispose of a separate major line of business or geographical area of operations or
- is a subsidiary acquired exclusively with a view to resale

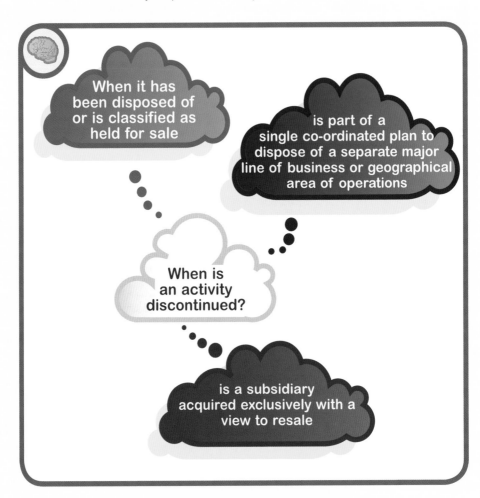

A component of an entity may be a segment (under IFRS 8), a cash-generating unit (IAS 36) or a subsidiary.

The revenue, expenses, pre-tax profit or loss and the income tax expense of the discontinued operations should be separately presented on the face of the income statement* or in the notes to the accounts. The face of the statement of profit or loss* must include, as a minimum, the profit or loss of discontinued operations.

* Statement of profit or loss = Income statement

The cash flows from operating, investing and financing should be separately disclosed on the face or in the notes.

Components of an entity that are abandoned are subject to the same disclosure requirements as those disposed when the abandonment occurs. Assets abandoned (as opposed to components of an entity) are not discontinued operations.

Conclusion

The analysis regarding discontinued activities is key if users of accounts are to be presented with relevant information. When a company discontinues an activity, a purchaser of shares needs to know about it if the results are to be understandable.

* Statement of financial position = Balance Sheet (see page 19)

(21) IAS 32 – Financial instruments: presentation

Introduction

> "There are three types of accountants - those who can count and those who can't".
>
> Anon

IAS 32 is a companion standard to IFRS 9: They both deal with financial instruments. Whenever a company raises finance, it issues a financial instrument. Sometimes they raise finance by issuing shares – equity finance; sometimes they issue loan notes or debentures or the like – debt finance.

The fundamental principle of IAS 32 is that when a company raises finance by issuing a financial instrument, the instrument should be classified as either a financial liability or an equity instrument according to the substance of the contract, not its legal form.

So ... when a company raises finance, we have to classify as debt or equity – is that it?

Well, it's actually a very big area and it covers the accounting from the other side also, i.e. for every company that raises finance some other company has to provide it. Every time somebody issues debentures, somebody purchases an investment. Financial instruments are assets as well as equity/liabilities. The definition of financial instruments is:

Any contract that gives rise to a financial asset of one entity and a financial liability or equity instrument of another entity.

However a good starting point for a student is with the raising of finance, and the need to classify as debt or equity.

Principle

In summary, when an issuer determines whether a financial instrument is a financial liability or an equity instrument, the instrument is an equity instrument **if, and only if,** both conditions (a) and (b) are met.

(a) The instrument includes no contractual obligation:

  (i) to deliver cash or another financial asset to another entity; or

  (ii) to exchange financial assets or financial liabilities with another entity under conditions that are potentially unfavourable to the issuer.

(b) If the instrument will or may be settled in the issuer's own equity instruments, it is:

  (i) a non-derivative that includes no contractual obligation for the issuer to deliver a variable number of its own equity instruments; or

  (ii) a derivative that will be settled by the issuer exchanging a fixed amount of cash or another financial asset for a fixed number of its own equity instruments. For this purpose, the issuer's own equity instruments do not include instruments that are themselves contracts for the future receipt or delivery of the issuer's own equity instruments.

> ## Note
>
> *The full rule from the standard is quite scary, for many exams you will just need to know the following:*
>
> ## The instrument is an equity instrument if it includes no contractual obligation
>
> *You will not usually need to understand derivatives until higher level papers - see the red section, once you have covered financial instruments at 'green' level!*

> ## So ... what's it trying to achieve?
>
> *The objective of the Standard is to establish principles for presenting financial instruments as liabilities or equity and for offsetting financial assets and financial liabilities. It applies to the classification of financial instruments, from the perspective of the issuer, into financial assets, financial liabilities and equity instruments; the classification of related interest, dividends, losses and gains; and the circumstances in which financial assets and financial liabilities should be offset.*

> ## Transactional example
>
> *Let us assume that MJF Inc issues preference (preferred) shares that pay a fixed rate of dividend and have a mandatory redemption feature at a future date.*

In some GAAP regimes, these would have been treated by their legal form as 'shares', although commonly disclosed separately as 'non-equity' shares.

Under IAS 32, the substance, not legal form, is reflected. In substance, there is a contractual obligation to deliver cash and, therefore, they should be recognised as a liability. The payment of this fixed rate dividend is not in fact a dividend, but should be treated as interest.

Compound financial instruments

The issuer of a financial instrument shall evaluate the terms of the financial instrument to determine whether it contains both a liability and an equity component. Such components shall be classified separately as financial liabilities, financial assets or equity instruments. Read the transaction, Sonya Inc below. It is a typical IAS 32 transaction. Look at the bubbles to help understand the terminology.

The word **issued** is important. This means Sonya Inc is raising finance. If they were providing finance, they would have purchased the instrument.

Sonya Inc can either issue these instruments:

At par - meaning they raise the face value of the instrument; or

At a discount - meaning they raise less than the nominal value

Transactional example

*Sonya Inc has **issued** 10,000 6% convertible bonds at a **par** value of $100 on 1st January 20X1. It is a two year instrument and interest is payable annually in arrears. The market rate of interest for similar debt without the conversion option is **8%**.*

Each bond is convertible into 4 shares in 2 years time.

Required

*Calculate the liability and equity element of the **convertible** bond.*

The fact the instrument is **convertible** means it is a compound instrument..

It is a liability and the purchasers can choose to have their $1,000,000 dollars back in 2 years, but the option to convert to shares means an equity element exists.

Without the option to convert Sonya Inc would have had to pay market interest on the loan, which is **8%**.

Because they built in a conversion option, they are only having to pay 6%

Splitting the proceeds (split accounting)

By issuing this instrument Sonya Inc has raised $1,000,000. 10,000 bonds issued at a par of $100 each equals $1,000,000. (10,000 x $100).

As this is clearly a compound instrument... you need to split the proceeds between the debt element and the equity element.

First of all you need to identify what cash flows you are now committed to:

1. It is a 2 year instrument paying 6% interest each year. This is known as 'coupon rate' and is a legal obligation for Sonya Inc.

   $1,000,000 x 6% = $60,000 for each of the two years.

2. At the end of the 2 years the holders can opt to have the principle repaid in cash (the conversion option, is just that..i.e. optional). It should not be anticipated.

   $1,000,000 is to be repaid on 31 December 20X2

These cash flows then need discounting to present value using the market rate of interest for similar loans, without the conversion option.

Date		Cash flow	Discounted	Present value
		$		$
31st December 20X1	Interest	60,000	$1/1.08$	55,556
31st December 20X2	Interest and capital repayment	1,060,000	$1/1.08^2$	908,779
Total liability component				964,335
Total proceeds				1,000,000
Equity element β				35,665
(equity is the residual, i.e. balancing figure (1,000,000 - 964,335))				

Note

Some examiners will give you discount factors for calculating the present value of a future cash flow. Some will not and you will need to default to using a '1 over 1 point the interest rate' style calculation (as in 1/1.08 here). As time elapses you will also need to take it on a year using your power button.

If financial instruments are examinable for you, make sure you use a scientific calculator.

Initial Recognition

Dr Bank (cash)	$1,000,000
Cr Liabilities	$964,335
Cr Equity β	$35,665

The issuer

If you raise finance you issue a financial instrument (bond, debenture, loan note, shares etc).

The holder

If you provide the finance you are the purchaser of the financial instrument (bondholder, debenture holder, noteholder, shareholder etc).

The issuer receives the cash.

The issuer records either a financial liability or equity.

The holder provides the cash.

The holder records a financial asset.

Sorry but you need to know ... DEFINITIONS

Financial instrument

Any contract that gives rise to a financial asset of one entity and a financial liability or equity instrument of another entity.

Financial asset

Any asset that is:

- cash
- a contractual right to receive cash or another financial asset from another entity
- a contractual right to exchange financial instruments with another entity under conditions that are potentially favourable; or
- an equity instrument of another entity.

Financial liability

A liability that is a contractual obligation:

- to deliver cash or another financial asset to another entity; or
- to exchange financial instruments with another entity under conditions that are potentially unfavourable.

Equity instrument

Any contract that evidences a residual interest in the assets of an entity after deducting all of its liabilities.

And the really important stuff ... accounting practice

Presentation

Equity and liabilities should be presented on the statement of financial position* following the substance of the instruments. If an instrument contains an obligation to pay out cash it is a financial liability. Preference shares are therefore often financial liabilities.

Compound instruments (those with both debt and equity elements) issued such as convertible debentures are 'split' accounted. This means the proceeds are recognised as debt and a separate equity option. The debt is measured by discounted cash flows and the equity is the residual of the proceeds.

Treasury shares

If an entity reacquires its own equity instruments, those instruments ('treasury shares') shall be deducted from equity. No gain or loss shall be recognised in profit or loss on the purchase, sale, issue or cancellation of an entity's own equity instruments. Such treasury shares may be acquired and held by the entity or by other members of the consolidated group. Consideration paid or received shall be recognised directly in equity.

Transactional example

Jupiter Inc has the following statement of financial position:

	$m
Assets	8,000
	8,000
Equity share capital $1	4,000
Share premium	1,000
Retained earnings	3,000
	8,000

Jupiter has decided to purchase 100,000 shares for $360,000 but has not cancelled them at the end of the reporting period.

The standard does not state exactly where the debit entry should go, just that it must be recognised in equity so some entities use a specially created reserve, they call 'treasury shares' or some other distributable reserve (i.e. retained earnings). If your examiner does not tell you in the exam question which reserve to use I suggest you create one and call it 'treasury shares'.

So here we would

Dr Treasury shares $360,000

    Cr Bank (cash) $360,000

So your statement of financial position would now look like this:

SOFP

Statement of financial position* (extract) as at 31 December 20X1

	$m
Assets	7,640
	7,640
Equity share capital $1	4,000
Share premium	1,000
Treasury shares	(360)
Retained earnings	3,000
	7,640

Interest, dividends, gains and losses

Interest, dividends, gains and losses treatment follow the presentation on the statement of financial position*. If a preference share is treated as a debt instrument, any dividends paid on that share are treated as interest charges.

Offsetting a financial asset and financial liability

Financial assets and liabilities should be offset on the statement of financial position* if:

(a) there is a legally enforceable right; and

(b) there is an intention to settle on a net basis, or to realise the asset and settle the liability simultaneously.

Conclusion

As mentioned, IAS 32 is really a companion standard to IFRS 9. You really need to study them both as a single topic. IAS 32 covers presentation issues, but in order to know about measurement we need to look at IFRS 9. Studying IAS 32 in isolation is therefore liable to give incomplete answers. All disclosures are now covered by IFRS 7.

---

* Statement of financial position = Balance Sheet (see page 19)

IFRS 9 – Financial instruments: the basics

Introduction

> "Annual income twenty pounds, annual expenditure nineteen nineteen and six, result happiness.
>
> Annual income twenty pounds, annual expenditure twenty pounds ought and six, result misery."
>
> Charles Dickens (1812-1876) David Copperfield

For a start, there is no point reading this chapter unless you have read the one on IAS 32. That chapter covered the issue of a company raising finance, and the need to classify the financial instrument as either a liability (debt finance) or equity (shares).

IFRS 9 does not address accounting for equity instruments issued by the reporting entity, but it does deal with accounting for financial liabilities, and therefore classification of an instrument as a liability or as equity is critical. **IAS 32 Financial instruments: presentation** addresses the initial classification question.

Some exam boards are still examining the old IAS 39 rules and for that reason the old standard continues to be included - see the red section of this book if that includes you (check your list of examinable documents).

So ... what's it trying to achieve?

The objective of this IFRS is to establish principles for the financial reporting of **financial assets** and **financial liabilities** that will present relevant and useful information to users of financial statements for their assessment of the amounts, timing and uncertainty of an entity's future cash flows.

Classification of financial liabilities

Once you have decided the company has raised finance and you will be classifying the instrument issued as a financial liability, then IFRS 9 will apply.

We then have a further classification issue:

IFRS 9 recognises two classes of financial liabilities:

- financial liabilities measured at amortised cost using the effective interest method.
- financial liabilities at fair value through profit or loss

Most financial liabilities are measured on the statement of financial position* using the standard amortised cost method.

However the fair value through profit and loss account** method may be appropriate if you are looking at liabilities created by a derivative contract (forward contracts, futures, options and swaps), or are experiencing an 'accounting mismatch'.

Note

This chapter covers the basics, including the common method of accounting for financial liabilities that is called amortised cost.

Derivative contracts and 'accounting mismatches'

If you are studying a more advanced paper that covers liabilities measured at fair value through profit or loss and the derivative contracts mentioned above you will need the more advanced chapter in the red section.

Other rules also apply to financial liabilities as a result of a financial guarantee contract or a commitment to provide a loan at a below-market interest rate. These exceptions are also covered in the 'red section' of this book.

Amortised cost using the effective interest rate method

A company will usually classify their borrowings as 'financial liabilities measured at amortised cost using effective interest rates'. This is a really important accounting transaction that you will be examined on in multiple situations.

One of the reasons why some students don't like these transactions is simply because the terminology can seem very confusing.

---

* Statement of financial position = Balance Sheet (see page 19)

** Statement of profit or loss = Income statement

Let us have a look at a standard transaction and make sure you are clear with regards to the language used.

Read through the transaction. This is a very standard exam style transaction.

The bubbles should then help you get to grips with what it is all about!

The word **issues** is very important. This is how you identify that Aidan Inc is raising finance and has a financial liability. If they had a financial asset they would have acquired a financial instrument.

Aidan Inc will not necessarily raise the **nominal** value in cash. They can either issue:
At par - meaning the nominal value is raised; or

At a discount - meaning they raise less than the nominal value.

Transactional example

Amortised cost

*Aidan Inc **issues** a financial instrument with a **nominal value** of $200,0000 for a cash injection of $157,763. It agrees to pay an annual **coupon rate** of 4% (i.e. **$200,000** x 4% = $8,000 each year) and it will be required to repay $200,000 in five years time.*

*The **effective** 'real' **interest rate** is 9.5%.*

$157,763 is the amount of cash Aidan Inc will receive. The instrument has been issued at a discount to its 'par' face value.

$200,000 is the amount Aidan Inc will have to repay.

The **coupon rate** is the legal requirement that an entity has to comply with. So Aidan Inc has to pay 4% x 200,000 (Coupon rate is applied to nominal value.) This is paid each year.

The **effective interest rate** is higher than the coupon rate of 4% because it takes into account the 'backloaded interest' that exists due to issuing the instrument for $157,763 but having to repay $200,000.

The 9.5% is usually given in the question but it represents an exact discounting of the future cash payments through the life of the instrument.

Do not worry about calculating it.

IAS 32 would classify the financial instrument issued by Aidan as a debt instrument – a liability, as Aidan Inc has an obligation to transfer economic benefit – both interest and on redemption. As it is a liability not equity, IFRS 9 also applies.

This will normally be classified by IFRS 9 as 'financial liability to be measured at amortised cost'. A company's borrowings are usually in this class.

Initial recognition

Financial assets and liabilities should be recognised when the company becomes party to the contractual provisions of the instrument. The asset or liability is measured at fair value – the actual transaction price on the reporting date, i.e. Aidan Inc would:

Cr Bank (cash)	$157,763
Cr Liability account	$157,763

Subsequent measurement – amortised cost

This financial liability would then be measured at 'amortised cost', This means the liability is remeasured at every reporting date. It is also very important to remember that coupon rate interest is not used for the finance charge in the statement of profit or loss*. Instead we apply substance over form and charge the effective rate of interest (9.5%). The first year's income statement is charged with $157,763 x 9.5% = $14,988 interest payable.

We are effectively divorcing the charge in the statement of profit or loss* with the amount going through the cash flow statement. The difference is what is called 'rolled up' or 'back loaded' interest' and is added to the loan account, i.e. Aidan would:

Dr Finance costs	$14,988
Cr Bank (cash)	$8,000 (4% x $200,000)
Cr Loan account – 'rolled up interest'	$6,988

At the reporting date the liability would show as $164,751 (157,763 + 6,988).

We would commonly use an 'amortised cost table' to calculate this:

Period	Amount borrowed	Finance cost (at 9.5%) for SOPL	Cash repayment 4% (200,000)	Rolled up interest	Bal c/fwd – liability for SOFP*
	$	$	$	$	$
1	157,763	14,988	(8,000)	6,988	164,751

For many questions, you only need one row in your table. If all you are asked for is an extract from this year's accounts, you now have information for both the statement of profit or loss* and the statement of financial position**. You might be asked to show

---

* Statement of profit or loss = Income statement

** Statement of financial position = Balance Sheet (see page 19)

the accounting over the life of the financial instrument however, and that would simply require that you completed the table. See below:

> **Note**
>
> *Amortised cost tables are not really a new learn at all. They were first introduced in the leasing chapter (although we called them 'leasing tables'). Finance leases do give rise to a financial liability after all.*

Period	Amount borrowed	Finance cost (at 9.5%) for SOPL	Cash repayment 4% (200,000)	Rolled up interest	Bal c/fwd – liability for SOFP*
	$	$	$	$	$
1	157,763	14,988	(8,000)	6,988	164,751
2	164,751	15,651	(8,000)	7,651	172,402
3	172,402	16,378	(8,000)	8,378	180,780
4	180,780	17,174	(8,000)	9,174	189,954
5	189,954	18,046	(8,000)	10,046	200,000

This is the amount you borrowed, cash wise

This is the amount you have to repay on redemption.

The redemption amount in year 5 is $200,000, which leaves a liability of nil when paid.

> **Note**
>
> *The rolled up interest column is included for explanation purposes. Most amortised cost tables will miss it out so the table just adds across to give the balance c/fwd for the statement of financial position*.*

Financial assets - providing finance

In addition to raising finance some companies also provide finance. In fact of course every time a company raises finance, some other entity must have provided it. This gives rise to a financial asset - an investment in a statement of financial position*.

Financial assets are examined as frequently as financial liabilities. Typical transactions are:

- parent company provides a loan to its subsidiary
- provide finance via the financial markets as a straightforward investment in quoted debt
- purchase of shares in a company (no control or significant influence gained).

---

* Statement of financial position = Balance Sheet (see page 19)

All of these various types of investment give rise to a financial asset and are now covered by IFRS 9

Remember receivables are also a financial asset. When you sell goods and allow a period of credit one company has a trade payable (a financial liability) and the other has a trade receivable (a financial asset).

Initial recognition of financial assets

IFRS 9 deals with recognition and measurement of financial assets. An entity should recognise a financial asset on its statement of financial position when, and only when, the entity becomes party to the contractual provisions of the instrument.

Initial measurement of financial assets

At initial recognition, all financial assets are measured at fair value. This is likely to be the purchase consideration paid to acquire the financial assets. Transaction costs are usually expensed unless the financial asset gets classified as Fair Value through Other Comprehensive Income (see later) when the transaction costs get capitalised.

Subsequent measurement of financial assets

Subsequent measurement then depends upon the type of financial asset.

There are three classes of financial asset:

- Fair Value through Profit and Loss (FVTPL)
- amortised cost
- Fair Value through Other Comprehensive Income (FVTOCI)

Accounting for each category is straightforward:

	Treatment in SOFP*	Treatment in Statement of profit or loss and other comprehensive income
Fair value through P&L	Fair Value (Market value)	Gains and losses in statement of profit or loss so they affect profit
Amortised cost	Remeasured Investment using amortised cost table (this will give a 'mirror image' of what we saw for financial liabilities; one company has a loan account, the other an investment account, one has finance costs, the other has finance income).	Finance income calculated using effective interest rates
Fair value through OCI	Fair Value (Market value)	Gains and losses taken to reserves and reported in 'Other comprehensive income' (OCI) so they don't affect profit but do affect 'Total Comprehensive income' (TCI)

Financial assets where the investment is in a debt instruments:

Investments in debt instruments (e.g. purchasing quoted debt, or a straight forward originating loan) would normally be measured at fair value through profit or loss (FVTPL), but would be measured at amortised cost provided the following two tests are passed:

The business model test

The objective of the entity's business model is to hold the financial asset to collect the contractual cash flows (rather than to sell the instrument prior to its contractual maturity to realise its fair value changes)

The contractual cash flow characteristics test

The contractual terms of the financial asset give rise on specified dates to cash flows that are solely payments of principal and interest on the principal amount outstanding.

Note

The issue of an 'accounting mismatch' is not covered here. See the red section for this complication.

Transactional example

Investment in a debt instrument (tests passed)

On 1st January 20X1 John Inc purchases a debenture off the market with a nominal value of $8,000. The coupon rate is 1%, but the market demands a return of 8%. The loan has four years to run. The intent is to hold the investment to maturity and John considers that the investment passes the business test model and the contractual cash flow test. John Inc prepare their accounts to 31 December each year.

Required

Calculate the amount that the company would be prepared to pay for the asset and show how it would be accounted for over the four years.

John will not be prepared to pay $8,000 for this investment which is only returning 1% when the market rate is 8%. As the interest rate rises this instrument will fall in value. Its market value can be calculated as the present value of the future cash flows. John will receive 1% interest each year for 3 years and then on redemption date they will receive $8,000 from the borrower.

The amount they are prepared to pay is the fair value as calculated below

Date		Cash flow	Discounted	Present value
31 December 20X1	Interest received	80	$1/1.08$	74.40
31 December 20X2	Interest received	80	$1/1.08^2$	68.80
31 December 20X3	Interest received	80	$1/1.08^3$	63.52
31 December 20X4	Interest and capital received	8,080	$1/1.08^4$	5,939.00
	FV on market			6,145.72

This is a debt instrument with the tests passed so the instrument is classified as 'amortised cost'.

Initial recognition

The investment is initially recognised at the fair value of the consideration, being $6,146.

	$	$
Dr Investment at cost	6,146	
Cr Bank (cash)		6,146

Subsequent measurement

At its year end the investment is remeasured on the amortised cost basis to $6,558.

SOFP

Statement of comprehensive income for the year ended 31 December 20X1(extract)

	$
Investment in debt instrument (W1)	6,558

SOCI

Statement of profit or loss* and other comprehensive income (OCI) (extract)

	$
Finance income (W1)	492

Date	Opening Balance $	Finance income 8% $	Cash Received $	Closing Balance $
The amount John Inc paid for the investment initially				
1 Jan X1 - 31 Dec X1	6,146	492	(80)	6,558
1 Jan X2 - 31 Dec X2	6,558	525	(80)	7,003
1 Jan X3 - 31 Dec X3	7,003	560	(80)	7,483
		Logic check at this point. This should be the amount of principle you are due to receive in 4 years time.		
1 Jan X4 - 31 Dec x4	7,483	597	(80)	8,000

As the amount you are getting back is 8,000, this has to be the figure the table finishes with. In the exam hall take any rounding differences through finance income in your amortised cost table

---

Transactional example

Investment in a debt instrument (tests not passed)

Robinson Inc has a year end of 31st December. On 15th December 20X1 they purchased some debenture loans on the stock exchange as a short term investment. The cost was $900 and the year end value was $800. Shortly after the new year start the debentures were sold for $850.

Required

Show how this financial asset will be initially recognised, subsequently remeasured and dealt with on disposal under IFRS 9.

This is a short-term investment in a debt instrument. As it is short term it is an asset held for trading. This is a financial asset at fair value with gains and losses to profit and loss.

*Statement of profit or loss = Income statement

Initial recognition

The investment is initially recognised at the fair value of the consideration, being $900.

	$	$
Dr Investment (debenture)	900	
Cr Bank (cash)		900

Subsequent measurement - at fair value

At its year end it is remeasured to its fair value of $800

Statement of financial position (extract) as at 31 December 20X1

	$
Investment - FVTPL	800

Investment - FVTPL

	$		$
Cash	900	Loss to statement of profit or loss	100
		Balance c/fwd	800
	900		900

Statement of profit or loss* (extract) for the year ended 31 December 20X1

	$
Finance costs (800 - 900)	(100)

On disposal

	$	$
Transfer carrying value to disposal account		
Dr Disposal	800	
Cr Investment		800
Post proceeds to disposal account		
Dr Bank (cash)	850	
Cr Disposal account		850
Take balance on disposal to statement of profit or loss*		
Dr Disposal	50	
Cr Statement of profit or loss* – financing		50

Investment in debt instrument

	$000		$000
Balance b/fwd	800	Transfer to disposal	800
	800		800

* Statement of profit or loss = Income statement

Disposal account			
	$000		$000
Carrying value	800	Cash proceeds	850
Profit on disposal to statement of profit or loss	50		
	850		850

Investment in a convertible

When we raised finance using the issue of a convertible per IAS 32 we used 'split accounting'. However we do not do the same in accounts of the company who purchases the convertible, as that would involve some anticipation of the conversion happening.

The purchase of the convertible must be treated as Fair value through profit and loss with amortised cost being unavailable due to the contractual cash flow test from above failing.

The convertible contains rights other than repayments of interest and capital, so FVTP&L is the only option.

Financial assets where the investment is in an equity instrument.

When you purchase shares (i.e. an equity instrument) a number of accounting standards may apply.

If you gain control then IFRS 10/IFRS 3 will apply, if you gain significant influence IAS 28 Investments in associates will apply. For these circumstances you will need the blue section of this book.

Here we are talking about investments in shares where we have no influence – IFRS 9 will apply.

Equity instruments are measured at either:

- fair value either through profit or loss*, or
- fair value through other comprehensive income

Any changes in fair value are normally recognised in profit or loss.

There is an exception to this rule where the financial asset is an investment in an equity instrument not held for trading. In this case the entity can make an irrevocable election to recognise changes in the fair value in other comprehensive income.

---

* Statement of profit or loss = Income statement

Transactional example

Investment in equity held for trading (FVTPL)

Gav Inc has a year end of 31 December and on 15th December 20X1 they purchased shares on the stock exchange for the purpose of speculating (making a profit) for $400. The value at the year-end is $330 and the value rises to $370 a few weeks later when the shares are sold.

Required

Show how this financial asset will be initially recognised and subsequently measured under IFRS 9.

This is a purchase of an equity instrument for speculation. As it speculation, this means it is held for trading, so the use of comprehensive income is not available. So it is a financial asset at fair value with gains and losses to profit and loss.

The investment is initially recognised at the fair value of the consideration, being $400.

Initial Recognition

	$	$
Dr Investment-	400	
Cr Bank (cash)		400

Subsequent measurement

At the year end it is remeasured to its fair value of $330.

SOFP	Statement of financial position* (extract) as at 31 December 20X1	
		$
	Investment in equity instruments	330

Investment - FVTPL

		$			$
Cash		400	Loss to statement of profit or loss		70
			Balance c/fwd		330
		400			400

SOCI	Statements of profit or loss** (extract) for the year ended 31 December 20X1	
		$
	Loss on financial asset (400 - 330)	(70)
	Profit	X

* Statement of financial position = Balance Sheet (see page 19)

** Statement of profit or loss = Income statement

Disposal

	$	$
Transfer carrying value to disposal account		
Dr Disposal account	330	
Cr Investment		330
Post proceeds to disposal account		
Dr Bank (cash)	370	
Cr Disposal account		370
Take balance on disposal to statement of profit or loss*		
Dr Disposal	40	
Cr Statement of profit or loss* - financing		40

Investment in equity instrument (shares)

	$000		$000
Balance b/fwd	330	Transfer to disposal	330
	330		330

Disposal account

	$000		$000
Carrying value	330	Cash proceeds	370
Profit on disposal to statement of profit or loss	40		
	370		370

Transactional example

Investment in equity held for long term (FVTOCI)

On 6th November 20X3 Exception Co acquired an equity investment with the intention of holding it in the long term. The investment cost $500. At Exception Co's year end of 31 December 20X3, the market price of the investment is $520. How is the asset initially and subsequently measured?

Exception Co has elected to present the equity investment in other comprehensive income.

Required

Show how this financial asset will be initially recognised and subsequently measured under IFRS 9.

---

* Statement of profit or loss = Income statement

Initial recognition

The asset is initially recognised at the fair value of the consideration, being $500.

	$	$
Dr Investment	500	
Cr Bank (cash)		500

Subsequent measurement

At the year end it is remeasured to fair value of $520,000

Statement of financial position* (extract) as at 31 December 20X3

SOFP

	$
Investments in equity instruments	520

A gain of $20 has arisen, this is taken directly to reserves and reported in OCI.

SOCI

Statement of profit or loss** and other comprehensive income (extract) for the year ended 31 December 20X3

	$
Profit for the year	X
Other comprehensive income (OCI):	
Gain on investment in FVTOCI equity instruments	20
Total comprehensive income	XX

Receivables

Receivables will pass the business model and contractual cash flow test, as we expect to simply collect the due amount on an agreed date, so amortised cost is appropriate.

Investments specifically purchased with a plan to 'trade'

This isn't really a separate category and we have already covered the issue, but just as a final confirmation. If any exam question says the financial asset is 'held for trading' whether it is an investment in a debt or equity instrument it must go in the FVTPL category.

Transaction costs

At initial recognition, all financial assets are measured at fair value. This is likely to be the purchase consideration paid to acquire the financial asset plus transaction costs that are directly attributable to the acquisition or issue of the financial asset...

However if the financial asset has been classified as **fair value through profit or loss*** then the transaction costs will be **expensed**.

* Statement of financial position = Balance Sheet (see page 19)

** Statement of profit or loss = Income statement

Transactional example - transaction costs

Moloney Inc bought an investment in equity for $40 million plus associated transaction costs of $1 million. The asset was designated upon initial recognition as fair value through other comprehensive income.

At the reporting date of 31 December 20X2 the fair value of the financial asset had risen to $60 million. Shortly after the reporting date the financial asset was sold for $70 million.

Required:

(a) How should this be accounted for?

(b) How would the answer have been different if the investment had been classified as fair value through profit and loss?

(a) Classified as Fair Value through Other Comprehensive Income

Initial Recognition

On purchase the investment is recorded at the consideration paid including, as the asset is classified as fair value through other comprehensive income, the associated transaction costs:

	$	$
Dr Investment account	41	
Cr Bank (cash)		41

Subsequent measurement

At the reporting date the asset is remeasured:

SOFP

Statement of financial position* (extract) as at 31 December 20X2

	$m
Investments in equity instruments	60

SOCI

Statement of profit or loss** and other comprehensive income for the year ended 31 December 20X2

	$
Profit for the year	X
Other comprehensive income (OCI):	
Gain on OCI equity instrument	19
60- 41	

Note the transaction costs were capitalised which is why we start with 41 (40 +1)

---

* Statement of financial position = Balance Sheet (see page 19)

** Statement of profit or loss = Income statement

On disposal

On disposal, the asset is derecognised, the gain or loss on disposal is determined by comparing disposal proceeds and carrying value, with the result taken to profit or loss.

	$	$
Transfer carrying value to disposal account		
Dr Disposal	60	
Cr Investment		60
Post proceeds to disposal		
Dr Bank (cash)	70	
Cr Disposal		70
Take balance on disposal to statement of profit or loss		
Dr Disposal	10	
Cr Statement of profit or loss		10

(b)   **Classified as Fair Value through Profit or loss**

If Moloney Inc had designated the investment as fair value through profit and loss, the transaction costs would have been recognised as an expense in profit or loss.

Initial recognition

	$	$
Dr Investment	40m	
Cr Bank (cash)		40m
Dr Expense	1m	
Cr Bank (cash)		1m

Subsequent measurement

At the year end, it is remeasured to fair value, being $60m:

> **SOFP***
>
> **Statement of financial position* (extract) as at 31 December 20X2**
>
> | | $m |
> |---|---|
> | Investments in equity instruments | 60 |
>
> *Note under both categories the SOFP shows the same answer.*

A gain of $20 has arisen, this is taken directly to reserves and reported in OCI

The transaction costs have been expensed directly.

> **SOPL**
>
> **Statement of profit or loss** and other comprehensive income (extract) for the year ended 31 December 20X2**
>
> | | $ |
> |---|---|
> | Transaction costs | (1) |
> | Gain on FVTPL equity instrument (60-40) | 20 |
> | Profit for the year | X |
> | **Other comprehensive income (OCI)** | |

* Statement of financial position = Balance Sheet (see page 19)

** Statement of profit or loss = Income statement

On disposal

On disposal the asset is derecognised with the gain taken to income

	$	$
Transfer carrying value to disposal account		
Dr Disposal	60	
Cr Investment		60
Post proceeds to disposal		
Dr Bank (cash)	70	
Cr Disposal		70
Take balance on disposal to statement of profit or loss*		
Dr Disposal	10	
Cr Statement of profit or loss		10

Derecognition of financial assets and liabilities

Derecognition is the removal of a previously recognised financial asset or financial liability from an entity's balance sheet.

Derecognition of a financial asset

Derecognition occurs when the contractual rights to the cash flows expire (e.g. a receivable would be derecognised when the customer pays their debt). It transfers the financial asset and the asset qualifies for derecognition.

Risks and rewards of ownership

When an asset is transferred, it will only qualify for derecognition if the entity has transferred substantially all the risks and rewards of ownership of the asset.

For example, if a company sells an investment in shares, but retains the right to repurchase the shares at any time at a price equal to their current fair value then it should derecognise the asset.

If the company sells an investment in shares and enters into an agreement whereby they buyer will return any increases in value to the company and the company will pay the buyer interest plus compensation for any decrease in the value of the investment, then the company should not derecognise the asset as it has retained substantially all the risks and rewards.

Transfers that do not qualify for derecognition

If a transfer does not result in derecognition because the entity has retained substantially all the risks and rewards of ownership of the transferred asset, the entity shall continue to recognise the transferred asset in its entirety and shall recognise a financial liability for the consideration received.

* Statement of profit or loss = Income statement

Transactional example - derecognition

Safiya Inc held a portfolio of trade receivables with a carrying amount of $4million at 31 May 20X2. At that date the entity entered into a factoring agreement with a bank, whereby it transfers the receivables in exchange for $3.6 million in cash. Safiya has agreed to reimburse the factor for any shortfall between the amount collected and $3.6million. Once the receivables have been collected any amounts above $3.6 million, less interest on this amount will be repaid to Safiya. Safiya has derecognised the receivables and charged $0.4million as a loss to profit or loss.

Safiya was wrong to derecognise the receivables as substantially all the risks and rewards were not transferred.

The primary risk associated with a receivable are that the debt is not paid (credit risk). Safiya has agreed to reimburse the factor for all credit losses. The risk is retained. The primary reward is the receipt of the cash. Safiya immediately benefits from $3.6 million and will receive benefit for those amount received above $3.6million in due course. Safiya continues to bear substantially all the risks and rewards and the receivables should be on the SOFP. The receipt of the 3.6million is in substance a short term loan secured on the receivables and should be treated as such.

	$m	$m
Dr Bank (cash)	3.6	
Cr Secured loan		3.6

Derecognition of a financial liability

A financial liability is derecognised (removed from the statement of financial position) when and only when, it is extinguished.

This could be because the obligation is:

- discharged
- cancelled or
- expires when an entity discharges the obligations specified in the contract or they expire.

There is no requirement to assess the extent to which the company has retained the risks and rewards in order to derecognise a financial liability, the derecognition focuses on whether the financial liability has been extinguished.

Sorry but you need to know ... DEFINITIONS

Financial instrument

Any contract that gives rise to both a financial asset of one enterprise and a financial liability or equity instrument of another enterprise.

Financial asset

Any asset that is:

- cash
- a contractual right to receive cash or another financial asset from another enterprise
- a contractual right to exchange financial instruments with another enterprise under conditions that are potentially favourable
- an equity instrument of another enterprise.

Financial liability

A liability that is a contractual obligation:

- to deliver cash or another financial asset to another enterprise; or
- to exchange financial instruments with another enterprise under conditions that are potentially unfavourable.

A **financial asset or financial liability at fair value through profit or loss** is a financial liability that meets either of the following conditions:

- it meets the definition of held for trading
- upon initial recognition it was designated as fair value through profit or loss (subject to restrictions).

Held for Trading

A financial asset or financial liability that:

(a) is acquired or incurred principally for the purpose of selling or repurchasing it in the near term

(b) on initial recognition is part of a portfolio of identified financial instruments that are managed together and for which there is evidence of a recent actual pattern of short-term profit-taking

(c) is a derivative (except for a derivative that is a financial guarantee contract or a designated and effective hedging instrument).

Note IFRS 9 is repeating the definitions you have already learnt for IAS 32...This page should be a quick skip through therefore!

Conclusion

This is an introduction to the basics of IFRS 9. It is a complex standard and first of all it is best to get solid on the initial recognition, subsequent measurement and derecognition rules for the main types of financial instruments.

Turn to the red section, if you need to get to grips with more complex transactions or indeed are still being examined on the IAS 39 rules (check your examinable documents).

Hedge accounting will eventually be covered by IFRS 9, but for now the rules are still covered by IAS 39. See the red section for IAS 39 and hedge accounting, if relevant to you.

IFRS 7 – Financial instruments: disclosures

Introduction

> "The Board believes that the introduction of IFRS 7 will lead to greater transparency about the risks that entities run from the use of financial instruments. This, combined with the new requirements in IAS 1, will provide better information for investors and other users of financial statements to make informed judgements about risk and return."
>
> Sir David Tweedie, IASB Chair

IFRS 7 is a companion standard to IAS 32 and 39. As it is purely a disclosure standard, it is not going to be a major issue in its own right – basically you just need an awareness of what it's all about.

So ... what's it trying to achieve?

IFRS 7 introduces new requirements to improve the information on financial instruments that is given in entities' financial statements. It replaces IAS 30 Disclosures in the **Financial Statements of Banks** and **Similar Financial Institutions** return.

IFRS 7 applies to all risks arising from all financial instruments, except those covered by another more specific standard such as interests in subsidiaries, associates and joint ventures, post-employment benefits, share-based payment and insurance contracts. Although IFRS 7 applies to all entities, the extent of disclosure required depends on the extent of the entity's use of financial instruments and of its exposure to risk.

Disclosures

The IFRS requires disclosures about the significance of financial instruments for an entity's financial position and performance. These disclosures incorporate many of the requirements previously in IAS 32 (whose title has been shortened to reflect the change). The IFRS also requires information about the extent to which the entity is exposed to risks arising from financial instruments, and a description of management's objectives, policies and processes for managing those risks. Together, these disclosures provide an overview of the entity's use of financial instruments and the exposures to risks they create.

Qualitative and quantitative information about exposure to risks arising from financial instruments is required, including specified minimum disclosures about credit risk, liquidity risk and market risk. The qualitative disclosures describe management's objectives, policies and processes for managing those risks. The quantitative disclosures provide information about the extent to which the entity is exposed to risk, based on information provided internally to the entity's key management personnel.

IFRS 7 includes mandatory application guidance that explains how to apply the requirements in the IFRS. It is accompanied by Implementation Guidance that describes how an entity might provide the disclosures required by the IFRS.

IFRS 7 is effective for annual periods beginning on or after 1 January 2007. Earlier application is encouraged.

Conclusion

When you are studying financial instruments it is probably best if you study IAS 32, IFRS 9 (or IAS 39) and IFRS 7 all together as they relate to the same topic.

Group accounts

"Things should be made as simple as possible but not any simpler."

Albert Einstein (1879-1955)

Introduction

Accountancy is really two quite separate topics. We tend to think of the double-entry bookkeeping records, leading to the individual company separate financial statements, as the 'real' accounts of a company. However, once we have a group of companies we may have to prepare from these 'real' accounts a set of consolidated financial statements. This is because the individual company accounts are not adequate for 'fair presentation' of the results of such groups.

A separate body of accounting standards exists for these group or consolidated accounts.

For those interested in group accounts:

- IFRS 3 (revised) Business combinations
- IFRS 10 Consolidated financial statements
- IAS 28 Investments in Associates
- IFRS 11 Joint arrangements
- IFRS 12 Disclosure of Interests in other entities
- IAS 27 Separate financial statements

"In individuals insanity is rare; but in groups, parties, nations and epochs it is the rule."

Friedrich Nietzsche (1844-1900)

Note

Many books on accounting standards start by giving you the aims and definitions from the standard. This book deliberately does not structure the chapters in that style. Instead the issue is generally explained, with the sort of transactions that the standard relates to being introduced. We do get to the aims and definitions and, for those of you who already feel comfortable with the standard, you may like to turn first to the definitions box – re-affirm those and then read the chapter.

IFRS 3 - Business combinations

Introduction

> **"The success combination in business is – do what you do better … and do more of what you do."**
>
> **David Joseph Schwartz**

IFRS 3 group accounts is a compulsory question featuring on many exam papers. It is really important that you have a sound technique and good understanding of IFRS 3 (revised) Business Combinations.

If one company owns more than 50% of the ordinary shares of another company this will usually give the first company 'control' of the second company.

This is because the first company, that is referred to as the holding or parent company (P say), has enough voting power to appoint all the directors of the second company that we call the subsidiary (S say). P is, in effect, able to manage S as if it were merely a department of P, rather than a separate entity. In strict legal terms P and S remain distinct, but in economic substance (commercial reality) they can be regarded as a single unit (a 'group').

The key principle underlying group accounts is the need to reflect the economic substance of the relationship. This issue of control is much more than just owning 50%+ of the shares and Chapter 26 IFRS 10 Consolidated Financial Statements covers the issue of 'control' in full. For this chapter we will assume that once a company has purchased at least 51% of another company that 'control' exists.

To reflect the true economic substance of a group of companies we need to produce group accounts in addition to the individual accounts prepared for each company within the group. One of the main methods of doing this is to prepare 'consolidated' accounts using the 'purchase' method and this is the main thrust of this chapter.

Consolidated accounts present the group as though it were a 'single economic entity'.

---

* Statement of financial position = Balance Sheet (see page 19)

So ... what's it trying to achieve?

The objective of IFRS 3 is to specify how to account when one entity combines with another.

The single entity concept

Business combinations consolidate the results and net assets of group members so as to display the group's affairs as those of a single economic entity. As already mentioned, this conflicts with the strict legal position that each company is a distinct entity. Applying the single entity concept is a good example of the accounting principle of showing economic substance over legal form.

The group as a single entity

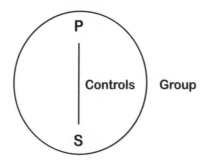

The mechanics of consolidation

When one company buys shares in another company the cash paid is recorded as an investment in the acquiring company's statement of financial position*.

A standard group accounting question will present you with the accounts of the parent company and the accounts of the subsidiary and will require you to prepare consolidated accounts. Consolidated statement of financial position* questions should be approached using the following set of standard workings.

 ## (W1) Establish the group structure

Date of acquisition — This indicates that P owns 80% of the ordinary shares of S and when they were acquired.

---

* Statement of financial position = Balance Sheet (see page 19)

(W2) Net assets of subsidiary

	At date of acquisition $	At the reporting date $
Equity shares	X	X
Reserves:		
Retained earnings	X	X
Other components of equity	X	X
	X	X

 # (W3) Goodwill on acquisition

	$
Cost of shares acquired	X
Non-controlling interest at date of acquisition**	X
Less	
100% Net Asset at date of acquisition (per W2) (net assets acquired)	(X)
Goodwill acquired	X
Less impairment to date	(X)
Goodwill to Consolidated Statement of Financial Position (CSOFP)	X

** Please note the standard allows NCI and therefore goodwill to be either measured at:

- fair value; or
- proportion of net assets.

If the accounting policy is fair value this will mean goodwill gets calculated on a full (gross) basis.

If the accounting policy is proportion of net assets this will mean goodwill gets calculated on a parent share only basis.

(W4) Non-controlling Interest (NCI)

	$
NCI at the date of acquisition (per W3)	X
NCI share of post acquisition profit (per W2)	X
Less NCI share of impairment	
loss (If policy is fair value) (per W3)	(X)
	———
NCI for Consolidated Statement of Financial Position (CSOFP)	X
	———

(W5) Group reserves

Retained earnings	$
P reserve (100%)	X
S group share of post-acquisition reserves (per W2)	X
Less: Goodwill impairments to date (W3)	(X)
(Parent share only if a fair value policy exists)	
	———
Group retained earnings for Consolidated Statement of Financial Position (CSOFP)	X
	———

Other components of equity	
	$
P reserve (100%)	X
S group share of post-acquisition (per W2)	X
	———
Other components of equity for Consolidated Statement of Financial Position (CSOFP)	X
	———

---

* Statement of financial position = Balance Sheet (see page 19)

These five workings are really key to consolidation of a statement of financial position*, so use the revise/cover/test approach.

This simply means you need to learn the five workings, then cover them up and see if you can correctly write them out without looking at the answers. Then you need to apply them to past exam questions.

Pre-acquisition reserves

The reserves that exist in a subsidiary company at the date when it is acquired are called its 'pre-acquisition' reserves. These are capitalised at the date of acquisition by including them in the goodwill calculation. We really need to look at some numbers.

Transactional example

Draft statements of financial position* of Pauline and Sophie on 31 December 20X1 are as follows:

	Pauline	Sophie
ASSETS	*$000*	*$000*
Property, Plant and Equipment (PPE)	90	100
Investment in Sophie at cost	110	
Current assets	50	30
	250	130
EQUITY AND LIABILITIES		
Capital and reserves		
Equity share capital $1	100	100
Retained earnings	120	20
	220	120
Current liabilities	30	10
	250	130

Pauline had bought 80% of the ordinary shares of Sophie on 1 January 20X1 when the retained earnings of Sophie had a balance of $10,000. No impairment of goodwill has occurred to date. The group accounting policy is to value non-controlling interest on the proportionate basis.

Required:

Prepare a consolidated statement of financial position* as at 31 December 20X1.

---

* Statement of financial position = Balance Sheet (see page 19)

First set out your answer booklet – you need a page for the consolidated statement of financial position* and then a separate page for the workings as shown below.

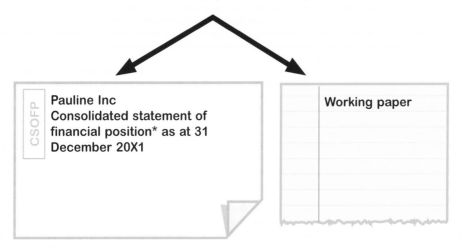

We are going to start with the working paper – use the five core workings from earlier in this chapter.

Workings

(W1) Group structure

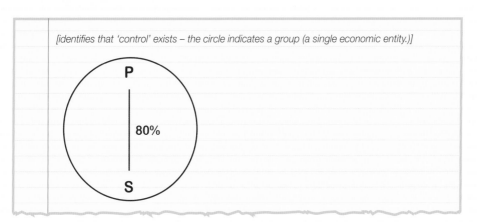

[identifies that 'control' exists – the circle indicates a group (a single economic entity.)]

---

* Statement of financial position = Balance Sheet (see page 19)

(W2) Net assets of Sophie

(Current reporting date is easy – tick off from Sophie's statement of financial position* in the question, and always assume a company's capital structure is unchanged since the date the company was incorporated unless the question tells you otherwise, i.e. equity shares is usually the same at both dates.)

	At date of acquisition $000	At the reporting date $000
$1 Equity shares	100	100
Retained earnings	10	20
Other components of equity	–	–
	110	120

Take this to (W3)	Deduct the net assets at the date of acquisition from the net assets at the reporting date. Take this to W4 and W5

(The reserves at the date of acquisition are ascertained by reading the supporting information in the question. If the reserves are NOT given in the supporting information, you will find there is enough information to allow you to calculate it.)

If the net assets have increased since the date of acquisition you have made gains. We call these 'post acquisition' gains. If net assets have reduced you have made losses in the post acquisition period.

(W3) Goodwill

(Pick up the cost of investment from the parent company's (Pauline) statement of financial position* - tick it off.)

	$000
Cost of Investment	110
NCI% x Net assets at acquisition (W2)	22
(For proportionate policy:	
this is NCI% x Net assets at acquisition) (W2)	
(20% x 110)	132
Less:	
100% Net Assets at the date of acquisition (W2)	(110)
Goodwill (to Consolidated Statement of Financial Position) *(as an intangible asset unless you are told it is impaired)*	**22**

---

* Statement of financial position = Balance Sheet (see page 19)

(W4) Non-controlling interest

	$000
NCI at the date of acquisition (W3)	22
NCI share of any profit created in the post acquisition period	2

(look back at W2. Remember net assets of a company increase if you make profits and reduce if you make losses. Sophie Inc has currently got net assets of $120,000 based on the current reporting date column. However $110,000 existed at the date of acquisition, so it is the difference between the two that we call post acquisition profit ($120,000- $110,000) x 20%)

NCI to Consolidated Statement of Financial Position (CSOFP)	**24**

(The non-controlling interest account only appears on a consolidated statement of financial position*, not an individual company statement of financial position*.)

(W5) Group retained earnings

(Always include 100% of any earnings that relate to the parent company – but think carefully about the subsidiary.)

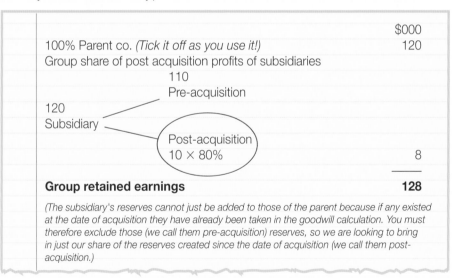

	$000
100% Parent co. *(Tick it off as you use it!)*	120

Group share of post acquisition profits of subsidiaries

110 — Pre-acquisition

120 Subsidiary

Post-acquisition 10 × 80% — 8

Group retained earnings	**128**

(The subsidiary's reserves cannot just be added to those of the parent because if any existed at the date of acquisition they have already been taken in the goodwill calculation. You must therefore exclude those (we call them pre-acquisition) reserves, so we are looking to bring in just our share of the reserves created since the date of acquisition (we call them post-acquisition.)

You would then be in a position to put together the answer. Start with the goodwill from W3. It appears on the consolidated statement of financial position*, unless it has been impaired, as an intangible asset. Do not forget to cross reference to your workings! Any numbers that are not already 'ticked' are then combined. Your answer should now look like this:

---

* Statement of financial position = Balance Sheet (see page 19)

Pauline group statement of financial position* as at 31 December 20X1

ASSETS	$000
Non-current assets	
Goodwill (W3)	22
Property, Plant and Equipment (90 + 100)	190
	212
Current assets (50 + 30)	80
Total assets	**292**
EQUITY AND LIABILITIES	$000
Capital and reserves	
$1 Equity shares (100% parent company only)	100
Retained earnings (W5)	128
Shareholders' capital	228
Non-controlling interest (W4)	24
	252
Current liabilities (30 + 10)	40
Total equity and liabilities	**292**

Please be aware this answer has calculated goodwill on a proportionate basis (parents share only). This was the only allowed approach traditionally under the original IFRS 3. If you are being examined on the revised IFRS 3 please be aware that although this 'partial basis' is still allowed companies using the new standard can choose to use the fair value (full) basis. If this was the case the question would state:

'The companies accounting policy is to value non-controlling interest on the fair value (or full) basis.'

In this circumstance we would have to be given the Fair Value of the Non-controlling interest at the date of acquisition or the share price of the acquired entity so that we can calculate it.

Let us say the share price of Sophie Inc at the date of acquisition was $1.25 per share. We can see that the parent company paid more than this to acquire their 80 shares. Pauline paid $110 to acquire 80 shares. This amounts to $1.375 per share (110/80), but this is normal because if a company wishes to gain control they may have to pay a premium. However there is a non-controlling interest in the other 20 shares. Valued at the date of acquisition this is 20 shares x $1.25= $25. If we use this figure to value the NCI at the date of acquisition we will get a different figure for goodwill and a different figure for NCI.

---

* Statement of financial position = Balance Sheet (see page 19)

The impact is as follows:

(W3) Goodwill

	$000
Cost of Investment	110
NCI at date of acquisition**	
(now valued at Fair Value) (20 x $1.25)	25
	135
Less	
100% of the net assets at the date of acquisition (W2)	(110)
Goodwill to CSOFP	**25**

** Please note the only thing that changes between the two calculations is the valuation of the NCI (both methods are acceptable under IFRS 3 (revised))

W4 will also have a different answer

(W4) Non-controlling interest

NCI at date of acquisition (at Fair Value) (W3)	25
NCI share of any profit created post acquisition	
($120,000-$110,000) x 20%	2
NCI to CSOFP	**27**

Pauline group statement of financial position* as at 31 December 20X1

ASSETS	$000
Non-current assets	
Goodwill (W3)	25
Property, plant and equipment (90 + 100)	190
	215
Current assets (50 + 30)	80
Total assets	**295**

EQUITY AND LIABILITIES	$000
Capital and reserves	
$1 Equity shares (100% parent company only)	100
Retained earnings (W5)	128
Shareholders' capital	228
Non-controlling interest (W4)	27
	255
Current liabilities (30 + 10)	40
Total equity and liabilities	**295**

Note

It is crucial therefore you read these questions very carefully to confirm if the accounting policy is fair value or proportionate. (parent share only).

Sorry but you need to know ... DEFINITIONS

Goodwill is an asset representing the future economic benefits arising from other assets acquired in a business combination that are not individually identified and separately recognised.

Intangible assets follow the definition in IAS 38.

Non-controlling interest is that portion of the profit or loss and net assets of a subsidiary attributable to equity interests that are not owned, directly or indirectly through subsidiaries, by the parent.

What if the goodwill is impaired?

We saw in Chapter 18 that the rule is 'assets must not be carried at more than their recoverable amount'. If the goodwill is impaired, it must not be shown as an asset, as it is not recoverable.

If an exam question tells you the goodwill is fully impaired, instead of taking it to the statement of financial position*, it becomes a negative adjustment to group reserves (remember an impairment loss on goodwill is a cost in the consolidated statement of profit or loss).

If the question above had told you the goodwill was fully impaired, (W3), (W4) and (W5) would look like this:

(W3) Goodwill

	Accounting policy - Proportionate $000	Accounting policy - Fair value $000
Cost of Investment	110	110
NCI at acquisition **	22	25
	132	135
Less 100% net assets at acquisition (W2)	(110)	(110)
Goodwill	22	25
Less goodwill impaired to date	(22)	(25)
Goodwill to CSOFP	**nil**	**nil**

---

* Statement of financial position = Balance Sheet (see page 19)

(W4) Non-controlling interest

	Accounting policy - Proportionate $000	Accounting policy - Fair value $000
NCI at acquisition (W3)	22	25
NCI share of post acquisition profits (W2) (120- 110) x 20)%	2	2
Less goodwill impairment *(note if on proportionate basis the goodwill is 100% group only so no impairment attributes to the NCI but if it is fair value goodwill it needs to be split between the NCI and the group. (25 x 20%)*	**24** (nil)	**27** (5)
NCI to CSOFP	**24**	**22**

(W5) Group retained earnings

	Accounting policy - Proportionate $000	Accounting policy - Fair value $000
100% Parent company	120	120
Group share of post acquisition reserve of subsidiary (120-110) x 80%	8	8
Less: goodwill impairment		
- proportionate policy = 100% group	(22)	
Fair value policy = 80% group (25 x 80%)		(20)
Group Retained earnings to CSOFP	**106**	**108**

So the consolidated statement of financial position* would look like this:

Pauline group statement of financial position as at 31 December 20X1

	Accounting policy – Proportionate $000	Accounting policy – Fair value $000
ASSETS		
Non-current assets		
Goodwill (W3)	nil	nil
Property, plant and equipment (90 +100)	190	190
	190	190
Current assets (50 + 30)	80	80
Total assets	**270**	**270**
EQUITY AND LIABILITIES		
$1 Equity shares (100% parent)	100	100
Retained earnings (W5)	106	108
Non-controlling interest (W4)	24	22
Current liabilities (30 +10)	40	40
Total equity and liabilities	**270**	**270**

Remember the goodwill may only be partially impaired so it may have a partial write off through (W5) and a partial intangible on the consolidated statement of financial position*.

Inter-company transactions

The single entity concept

 A common mistake in 'consolidation' questions is to fail to understand the true objective of group accounts is to present the group as a single entity. Hence the effects of transactions between group members need to be eliminated as the group has not transacted with any third party.

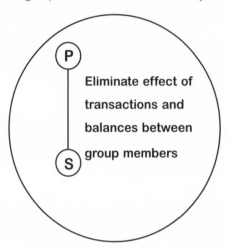

Reflecting the group as a single entity means that items which are assets in one group company and liabilities in another need to be cancelled out; otherwise group assets and liabilities could be overstated.

Intra-group balances result from, for example:

- loans and debentures between group companies
- intra-group trading.

To eliminate such balances, cancel the credit balance in one company against the debit balance in the other, before summing net assets line-by-line.

Transactional example

Draft statements of financial position* of Henry and Suzi on 31 March 20X7 are as follows.

	Henry $000	Suzi $000
ASSETS		
Property, plant and equipment	100	140
Investment in Suzi at cost	180	
Current assets		
Inventory	30	35
Trade receivables	20	10
Cash	10	5
	340	190
EQUITY AND LIABILITIES		
Capital and reserves		
$1 Equity shares	250	100
Share premium	–	30
Retained earnings	–	20
Other components of equity	–	–
	250	150
Non-current liabilities		
10% loan notes	65	–
Current liabilities	25	40
	340	190

Notes:

1 *Henry bought 80,000 shares in Suzi in 20X1 when Suzi's reserves included a share premium of $30,000 and retained earnings of $5,000. There were no other components of equity.*

2 *Henry owes Suzi $8,000 and this is reflected in both their accounts.*

3 *No impairment of goodwill has occurred to date. The group accounting policy is to value non-controlling interest on the partial (proportionate) basis. The fair value of the NCI at the date of acquisition is $43,000.*

Required:

Prepare a consolidated statement of financial position* as at 31 March 20X7.

---

* Statement of financial position = Balance Sheet (see page 19)

Note

Because of the inter-company debt you will have to:

Dr Group payables $8,000

Cr Group receivables $8,000

(deduct $8,000 from both lines)

Henry group consolidated statement of financial position*
as at 31 March 20X7

	$000	$000
ASSETS		
Non-current assets		
Intangible assets (W3)		88
Property, plant and equipment (100+140)		240
		328
Current assets		
Inventory (30 + 35)	65	
Trade receivables (20 + 10 – **8**)	22	
Cash (10 + 5)	15	
		102
		430
EQUITY AND LIABILITIES		
Capital and reserves		
Share capital (100% parent only)		250
Retained earnings (W5)		12
		262
Non-controlling interests (W4)		46
		308
Non-current liabilities		
10% loan notes		65
Current liabilities		
Payables (25 + 40 – **8**)		57
		430

(W1) Group structure

Henry

80%

Suzi

Date of acquisition = 20X1

(W2) Net assets of Suzi

(Note all reserves go into this working.)

	At date of acquisition $000	At the reporting date $000
$1 Equity shares	100	100
Share premium	30	30
Retained earnings	5	20
Other components of equity	–	–
Net assets	135	150

(W3) Goodwill

	$000
Cost of Investment	180
NCI at acquisition (per question)	43
	223
Less	
100% Net assets acquired (W2)	(135)
Goodwill	88
Impairment to date	(nil)
Goodwill to Consolidated Statement of Financial Position (CSOFP)	**88**

---

* Statement of financial position = Balance Sheet (see page 19)

(W4) Non-controlling interest

NCI at date of acquisition (W3)	43
NCI share of post acquisition profit	
(150,000- 135,000) x 20%	3
Less	
NCI share of impairment (if full/fair value goodwill)	(nil)

(W5) Group reserves

Group retained earnings	$000
100% Henry	Nil
Pre-acquisition 135,000	
S 150,000	
15,000 x 80% Post-acquisition to CSOFP	12
Group retained earnings	**12**

Group share premium account	
	$000
100% P	Nil
Pre-acquisition 30,000	
S 30,000	
Nil x 80% Post-acquisition to CSOFP	Nil
Group share premium to CSOFP	**Nil**

The consolidated statement of profit or loss and other comprehensive income

Control and ownership

A statement of profit or loss and other comprehensive income shows the gains generated by resources disclosed in the related statement of financial position*.

- P's individual statement of profit or loss (SOPL) includes dividend income receivable from S.
- The consolidated statement of profit or loss (CSOPL) shows all income generated by the group's resources (i.e. by the net assets shown in the consolidated statement of financial position*).

To reflect this we must prepare the CSOPL on a basis consistent with the consolidated statement of financial position*. In particular, the CSOPL must show incomes generated from the net assets under P's control.

To do this, we include in the CSOPL all of S's income and expenses (100%), line by line, down to and including net profit for the period (profit after tax). This is the case even if the equity share in S is less than 100%.

To reflect the ownership in S we must then show the amounts attributable to the 'equity holders of the parent' (the parent's shareholders) and the amount attributable to the 'non-controlling interest'.

If S has paid dividends to P these should be cancelled against P's investment income. Indeed, this is just one example of intra-group transactions that must be eliminated from the consolidated accounts. We have already dealt with such transactions in the consolidated statement of financial position* (e.g. unrealised profit in closing inventories). We now look at the impact of intra-group transactions on the CSOPL.

Intra-group transactions

Intra-group transactions are those which take place within the group and do not involve outside entities. An equivalent term is inter-company transactions (inter = between): transactions between members of the group, not involving outsiders.

The objective of consolidated accounts is to display the group as a single entity. Intra-group transactions have a nil effect on the group as a whole and must be excluded from the consolidated accounts. We have just seen one example of this, the example of Henry and Suzy: payment of a dividend by S to P. Similarly, if S pays loan interest to P this too must be excluded.

The effect of this on the CSOPL is any dividend income shown in the CSOPL must arise from trade investments, not investments in S or P.

The non-controlling interest in S is calculated on the profit after tax and before dividends. The figure therefore includes the NCI's share of S's dividends and S's retained earnings.

Inter-company trading must also be eliminated from the CSOPL. Such trading will be included in the sales revenue of one group company and the purchases of another.

* Statement of financial position = Balance Sheet (see page 19)

To cancel these transactions on consolidation:

- add across P and S sales revenue and cost of sales to get the consolidated figure
- deduct the value of the inter-company sale from consolidated sales revenue and cost of sales.

If any items sold by one group company to another are included in closing inventories, their value must be adjusted to the lower of cost and net realisable value to the group. If the subsidiary pays a dividend to the parent, the parent, will have included the dividend received as finance income, this must be excluded from the consolidated statement of profit or loss.

Transactional example

Below are the statements of profit or loss of the Binbrook Group, as at 31 December 20X8.

	Binbrook	**Earlswood**
	$000	*$000*
Revenue	*385*	*100*
Cost of sales	*(185)*	*(60)*
Gross profit	*200*	*40*
Distribution costs	*(10)*	*(10)*
Administration expenses	*(40)*	*(5)*
Profit from operations	*150*	*25*
Tax	*(50)*	*(12)*
Profit for the year	*100*	*13*

You are also given the following information:

- *Binbrook acquired 45,000 ordinary shares in Earlswood. Earlswood has 50,000 $1 ordinary shares*
- *Binbrook sold $10,000 of goods to Earlswood. None was in inventory as at the year end.*

Draft a consolidated statement of profit or loss for Binbrook for the year ended 31 December 20X8.

Note

We are going to combine the results of the two companies, making sure we exclude any internal transactions. As we do not own 100% of the shares in Earlswood we will need to express a non-controlling interest in the profits of Earlswood – two figures exist for non-controlling interest, the statement of financial position* one is based on net assets and the consolidated statement of profit or loss one is based on profit – don't confuse the two.

See overleaf:

---

* Statement of financial position = Balance Sheet (see page 19)

Binbrook Group

Consolidated statement of profit or loss for the year ended 31 December 20X8

	$000
Revenue (385 + 100) – 10	475
Cost of sales (185 + 60) – 10	(235)
Gross profit	240
Distribution costs (10 + 10)	(20)
Administration expenses (40 + 5)	(45)
Profit from operations	175
Taxation (50 + 12)	(62)
Profit for the year	113
Amount attributable to:	
Equity holders of the parent	111.7
Non-controlling interests	
(10% of Earlswood's profit after tax)	1.3
(10% x 13)	113

This is consistent with our treatment of inventories in the consolidated statement of financial position*.

(W1) Group structure

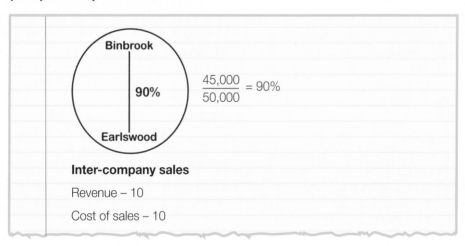

Inter-company sales

Revenue – 10

Cost of sales – 10

Provisions for unrealised profit (PURP)

It is normal commercial practice for group companies to sell goods to each other. This could be the parent (P) selling goods to the subsidiary or the subsidiary (S) selling goods to the parent.

For the purpose of the consolidated income statement as we have just seen in Binbrook you cannot sell goods to yourself (which is what is effectively happening in

* Statement of financial position = Balance Sheet (see page 19)

a group structure when one company sells to the other). We have therefore excluded the total of inter company sales from both revenue and cost of sales.

However if any of these goods are still held by the purchasing company at the year end (i.e they have goods in the warehouse counting as inventory at the year-end) there may be a second issue. This is that these goods now include a profit element. We know from IAS 2 that inventory must be carried at the lower of cost and NRV. The cost of these goods from the group's perspective is now being overstated. The selling company is also claiming a profit, which simply is not a real profit from the point of view of the group. We call this an 'unrealised profit' situation. We will therefore need to create a 'Provision for Unrealised Profit' (PURP) to ensure this overstatement of both the cost of inventory and the profit is corrected.

 Transactional example

Ellie Inc purchased an 80% holding in Hannah Inc. Ellie sold goods to Hannah for $400 at cost plus 25% (this is a mark up as it is based on cost).

All these goods remain in Hannah's inventory as at the reporting date.

As Ellie and Hannah are effectively the same company this cannot be claimed as a sale in the consolidated statement of profit or loss and must be excluded from both revenue and from cost of sales. This should be considered in (W1).

(W1) Group structure

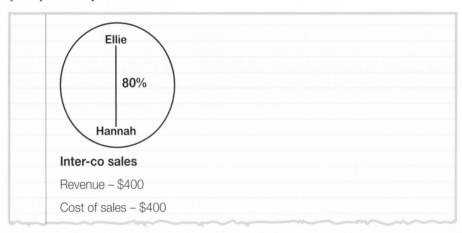

Ellie

80%

Hannah

Inter-co sales

Revenue – $400

Cost of sales – $400

However, as the goods are still in the warehouse (inventory) at year end a provision for unrealised profit will also need to be created.

Step 1 is to calculate the profit element in the goods based on the pricing structure given in the question. Here it is a mark-up of 25%.

So selling price x $\dfrac{\text{mark-up}}{100 + \text{mark-up}}$

will calculate the profit element as the cost is being treated as 100%. 25% is being added to that cost to give you 125% below the line. You need to know 25% out of the total of 125%.

So:

$400 x $\dfrac{25}{125}$ = $80 profit element included in that inventory. A provision for unrealised profit (PURP) is needed for the group accounts of $80.

Step 2 is to identify the adjustments needed. This will depend on who sells to whom i.e. if the parent sells to the subsidiary the profit is made by the parent so the adjustment is:

Dr Group reserves (W5) $80

W5 means assuming we are completing a full CSOFP
    Cr Inventory (face of CSOFP) $80

If the subsidiary sells to the parent the profit is made by the subsidiary so the adjustment is:

Dr Net Assets of subsidiary (W2) at reporting date $80

    Cr Inventory (face of CSOFP) $80

For Ellie as the parent sold to the subsidiary the adjustment is

Dr Group reserves (W5) $80

    Cr Inventory (face of CSOFP) $80

This calculation can be done as part of a standard (W1) so that you know before (W2) if a PURP adjustment is required.

Transactional example

Summarised statements of financial position* for the year to
31 December 2008

	Mike	Susan
ASSETS	$	$
Non Current Assets		
Property, Plant and Equipment	1,800	1,000
Investment in Susan	1,600	-
Current Assets	1,400	1,200
	4,800	2,200
EQUITY AND LIABILITIES		
$1 Equity Shares	1,000	400
Retained earnings	1,600	800
Current liabilities	2,200	1,000
	4,800	2,200

1   Mike purchased 80% of the ordinary shares of Susan for $1,600 two years ago when Susan retained earnings showed a balance of $400.

2   Mike and Susan traded with each other during the year. At the end of the year Susan owed Mike $300. This is included in both sets of individual company figures. Also included in the inventory of Mike was $60 of goods purchased from Susan at mark up on cost of 25%.

3   The fair value of the non-controlling interest at the date of acquisition was $400

Required

Prepare the consolidated statement of financial position* for the Mike Group as at 31 December 2008 using the fair value method where an impairment of $400 has occurred on goodwill.

---

* Statement of financial position = Balance Sheet (see page 19)

Mike group statement of financial position as at 31 December 2008

	$
ASSETS	
Goodwill (W3)	800
Property, Plant and Equipment (1,800 + 1,000)	2,800
Current Assets (1,400 + 1,200 – 300 – 12PURP)	2,288
	5,888
EQUITY AND LIABILITIES	
$1 Equity Shares	1,000
Retained earnings (W5)	1,590
Non-controlling Interest (W4)	398
Current liabilities (2,200 + 1,000 – 300)	2,900
	5,888

(W1) Group Structure and PURP

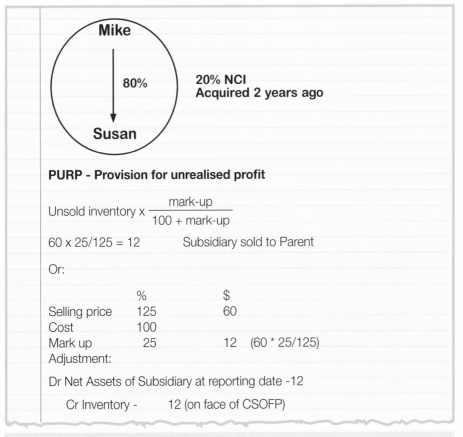

Mike

80%

20% NCI
Acquired 2 years ago

Susan

PURP - Provision for unrealised profit

$$\text{Unsold inventory} \times \frac{\text{mark-up}}{100 + \text{mark-up}}$$

60 x 25/125 = 12   Subsidiary sold to Parent

Or:

	%	$
Selling price	125	60
Cost	100	
Mark up	25	12 (60 * 25/125)

Adjustment:

Dr Net Assets of Subsidiary at reporting date -12

   Cr Inventory -   12 (on face of CSOFP)

(W2) Net assets of Susan

	At date of acquisition $	At reporting Date $
Share Capital	400	400
Retained earnings	400	800
Less: unrealised profit (PURP) (W1)		(12)
	800	1,188

(W3) Goodwill

	$
Parent holding (investment) at fair value	1,600
NCI value at acquisition (given)	400
	2,000
Less:	
100% fair value of net assets at acquisition (W2)	(800)
Goodwill on acquisition	1,200
Impairment (given)	(400)
Carrying value of **Goodwill** in **CSOFP**	800

NB Impairment of $400 is split between group and NCI in the same proportion as profits and losses of the subsidiary.

(W4) Non-controlling interest

	$
NCI value at acquisition (W3)	400
NCI share of post-acquisition reserves (W2) 20%(1,188-800)	77.6
NCI share of impairment (fair value method only) (400 x 20%) (W3)	(80)
NCI for CSOFP	**397.6**

(W5) Retained earnings

	$
100% Mike	1,600
Group share of post-acquisition reserves (W2)	
80% (1,188-800)	310.4
Less group share of impairment (400 x 80%)	(320)
Group retained earnings for CSOFP	**1,590.4**

Unrealised profit – non-current assets

It is not just inventory that can be sold between group companies. It's possible that non-current assets could also be transferred between group companies. Exactly the same principles apply – any profit made on the transfer should be cancelled and the non-current asset reduced to cost to the group.

The additional consideration would be depreciation.

You must remember that the depreciation needs to be based on cost to the group. An adjustment to the Carrying Value/Net Book Value (CV/NBV) of the asset and profit may be necessary.

Transactional example

On 1 July 2011 Max acquired 80% of the equity share capital of Bruce. The Max Group are now preparing group financial statements for the year ended 30 June 2012.

On the acquisition date Max sold an item of equipment to Bruce for $84,000. The asset originally cost $96,000 and has been written down to $64,000 as at 30 June 2011. Both companies depreciate plant and equipment on a straight line basis over 6 years. Bruce depreciated the cost of the asset over its remaining useful life of 4 years.

The principles are exactly the same in that a Provision for unrealised profit (PURP) will need creating when Property Plant or Equipment (PPE) is transferred between members of a group.

(W1) Group Structure

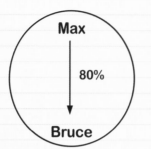

Max

80%

Bruce

20% NCI
Acquired 1 year ago

PURP

Provision created on transfer at 1st July 2011

Transfer Price	$84,000
Carrying value	$64,000

Profit on transfer $20,000
Parent sells to subsidiary so provision is created

Dr Retained Earnings (W5)

   Cr Plant (PPE) on face of CSOFP

But time has elapsed and it is now one year later. An additional step is required if it is a depreciating asset to eliminate additional depreciation.

Depreciation if the transfer had not occurred: (64,000/4)	$16,000
Depreciation as a result of the transfer : (84,000/4)	$21,000
Additional depreciation charged:	$5,000

Net impact

Plant (PPE) -20,000 + 5,000 = -15,000
Retained earnings -20,000 + 5,000 = -15,000

OR

Compare:

NBV if no transfer	(64,000 – (64,000/4 * 1))	$48,000
NBV with transfer	(84,000 – (84,000/4 * 1))	$63,000
Difference		$15,000

Plant (PPE) - 15,000

Retained earnings - 15,000

---

* Statement of financial position = Balance Sheet (see page 19)

Fair values

The accounting problem

So far in dealing with the acquisition of a subsidiary we have assumed that the net assets shown in the subsidiary's statement of financial position* are stated at fair value. This is not always the case, owing to the limitations of historical cost accounting. It is important that the financial results reported following acquisition accurately show the performance of the new management.

Therefore IFRS 3 (revised) requires that at the date of acquisition the identifiable assets and liabilities and contingent liabilities of the subsidiary that meet its recognition criteria must be stated at fair value on that date.

Group accounting questions may therefore include a requirement to put through fair value adjustments. The fair values, not the book values, will be used in the calculation of goodwill.

You will also have taken account of the impact of these adjustments on the post-acquisition reserves and assets and liabilities in the consolidated statement of financial position*.

Accounting treatment

The parent should recognise separately at fair value the acquiree's identifiable assets, liabilities and contingent liabilities at the acquisition date only if they satisfy the following criteria at that date:

- for an asset other than an intangible asset, it is probable that any associated future economic benefits will flow to the acquirer, and its fair value can be measured reliably
- for a liability other than a contingent liability, it is probable that an outflow of resources embodying economic benefits will be required to settle the obligation, and its fair value can be measured reliably
- in the case of an intangible asset or a contingent liability, its fair value can be measured reliably.

Identifiable assets and liabilities recognised in the accounts are those of the acquired entity that existed at the date of acquisition. The following specifically do not meet the criteria listed above and therefore must be dealt with as post-acquisition items:

- changes resulting from the acquirer's intentions or future actions
- changes resulting from post-acquisition events
- provisions for future operating losses or reorganisation costs incurred as a result of the acquisition.

---

* Statement of financial position = Balance Sheet (see page 19)

Calculating fair values

The revised IFRS 3 uses the same definition of fair value that the IASB and the FASB respectively use in their other standards. IFRS 3 offers guidelines in determining the fair value of specific classes of assets and liabilities:

- marketable securities (i.e. those traded on an active market) should be valued at current market value (quoted price)
- non-marketable securities should be valued at estimated value. Looking at comparable securities of similar quoted enterprises may be helpful
- receivables should be valued at the present value of amounts expected to be received, determined at appropriate current interest rate, less allowance for uncollectability and collection costs if necessary. Discounting is unlikely to be necessary for short-term receivables
- inventories:
  - finished goods should be valued at selling prices less the sum of disposal costs and a reasonable profit allowance
  - work in progress should be valued at ultimate selling prices less the sum of completion costs, disposal costs and a reasonable profit allowance
  - raw materials should be valued at current replacement costs
- property, plant and equipment should be valued at market value. If there is no evidence of market value, depreciated replacement cost should be used.
- intangible assets as per IAS 38
- payables should be valued at the present value of amounts expected to be paid. As with receivables, discounting will not be necessary for short-term payables.

An acquirer is no longer permitted to recognise contingencies acquired in a business combination that do not meet the definition of a liability.

The fair value exercise should be completed, if possible, by the date on which directors approve the first post-acquisition financial statements of the acquirer. If this is not possible there is a 12-month window to make fair value adjustments to the assets, liabilities and therefore goodwill. After this 12-month period, changes may only be made if errors occurred in accordance with IAS 8.

The mechanics of dealing with fair value adjustments

To process a fair value adjustment in a consolidation question you must consider the impact both at the acquisition and the statement of financial position* date.

At acquisition put an adjustment into the net assets working of the subsidiary to bring the net assets to fair value.

At the statement of financial position* date, any adjustments remaining from the acquisition must be accounted for both on the face of the consolidated statement of financial position* and in the net assets working as shown in the comprehensive illustration below.

---

* Statement of financial position = Balance Sheet (see page 19)

(W2) Net assets

	At date of acquisition $000	At the reporting date $000
Equity share capital + reserves	X	X
Fair value adjustments:		
Land *(no dep'n to consider from acq to reporting date)*	X	X
Other tangibles *(depreciate the FV adj from acq to reporting date using policy given)*	X	X
Less depreciation		(x)
Intangible assets meeting the IAS 38 criteria *(amortise the FV adj from acq to reporting date using policy given)*	X	X
Less amortisation		(x)
Inventory *(probably sold by the reporting date so no adj)*	X	–
Long-term payables *(discount to present value if an interest rate is given at acq and reporting date)*	X	X
Contingent liabilities *(include in the net assets of sub even though they would not normally be included in the financial statements)*	x/(x)	x/(x)
Net assets at fair value	X	X
PURP adjustment		(x)
	XX	XX

Note ⚠️

Other factors to consider:

Common accounting policies (it may be necessary to bring the subsidiary in line with group policy on such items as capitalisation of finance costs).

The cost of the acquisition

The cost of acquisition includes the following elements:

- cash paid
- fair value of any other consideration (which can often be in the form of shares)
- (Note under the revision of IFRS 3 professional fees and similar incremental costs will no longer be capitalised as part of the cost of acquisition, but will instead be written off to profit or loss.)

Issue costs of shares or other securities must be deducted from the proceeds of the issues not included in the cost of the acquisition.

Deferred consideration should be discounted, using a rate at which the acquirer could obtain similar borrowing (see example below).

Any contingent consideration should be included. Adjust the cost of acquisition and goodwill when estimates are revised. (Note under the revised IFRS 3 contingent consideration is to be measured at fair value and changes are most likely to be recognised in income unless they actually arise from additional information arising about conditions at the date of acquisition).

Where contingent consideration involves the issue of shares there is no liability (obligation to transfer economic benefits). Recognise this as part of the equity under a separate caption representing shares to be issued.

Consideration	Fair value	Entry in parent's accounts
Immediate transfer of cash	Cash value	DR Investment CR Cash
Immediate transfer of shares	Current market value	DR Investment CR Equity share capital CR Share premium
Deferred cash	Cash is discounted to present value	DR Investment CR Liability
Deferred shares	Current market value	DR Investment CR Other components of equity (shares to be issued reserve)
Contingent deferred cash	Regardless of the likelihood of the contingent event to occur, consideration is measured at its fair value at the acquisition date.	DR Investment CR Liability
Contingent deferred shares		DR Investment CR Other components of equity (shares to be issued reserve)

Transactional example

John Inc acquired 60% of the ordinary share capital of Robbie Inc four years ago, when the balance of Robbie Inc's reserves were $1,000,000.

At the date of acquisition the total of the fair value of the net assets of Robbie was $5,000,000.

There were three fair value adjustments at the date of acquisition, one for $200,000 related to inventory that has since been sold, one for land which the company still holds of $200,000, and the other fair value adjustment relating to plant with an original estimated life of ten years, which was two years old at the date of acquisition.

Goodwill arising on consolidation is capitalised and no impairment has occurred.

	John Inc	Robbie Inc
Statements of profit or loss	*$000*	*$000*
Revenue	*10,000*	*10,000*
Operating costs	*(8,000)*	*(9,000)*
Operating profit	*2,000*	*1,000*
Tax	*(500)*	*(400)*
Profit for the year	*1,500*	*600*

Statements of financial position*		
ASSETS		
Property, Plant and Equipment	*9,000*	*7,000*
Investment in Robbie Inc	*5,000*	
Total Assets	*14,000*	*7,000*
EQUITY AND LIABILITIES		
$1 Equity shares	*8,000*	*3,000*
Retained earnings	*5,000*	*3,000*
Liabilities	*1,000*	*1,000*
	14,000	*7,000*

Required

Prepare the consolidated statement of profit or loss and statement of financial position* for the John Inc group. The group accounting policy is to value goodwill and non-controlling interest on the fair value basis. Robbie's share price just before the acquisition was $2.5 so the fair value of the NCI was 3,000 shares x 40% = 1,200 x $2.5 =$3,000,000).

---

* Statement of financial position = Balance Sheet (see page 19)

First you would set up your answer booklet – leave a page for preparation of the statement of financial position* and a page for preparation of the income statement**.

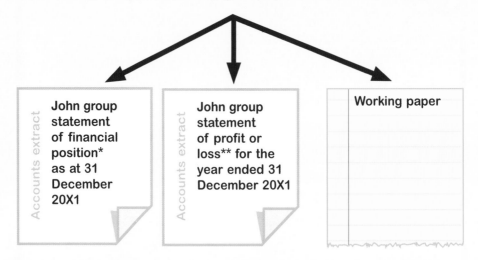

| Accounts extract | John group statement of financial position* as at 31 December 20X1 | | Accounts extract | John group statement of profit or loss** for the year ended 31 December 20X1 | | Working paper |

Then prepare a working paper. First do the standard statement of financial position* workings. However, this time as we have got fair value adjustments we will have to be prepared to adjust the (W2) net assets to fair value as per the requirements of IFRS 3.

(W1) Group structure

John
| 60%   4 years ago
Robbie   No inter company sales or PURP

(W2) Net assets at fair value

(This will need a bit of thinking about – first put a basic working together at book value but note you are given fair value information. You will have to put through fair value adjustments – set up a skeleton working as below:)

	Net assets at acquisition $	Net assets at reporting date $
Share capital	3,000	3,000
Reserves	1,000	3,000
Net assets at book value	4,000	6,000
Fair value adjustments		

---

* Statement of financial position = Balance Sheet (see page 19)

**Statement of profit or loss = Income statement

You are told the net assets at fair value at the date of acquisition were $5,000. This becomes your bottom line in the date of acquisition column – see below – it's a bit like fitting a jigsaw of numbers together.

(W2) Net assets at fair value

(your skeleton working now looks like this:)

	Net assets at acquisition $	Net assets at reporting date $
Share capital	3,000	3,000
Reserves	1,000	3,000
Net assets at book value	4,000	6,000
Fair value adjustments		
Net assets at fair value	5,000 *(given)*	

You then need to read what assets it relates to: it could be land (easy as non-depreciating); inventory (usually easy as inventory is a current asset and is usually gone by the statement of financial position* date) and property, plant and equipment (depreciating non-current assets need most thinking about due to the time lapse between the date of acquisition and the statement of financial position* date). Complete the date of acquisition column from the information in the question as overleaf.

---

* Statement of financial position = Balance Sheet (see page 19)

(W2) Net assets at fair value

(skeleton working continued)

	Net assets at acquisition $	Net assets at reporting date $
Share capital	3,000	3,000
Reserves	1,000	3,000
Net assets at book value	4,000	6,000
Fair value adjustments		
Land *(doesn't depreciate (given))*	200	
Inventory *(current asset – gone at reporting date (given))*	200	–
Plant *(depreciating asset (see below))*	600	
	–	
	5,000	

You can now complete the current reporting date column. If you have a fair value adjustment on a depreciating asset you will need to know how many years have elapsed between the date of acquisition and the current reporting date, so you can adjust the fair value – **WATCH THE DATES!!** Here the date of acquisition was four years previously and there is a depreciating fair value adjustment on an asset (plant) which had a useful economic life of eight years (10 – 2) at the date of acquisition. It now, therefore has a remaining useful economic life of four years (8 – 4). The working can now be completed – see overleaf.

(W2) Net assets at fair value (complete working)

	Net assets at acquisition	Net assets at reporting date
	$	$
Share capital	3,000	3,000
Reserves	1,000	3,000
Net assets at book value	4,000	6,000
Fair value adjustments		
Land *(doesn't depreciate)*	200	200
Inventory *(current asset – gone at statement of financial position* date)*	200	–
Plant *(depreciating asset)*	600	600
less depreciation (600 x 4/8)		(300)
	–	
	5,000	6,500

Note

The fair value adjustment on land is the same in both columns, on inventory it has gone by the statement of financial position* date and on the plant it is in both columns but at a reduced amount to reflect the elapse of time. These fair value figures are then the figures used in the other workings. Your next step will be to calculate goodwill at (W3) based on the fair value of the net assets at the date of acquisition.

(W3) Goodwill

	$
Cost of Investment	5,000
NCI at acquisition *(given)*	3,000
	8,000
Less	
100% Net assets acquired (W2)	(5,000)
Goodwill	3,000
Impairment to date	nil
Goodwill for CSOFP	**3,000**

---

* Statement of financial position = Balance Sheet (see page 19)

Calculate non-controlling interest for the statement of financial position* also using the net assets at fair value, but this time use the reporting date figure.

(W4) Non-controlling interest

	$
NCI at acquisition (W3)	3,000
NCI share of post acquisition profit(6,500- 5,000) x 40%	600
Less impairment to date *(if fair value/full policy)*	(nil)
NCI for CSOFP	**3,600**

When you calculate group reserves in a question with a depreciating fair value adjustment, you need to calculate post-acquisition profit by using the 'CHANGE IN NET ASSETS' approach. If you consider the net assets at fair value at the current statement of financial position* date (i.e. $6,500), and deduct the net assets at the date of acquisition at fair value (i.e. $5,000), the difference must be reserves created in the post-acquisition period (unless new share capital was introduced). This is a quick and easy way of doing the calculation – essential when you have a depreciating fair value adjustment in the question, and will work for all questions. See example below:

(W5) Group retained earnings

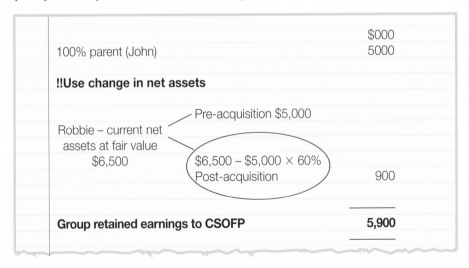

	$000
100% parent (John)	5000
!!Use change in net assets	
Pre-acquisition $5,000	
Robbie – current net assets at fair value $6,500	
$6,500 – $5,000 × 60% Post-acquisition	900
Group retained earnings to CSOFP	**5,900**

You can now prepare the consolidated statement of financial position*!! **Check the net assets at fair value at current reporting date. You need to remember to bring in the fair values to the consolidated statement of financial position*.** You do **the whole thing** by reference to fair values when they come up.

---

* Statement of financial position = Balance Sheet (see page 19)

John group statement of financial position*

	$
Goodwill (W3)	3,000
Property, Plant and Equipment 9,000 + 7,000 + 300 (W2) + 200 (W2)	16,500
	19,500
Share capital (100% parent)	8,000
$1 Equity shares (W5)	5,900
Non-controlling interest (W4)	3,600
Liabilities 1,000 + 1,000	2,000
	19,500

CSOFP*

When you put together the income statement, remember you will have an expense that doesn't exist in the real company accounts – the additional depreciation expense re Robbie's plant (the depreciating fair value adjustment. A one year (current year effect) charge will need to be shown as an expense in the income statement $[(600 \times 1/8) = 75]$ based on the eight years remaining useful economic life. This will also need to be reflected at the non-controlling interest line as it relates to the subsidiary. The income statement will look like this:

John group statement of profit or loss

Revenue 10,000 + 10,000	20,000
Operating costs (8,000 + 9,000) + 75 additional depreciation (W2)	(17,075)
Operating profit	2,925
Tax 500 + 400	(900)
Profit for the year	2,025
Profit attributable to:	
Equity shareholders of the parent	1,815
NCI (40%(600-75)	210
Robbie profit after tax-additional depreciation expense	
	2,025

Consolidated statement of profit or loss

Complex groups

It is possible to gain control without directly purchasing a single share in a company. If a company controlled by the parent (a subsidiary) purchases enough shares to control a third company, we have a 'control gained indirectly' situation.

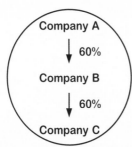

For example where the parent (Company A) owns a 60% share in a subsidiary (Company B) and then Company B has a 60% share in another company (Company C).

In this situation, despite company A not directly owning any shares in Company C, the control of the financial and operating policies' of Company C lies with Company A, via the controlled entity Company B.

In this case Company A is actually the ultimate parent of Company C and Company C will be treated as a subsidiary. These indirectly held subsidiaries are often referred to a sub-subsidiaries.

Impact on consolidation technique

Assets and liabilities are still added together (to show what the group controls).

Equity shows the ownership of the assets and liabilities and the reserves will be based on the effective holding.

Vertical groups

Acquisition of sub-subsidiary pre acquisition

In this situation the parent acquires a subsidiary, which has already a subsidiary, so effectively the parent is acquiring an interest in the group.

Acquisition of sub-subsidiary post acquisition

In this situation the parent acquires a subsidiary and then at a later stage the subsidiary (as part of the group effectively) acquires an interest in another subsidiary.

The most important thing is to watch the dates of acquisition and remember the date of acquisition is the date the ultimate parent gains control. This is not necessarily the date that the shares were purchased.

Transactional example

The financial statements of 3 companies as at 31 December 2010 are as follows:

	America $'000	Bali $'000	Germany $'000
ASSETS			
Investments			
300,000 shares in Bali	450		
240,000 shares in Germany		320	
Current assets	890	610	670
	1,340	930	670
EQUITY AND LIABILITIES			
$1 Equity shares	600	400	300
Retained earnings	400	300	100
Current liabilities	340	230	270
	1,340	930	670

There is also some additional information available:

1 On 1 January 2008 America acquired its interest in Bali, a public limited company. The purchase consideration comprised cash of $450,000 and the fair value of the identifiable net assets was the same as the book value. The fair value of the non-controlling interest in Bali was $125,000 on 1 January 2008. America wishes to use the 'full goodwill' method for all acquisitions.

2 Bali acquired its interest in Germany, a public limited company on 1 January 2008. The purchase consideration was cash of $320,000. Germany's net assets had a fair value equivalent to the book value and the NCI of Germany attributable to America had a fair value of $144,000.

3 The retained earnings of Bali and Germany are as follows:

	1st Jan 2008 $'000	1st Jan 2010 $'000
Bali	100	300
Germany	60	100

4 An impairment review carried out at 31 December 2010 showed an impairment loss of:

- Bali $50,000
- Germany $15,000.

Required.

(a) Prepare the consolidated statement of the financial position of America and its subsidiary companies at 31 December 2010

---

* Statement of financial position = Balance Sheet (see page 19)

Working paper – with indirect held entity

(W1) Group structure and PURP

PURP

There have been no inter-company sales in this period.

When there is a indirectly held entity in the group (such as Germany here) in order to do the W4 and W5 split (between NCI and group) you need to work out the effective interest from the point of view of the ultimate parent - here America. America owns 75% of a company who owns 80% of Germany.

For the purpose of W5 the group effectively own 75% of the 80% owned by Bali = 60%

For the purpose of W4 the NCI is the difference between 100% and the 60% effectively owned by the group. 100% - 60% = 40%. The NCI **percentage**, therefore is a balancing figure.

(W2) Net assets of subsidiary

Bali	At acquisition date $000	At reporting date $000
$1 Equity Share Capital	400	400
Retained earnings	100	300
	500	700
Germany	**At acquisition date $000**	**At reporting date $000**
$1 Equity Share Capital	300	300
Retained earnings	60	100
	360	400

(W3) Goodwill – Bali

	$000
Cost of Investment (given)	450
NCI value at acquisition (given)	125
	575
Less:	
Fair value of net assets at acquisition (W2)	(500)
Goodwill on acquisition	75
Impairment	(50)
Carrying value of Goodwill in CSOFP	**25**

Indirect holding adjustment

So far the workings in this complex group have been pretty much the same as doing a simple group (a simple group is a group for which there are only directly held entities).

However if the subsidiary is indirectly held then there is an additional consideration when you try to calculated the goodwill. This is the **indirect holding adjustment.**

An indirect holding adjustment is required because if we pick up the cost of investment in Germany in the normal way (see goodwill working below) we will calculate goodwill incorrectly.

America illustrates this: the cost of the shares in Germany was $320,000. However America did not pay the $320,000, Bali paid the $320,000 not America.

America owns 75% of Bali and so has effectively paid 75% of the $320,000.

This is why the indirect holding adjustment is needed. It is deducted from the cost of investment to reduce to the effective 75% of the $320,000.

It is calculated, therefore, by multiplying the cost of investment by the NCI percentage for the directly held subsidiary.

Here America effectively paid 75% of the $320,000 so the other 25% was effectively paid by the NCI.

The required indirect holding adjustment is therefore 25% of the $320,000 - the NCI share of the cost of investment.

(W3) Goodwill – Germany

	$000
Cost of Investment (given)	320
Less:	
Indirect holding adjustment 25% (320)	(80)
NCI value at acquisition (given)	144
	384
Less:	
Fair value of net assets at acquisition (W2)	(360)
Goodwill on acquisition	24
Impairment (given)	(15)
Carrying value of Goodwill in SOFP	9

This indirect holding adjustment line only occurs in a complex group. The other side of the entry is in W4

Note

The indirect holding adjustment

This will always be needed when you have an indirectly held entity in the group

(W4) Non-controlling Interest

	$000
NCI value at acquisition (W3) - Bali	125
NCI share of post-acquisition reserves (W2) - Bali (700-500) *25%	50
NCI value at acquisition (as in W3)- Germany	144
NCI share of post-acquisition reserves (W2) - Germany (400-360)*40%	16
Indirect holding adjustment (W3)	(80)
NCI share of impairment (fair value method only) - Bali (50*25%)	(12.5)
NCI share of impairment (fair value method only) - Germany (15*40%)	(6)
Non-controlling interest in CSOFP	**236.5**

This is the other side the entry from working 3

Note

The standard working has doubled up with both companies now being included and the other side of the entry for the indirect holding adjustment also being deducted here.

(W5) Group retained earnings

	$000
100% Parent retained earnings	400
Parent's share of Bali's post acquisition retained earnings (700- 500) *75%	150
Parent's share of Germany's post acquisition retained earnings (400-360) *60%	24
Less goodwill impairment (W3) Bali (50 *75%) Germany (15*60%)	(37.5) (9)
Total Group reserves for CSOFP	**527.5**

America group statement of financial position as at 31 December 2010

ASSETS	$000	$000
Non-current assets		
Goodwill (W3) (25+9)		*34*
Current assets (890+610+670)		*2,170*
Total assets		**2,204**
EQUITY AND LIABILITIES		
Equity attributable to the parent		
Equity share capital	*600*	
Retained earnings (W5)	*527.5*	
		1,127.5
Non-controlling interest (W4)		*236.5*
Current liabilities (340+230+270)		*840*
Total equity and liabilities		**2,204**

D shaped groups

In this situation a parent company (P) has direct control over a subsidiary (A1) and then both the parent and the subsidiary invest in another company (A2). In this case the parent now has direct control over the initial subsidiary (A1) plus direct control over the other subsidiary (A2) and indirect control through its control of the first subsidiary (A1).

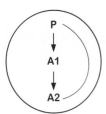

This is just like you have a mix of a simple and a vertical group.

i.e. this effects the goodwill calculation of the company where you have a direct and an indirect holding.

(W3) Goodwill – for a company with a direct and an indirect holding

	$
Cost of Investment - Direct	X
Cost of Investment - Indirect	X
Less:	
Indirect holding adjustment	(x)
NCI value at acquisition	X
	X
Less:	
Fair value of net assets at acquisition (W2)	(x)
Goodwill on acquisition	X
Impairment	(x)
Carrying value of Goodwill in CSOFP	**xx**

An indirect holding adjustment is needed in a D shaped group as well as a vertical group

Transactional example

The financial statements of 3 companies as at 31 December 2011 are as follows:

	Oak $'000	Beech $'000	Gold $'000
ASSETS			
Investments			
300,000 shares in Beech	450		
25,600 shares in Gold	35		
230,400 shares in Gold		316	
Current assets	869	660	574
	1,354	976	574
EQUITY AND LIABILITIES			
$1 Equity share capital	600	400	320
Retained earnings	400	356	180
	1,000	756	500
Current liabilities	354	220	74
	1,354	976	574

Further additional information available is as follows:

(1) Oak bought its shares in Beech on 1 January 2009 when Beech's retained earnings were $140,000.

(2) Oak and Beech bought their shares in Gold on 1 January 2010 when the balance on retained earnings was $80,000.

(3) It is group policy to value the NCI at FV at the date of acquisition, the FV of the NCI in Beech on 1 January 2009 was $145,000 and the FV of the 38% NCI in Gold on 1 January 2010 was $160,000.

(4) Goodwill has been tested for impairment and it is not impaired.

Required
Prepare the consolidated statement of financial position as at 31 December 2011.

Oak group statement of financial position* as at 31 December 2011
Oak, Beech and Gold

ASSETS	$000	$000
Non-current assets		
Goodwill (W3) (55 +32)		87
Current assets (869+660+574)		2,103
Total assets		**2,190**
EQUITY AND LIABILITIES		
Equity attributable to the parent		
Equity share capital	600	
Retained earnings (W5)	624	
		1,224
Non-controlling interest (W4)		318
Current liabilities (354+220+74)		648
Total equity and liabilities		**2,190**

SOFP standard workings

(W1) Group structure

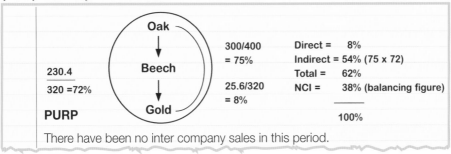

Oak

Beech

Gold

PURP

300/400 = 75%

25.6/320 = 8%

230.4 / 320 = 72%

Direct = 8%
Indirect = 54% (75 x 72)
Total = 62%
NCI = 38% (balancing figure)
100%

There have been no inter company sales in this period.

(W2) Net assets of subsidiary

Beech	At acquisition date $000	At reporting date $000
$1 Equity Share Capital	400	400
Retained earnings	140	356
	540	756
Gold	**At acquisition date $000**	**At reporting date $000**
$1 Equity Share Capital	320	320
Retained earnings	80	180
	400	500

(W3) Goodwill – Beech

	$
Cost of Investment *(given)*	450
NCI value at acquisition *(given)*	145
	595
Less	
Fair value of net assets at acquisition (W2)	(540)
Goodwill on acquisition	55
Impairment	nil
Carrying value of goodwill in CSOFP	**55**

(W3) Goodwill – Gold (remember there is a direct as well as an indirect holding

	$000
Cost of Investment - Direct *(given)*	35
Cost of Investment - Indirect	316
Less	
Indirect holding adjustment 25% (316)	(79)
NCI value at acquisition *(given)*	160
	432
Less	
Fair value of net assets at acquisition (W2)	(400)
Goodwill on acquisition	32
Impairment	(nil)
Carrying value of goodwill in SOFP	**32**

Remember you need an indirect holding adjustment in both vertical and D shaped groups. The other side of the entry is in W4 Non-controlling Interest

(W4) Non-controlling interest

	$000
NCI value at acquisition (W3) - Beech	145
NCI share of post-acquisition reserves (W2) - Beech (756-540) *25%	54
NCI value at acquisition (as in W3)- Gold	160
NCI share of post-acquisition reserves (W2) - Gold (500-400)*38%%	38
Indirect holding adj (W3)	(79)
NCI share of impairment (fair value method only) -Beech	nil
NCI share of impairment (fair value method only) - Gold	nil
Non-controlling interest in CSOFP	**318**

This is the other side of the adjustment from (W3)

(W5) Group retained earnings

100% Parent retained earnings		400
Parents share of Beech's post acquisition retained earnings (756-540) *75%		162
Parents share of Gold's post acquisition retained earnings (500-400)*62%		62
Less goodwill impairment (W3)		
Beech		Nil
Gold		Nil
Total group reserves for CSOFP		**624**

Step Acquisition

Acquisition accounting (accounting for recognition of goodwill and non-controlling interests) is only applied at the date when control is achieved.

Any pre-existing equity interest in an entity is accounted for according to:

* IFRS 9 in the case of simple investments
* IAS 28 in the case of associates
* IFRS 11 in the case of joint ventures.

At the date when equity interest is increased and control achieved:

* remeasure the previously held equity interest to fair value
* recognise any resulting gain or loss in profit or loss
* calculate goodwill and non-controlling interest on either a partial (i.e. proportionate) or full (i.e. fair value) basis in accordance with IFRS 3 Revised. The cost of acquiring control will be the fair value of the previously held equity interest plus the cost of the most recent purchase of shares at acquisition date
* if there has been re-measurement of any previously held equity interest that was recognised in other comprehensive income, any changes in value recognised in earlier years are now reclassified from equity to profit or loss
* the situation of a further purchase of shares in a subsidiary after control has been acquired (for example taking the group interest from 60% to 75%) is regarded as a transaction between equity holders; goodwill is not recalculated. This situation is covered by IFRS 10.

Transactional example

Jay, a public limited company, has acquired the following shareholdings in Gee a public limited company.

Date of acquisition	Holding acquired	Fair value of net assets	Purchase consideration
Gee		$m	$m
1 June 20X3	30%	40	15
1 June 20X4	50%	50	30

The following statements of financial position relate to Jay and Gee at 31 May 20X5:

	Jay $m	Gee $m
ASSETS		
Property, plant and equipment	300	40
Investment in Gee	45	–
Current assets	122	20
Total assets	467	60
EQUITY AND LIABILITIES		
$1 Equity share capital	100	10
Share premium account	50	20
Retained earnings	132	16
Other components of equity	15	–
Total equity	297	46
Non-current liabilities	60	4
Current liabilities	110	10
Total equity and liabilities	467	60

The following information is relevant to the preparation of the group financial statements of the Jay Group.

(a) Gee has not issued any new share capital since the acquisition of the shareholdings by Jay. The excess of the fair value of the net assets of Gee over their carrying amounts at the dates of acquisition is due to an increase in the value of Gee's non-depreciable land of $10 million at 1 June 20X3 and a further increase of $4 million at 1 June 20X4. There has been no change in the value of non-depreciable land since 1 June 20X4.

---

* Statement of financial position = Balance Sheet (see page 19)

(b) Before obtaining control of Gee, Jay did not have significant influence over Gee. Jay has accounted for the investment in Gee at market value with changes in value being recorded in profit or loss. The market price of the shares of Gee at 1 June 20X4 had risen to $6 per share as there was speculation regarding a takeover bid. This impact has not yet been accounted for.

(c) At 1 June 20X4 the fair value of the non-controlling interest in Gee was $11m.

(d) Goodwill has been tested for impairment and is not impaired.

Required:

Prepare the consolidated statement of financial position* of the Jay Group as at 31 May 20X5 in accordance with IFRS 3 Business Combinations.

Jay group statement of financial position* as at 31 May 20X5

ASSETS	$000
Non-current assets	
Goodwill (W3)	9
Property, plant and equipment	
(300+40) + 14 (W2)	354
Current assets (122 + 20)	142
Total assets	**505**
EQUITY AND LIABILITIES	
Equity attributable to the parent	
Equity share capital	100
Share premium account	50
Retained earnings (W5)	143
Other components of equity	15
	308
Non-controlling interest (W4)	13
Non-current liabilities (60 + 4)	64
Current liabilities (110 + 10)	120
Total equity and liabilities	**505**

* Statement of financial position = Balance Sheet (see page 19)

SOFP Standard Workings – with step acquisition

(W1) Group structure and PURP

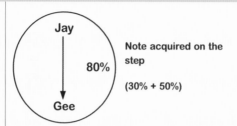

Jay
80%
Gee

Note acquired on the step

(30% + 50%)

Due to acquisition on the step: remember to revalue the original cost of investment to fair value:

Originally Jay paid $15m for 3 million shares in Gee. This was a 30% holding (3m /10m shares).

To acquire those same 3 million shares on 1st June 20X4 (date control is achieved) would require an investment of 3m shares x $6 = $18m. There is a need to revalue.

Dr Investment in Gee $3m (18m -15m purchase price)

   Cr Profit (income Statement) $3m

PURP

There have been no inter-company sales in this period.

(W2) Net assets of subsidiary – initial skeleton working

Remember date of acquisition is date you gained control.

Gee	At acquisition date $m	At reporting date $m
$1 Equity Share Capital		10
Share Premium		20
Retained earnings		16
		46

Note

The reporting date information is given on the SOFP and the fair value adjustment info is in note (a). The opening table has the total fair value at the date of acquisition.

(W2) Net assets of subsidiary - skeleton working continued

Gee	At acquisition date $m	At reporting date $m
$1 Equity share capital		10
Share premium		20
Retained earnings		16
		46
Fair value adjustments		
Land	14	14
Less depreciation		(nil)
Net assets at fair value	50	60

The rest can be deduced – you are told Gee has not issued any new shares since the date of acquisition. The 6 is therefore the balancing figure.

(W2) Net assets of subsidiary - complete

Gee	At acquisition date $m	At reporting date $m
$1 Equity Share Capital	10	10
Share Premium	20	20
Retained earnings (balancing figure)	6	16
	36	46
Fair value adjustments		
Land	14	14
Less depreciation		(nil)
Net assets at fair value	50	60

(W3) Goodwill – Gee

	$
Cost of Investment (45+3)	48
NCI value at acquisition *(given)*	11
	59
Less	
100% Fair value of net assets at acquisition (W2)	(50)
Goodwill on acquisition	9
Impairment	nil
Carrying value of Goodwill in CSOFP	**9**

(W4) Non-controlling interest

	$000
NCI value at acquisition (W3) - Gee	11
NCI share of post-acquisition reserves (W2) - Gee (60-50) *20%	2
NCI share of impairment (fair value method only) - Gee	(nil)
Carrying value of NCI in CSOFP	**13**

(W5) Group retained earnings

	$000
100% Parent retained earnings	132
Revaluation due to step acquisition (18-15) (W1)	3
Parents share of Gee's post acquisition retained earnings (60-50)*80%	8
Less: goodwill impairment (W3)	
Gee	(nil)
Total Group reserves for CSOFP	**143**

And the really important stuff … accounting practice

All business combinations must be accounted for under the acquisition method. The pooling of interests method (merger method) that was available in IAS 22 has been abolished.

If a business combination is by exchange of shares and control passes to the party that has not issued the shares, the acquisition is a reverse acquisition. The controlling party (the legal subsidiary) is treated as the acquirer.

The cost of a business combination is the aggregate of:

- the fair values of assets given, liabilities incurred, and equity instruments issued.

PLEASE NOTE:

The costs directly attributable to the business combination must be taken directly to profit (statement of profit or loss) per the revised IFRS 3.

Contingent costs are included when at fair value, with changes in income (unless they arise from additional information arising about conditions at the date of acquisition).

The acquirer recognises separately the acquiree's identifiable assets, liabilities and contingent liabilities if they satisfy the following criteria:

- for assets other than intangibles, it is probable that economic benefits will flow and they can be measured reliably

- for liabilities (other than contingent liabilities), it is probable that an outflow of economic benefits will be required and they can be measured reliably

- it is an intangible (including in-progress R&D) that meets the criteria in IAS 38 and is not the value of the assembled workforce (it is presumed in IAS 38 that these can be measured reliably if they have a finite life)

- for contingent liabilities, its fair value can be measured reliably.

Goodwill should initially be measured either at cost or at fair value.

Positive goodwill is not amortised but instead is subject to an annual impairment review (following IAS 36).

Negative goodwill is immediately recognised as income in the statement of profit or loss.

Disclosures

An acquirer should disclose information that enables users of its financial statements to evaluate the nature and financial effect of business combinations that were effected:

(a) during the reporting period

(b) after the reporting date but before the financial statements are authorised for issue.

Conclusion

If group accounts are on your syllabus they will be a very important part of most exams. In fact, once they are on your syllabus it is quite rare for them to go unexamined. You must make sure you practise many questions set previously by your examiner to ensure you understand the standard to which you are being examined. There are many different potential complications in group accounting questions. Find out which ones your examiner includes and … **practise, practise, practise!!**

IFRS 10 – Consolidated financial statements

Introduction

> **"I believe I was extremely greedy. I've lost my moral compass and did things I regret."**
>
> **Andrew Fastow, Chief Financial Officer (CFO) of Enron**

Andy Fastow was the Chief Financial Officer of Enron, the most famous bankruptcy of all time. One of the 'things' that Andy Fastow 'did' (he went to prison for six and a half years by the way) was to set up a deliberate network of over 4,000 companies that, despite being controlled entities in substance, were not included in the consolidated financial statements of Enron. This was because they were deliberately established to fall outside the US GAAP definition of a subsidiary. This was a deliberate plan to mislead the readers of the main Enron accounts about the amount of cash that Enron was borrowing and to cover up the true level of its debt.

Consolidated accounts are pretty important then?

Absolutely! All companies may be separate legal entities but often one company owns enough shares to appoint the board of another company. This means that, although the second company is a separate legal entity, in substance it is merely like a division of the first. The two companies together are commercially a 'single entity'. Just preparing separate financial statements will not present fairly. We call the company that owns the shares the 'parent' and the second company the 'subsidiary'. All subsidiaries (subject to some limited exemptions) should have their accounts consolidated with those of the parent. Only in this way the true commercial reality is being reflected.

So ... what's it trying to achieve?

IFRS 10 establishes principles for the presentation and preparation of consolidated financial statements when an entity controls one or more other entities.

Sorry but you need to know ... DEFINITIONS

Consolidated financial statements are the financial statements of a **group** presented as those of a single economic entity.

Control of an investee
An investor controls an investee when the investor is exposed, or has rights, to variable returns from its involvement with the investee and has the ability to affect those returns through its power over the investee.

A **group** is a parent and its subsidiaries.

A **parent** is an entity that **controls** one or more entities.

A **subsidiary** is an entity that is controlled by another entity.

Power
Existing rights that give the current ability to direct the **relevant activities.**

Relevant activities
For the purpose of this IFRS, relevant activities are activities of the investee that significantly affect the investee's returns.

Control

In a change from the structural approach previously required by IAS 27, control is identified by IFRS 10 Consolidated Financial Statements as the sole basis for consolidation and comprises the following three elements:

1   power over the investee, where the investor has existing rights that gives it the ability to direct activities that significantly affect the investee's returns

2   exposure, or rights to, variable returns from involvement in the investee; and

3   the current ability to use power over the investee to affect the amount of the investor's returns.

IFRS 10 adopts a principles-based approach to determining whether or not control is exercised in a given situation, which may require the exercise of judgement. One outcome is that it should lead to more consistent judgements being made, with the consequence of greater comparability of financial reporting information.

IFRS 10 states that investors should periodically consider whether control over an investee has been gained or lost. It goes on to identify a range of circumstances that may need to be considered when determining whether or not an investor has power over an investee.

Exercise of the majority of voting rights in an investee

Most parent and subsidiary relationships are easy to identify as, once an investor holds more than half of the voting rights in an investee, they usually gain control as the ordinary shares usually come with matching voting rights, so 80% of the equity shares equals 80% of the votes.

This allows the investor to appoint the board and direct the relevant activities of the investee.

 Transactional example

Retallack acquires 80% of the equity shares of Obrey.

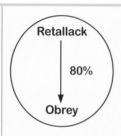

But... this is actually assuming the relevant activities are directed by a vote of the holder of the majority of the equity shares and that a majority of the board are appointed by the holder of the majority of the equity shares.

Note

Substantive rights

When assessing the power to control, you must only consider substantive rights - i.e. the holder must have the practical ability to exercise that right.

Majority of the voting rights but no power

 Beware of circumstances where you have more than half the voting rights but no power because another entity has the right to direct the relevant activities, this could be due to the company's actions being subject to direction by government, court administrator, receiver, liquidator or regulator.

Power without a majority of the voting rights

An investor can have power even if it holds less than a majority of the voting rights of an investee. An investor can have power with less than a majority of the voting rights of an investee, for example, through:

(a) a contractual arrangement between the investor and other vote holders

(b) rights arising from other contractual arrangements

(c) the investor's voting rights

(d) potential voting rights; or

(e) a combination of (a) – (d).

Transactional example

Aston (investor) acquired 48% of the voting shares of Villa (investee) on 1 March 2006.The remaining voting rights are held by thousands of shareholders, none individually holding more than 1 per cent of the voting rights. None of the shareholders has any arrangements to consult any of the others or make collective decisions. When assessing the proportion of voting rights to acquire, on the basis of the relative size of the other shareholdings, the investor determined that a 48 per cent interest would be sufficient to give it control.

In this case, on the basis of the absolute size of its holding and the relative size of the other shareholdings, the investor concludes that it has a sufficiently dominant voting interest to meet the power criterion without the need to consider any other evidence of power.

A typical error that students make in questions concerning consolidation relates to determining the status of the company. Students often apply a blanket percentage approach, i.e. if it is above 50% they consolidate and if it is below they don't. Remember the decision should be made by ability to control, not the percentage held. Here Villa should be consolidated.

Transactional example

Investor Roy Slaney holds 40% of the voting rights of an investee and twelve other investors each hold 5 per cent of the voting rights of the investee. A shareholder agreement grants investor Roy Slaney the right to appoint, remove and set the remuneration of management responsible for directing the relevant activities. To change the agreement, a two-thirds majority vote of the shareholders is required.

In this case, investor Roy Slaney concludes that the absolute size of the investor's holding and the relative size of the other shareholdings alone are not conclusive in determining whether the investor has rights sufficient to give it power. However, investor Roy Slaney determines that its contractual right to appoint, remove and set the remuneration of management is sufficient to conclude that it has power over the investee. The fact that investor Roy Slaney might not have exercised this right or the likelihood of investor Roy Slaney exercising its right to select, appoint or remove management shall not be considered when assessing whether investor Roy Slaney has power.

Relevant activities and direction of relevant activities

For many investees, a range of operating and financing activities significantly affect their returns. Examples of activities that, depending on the circumstances, can be relevant activities include, but are not limited to:

(a) selling and purchasing of goods or services

(b) managing financial assets during their life (including upon default)

(c) selecting, acquiring or disposing of assets

(d) researching and developing new products or processes; and

(e) determining a funding structure or obtaining funding.

Examples of decisions about relevant activities include but are not limited to:

(a) establishing operating and capital decisions of the investee, including budgets; and

(b) appointing and remunerating an investee's key management personnel or service providers and terminating their services or employment.

Transactional example

The Finance Director of Place, a public limited company has set up a company, Wilton, through which Place is to conduct some investment activities. Place has paid $400 million to Wilton during the year.

Wilton invested the money in a specified portfolio of investments. Ninety five per cent of profits and one hundred percent of the losses in the specified portfolio are transferred to Place.

An investment manager has charge of the company's investments and owns all of the equity share capital of Wilton. An agreement between the investment manager and Place sets out the operating guidelines and prohibits the investment manager from obtaining access to the investments for the manager's benefit. An annual transfer of the profit/ loss will occur on 30th June annually. The transfer of cash occurred on 1st January 2012 but no transfer of profit/loss has occurred. The statement of financial position as at 30 June 2012 is as follows:

Wilton - statement of financial position as at 30th June 2012

	$m
Investment – FVTP&L	390
	390
Equity share capital	400
Retained earnings	(10)
	390

Application of IFRS 10 to Place and Wilton

Power

An investor has power over an investee when the investor has existing rights that give it the current ability to direct the relevant activities, i.e. the activities that significantly affect the investee's returns.

Returns

An investor is exposed, or has rights, to variable returns from its involvement with the investee when the investor's returns from its involvement have the potential to vary as a result of the investee's performance. The investor's returns can be only positive, only negative or wholly positive and negative.

Link between power and returns

An investor may delegate its decision-making authority to an agent on some specific issues or on all relevant activities. When assessing whether it controls an investee, the investor shall treat the decision-making rights delegated to its agent as held by the investor directly.

---

* Statement of financial position = Balance Sheet (see page 19)

A decision maker shall consider the overall relationship between itself, the investee being managed and other parties involved with the investee, in particular all the factors below, in determining whether it is an agent:

(a) the scope of its decision-making authority over the investee

(b) the rights held by other parties

(c) the remuneration to which it is entitled in accordance with the remuneration agreement(s)

(d) the decision maker's exposure to variability of returns from other interests that it holds in the investee.

Conclusion

The investment manager of Wilton is merely an agent as they do not control the fund.

Place is the principal and controls Wilton, and Wilton will need to be included in the consolidated accounts of Place. Place has power of the investee via the operating guidelines. The investment manager manages the fund within the guidelines and receives 5% of any profits earned. This amounts to remuneration for services.

The investment manager cannot earn more than 5% of the profits and has no exposure to losses (negative returns).

Under IFRS 10 Wilton will need to be consolidated into the group accounts of Place.

And the really important stuff ... accounting practice

An entity that is a parent shall present consolidated financial statements.

This IFRS applies to all entities except as follows:

(a) a parent need not present consolidated financial statements if it meets all the following conditions:

   (i) it is a wholly-owned subsidiary or is a partially-owned subsidiary of another entity and all its other owners, including those not otherwise entitled to vote, have been informed about, and do not object to, the parent not presenting consolidated financial statements

   (ii) its debt or equity instruments are not traded in a public market (a domestic or foreign stock exchange or an over-the-counter market, including local and regional markets)

   (iii) it did not file, nor is it in the process of filing, its financial statements with a securities commission or other regulatory organisation for the purpose of issuing any class of instruments in a public market; and

(iv) its ultimate or any intermediate parent produces consolidated financial statements that are available for public use and comply with IFRSs.

(b) post-employment benefit plans or other long-term employee benefit plans to which IAS 19 Employee Benefits applies.

Consolidation procedures

Intra-group (intra=within) balances and transactions must be eliminated in full.

If they have different year-ends the parent and subsidiary accounts can be consolidated if they are within three months of each other.

Parents and subsidiaries must use uniform accounting policies.

Non-controlling interests should be presented in equity, but separate from the parent shareholder's equity. Non-controlling interests should also be separately presented in the income statement*.

Loss of control

If a parent loses control of the subsidiary, the parent:

(a) derecognises the assets and liabilities of the former subsidiary from the consolidated statement of financial position

(b) recognises any investment retained in the former subsidiary at its fair value when control is lost and subsequently accounts for it and for any amounts owed by or to the former subsidiary in accordance with relevant IFRSs

(c) recognises the gain or loss associated with the loss of control attributable to the former controlling interest.

* Statement of profit or loss = Income statement

Transactional example

The statements of profit or loss for Hop, Skip and Jump for the year ended 30 September 2010 are as follows:

	Hop $m	Skip $m	Jump $m
Revenue (Note 1)	500	400	300
Cost of sales	(200)	(150)	(120)
Gross Profit	300	250	180
Distribution and admin costs	(150)	(130)	(90)
Profit from operations	150	120	90
Investment income (Notes 2 and 3)	24	-	-
Finance costs	(60)	(40)	(30)
Profit before tax	114	80	60
Income tax expense	(40)	(28)	(15)
Profit for the period	74	52	45

The retained earnings of the three companies at 1 Oct 2009 are as follows:

	$
Hop	250m
Skip	160m
Jump	165m

Dividends were paid by all 3 companies on 30 September 2010 as follows:

	$
Hop	50m
Skip	32m
Jump	25m

Profits are assumed to accrue evenly.

Notes

1   Hop supplies a product used by Skip (but not by Jump). During the year ended 30 September 2010, sales of the product by Hop to Skip (all at cost to Hop plus a mark up of 25%) totalled $48 million. At 30 September 2010, the inventories of Skip included $18 million ($9 million as at 30 September 2009) in respect of goods supplied by Hop.

2   Investments made by Hop in Skip and Jump were as follows:

(a) On 1 October 2000, Hop purchased 75% of the equity shares of Skip . The purchase consideration comprised cash of $100 million. The fair value of the non-controlling interest in Skip was £35m on 1 October 2000. The statement of financial position* of Skip at that date showed the following:

	$m
Equity share capital ($1 shares)	60
Retained earnings	60
	120

The fair values of the net assets of Skip on 1st October 2000 were the same as their book values

(b) On 1 October 1998, Hop purchased 80% of the equity shares of Jump. The purchase consideration was cash of $120 million. The fair value of the NCI at that date was $30m. The statement of financial position* of Jump at that date showed the following:

	$m
Equity share capital ($1 shares)	50
Retained earnings	75
	125

The fair values of the net assets of Jump on 1 October 1998 were the same as their book values.

The policy of Hop is to value goodwill using the 'full goodwill' method for all acquisitions.

3   On 31 May 2010, Hop disposed of the whole of its investment in Jump for $245 million. The taxation payable by Hop in connection with this disposal was estimated at $20 million. The effects of this disposal have NOT been incorporated into the income statement of Hop, which appears above. The business of Jump is very similar to the business of Hop and the directors of Hop are reasonably confident that the revenue of Hop will increase following the disposal to the extent that the revenue of the Group as a whole will not be materially affected.

4   Goodwill has been impairment tested annually and as at 30 September 2009 for Skip had reduced in value by 20% and as at 30 September 2010 had lost a further 20% of its original value. The goodwill impairment should be allocated between the group and NCI on the basis of equity shareholding. The goodwill of Jump had not been impaired.

* Statement of financial position = Balance Sheet (see page 19)

Required

(a) *Prepare the consolidated statement of profit or loss and other comprehensive income for the Hop Group for the year ended 30 September 2010.*

(b) *Calculate the goodwill that arose on the acquisition of:*

- Skip
- Jump

Consolidated statement of profit or loss and other comprehensive income for the year ended 30 September 2010

Hop, Skip and Jump

	$	$
Revenue (500 + 400 + (300*8/12)) - 48 (W1)		1,052
Costs of sales (200 +150 + (120*8/12) - 48+1.8 (W1)		(383.8)
Gross profit		668.2
Distribution and admin costs (150 +130 + (90*8/12)) + 3 (W3)		(343)
Profit from operations		325.2
Profit on disposal (W6)		29
Investment income (all inter co) (24 - (32*75%))		nil
Finance costs (60+40+(30*8/12))		(120)
Profit before tax		234.2
Income tax expense (40+28+(15*8/12) + 20)		(98)
Profit for the year		**136.2**
Other comprehensive income		
Gain on revaluation	nil	nil
Total comprehensive income for the year		**136.2**
Profit attributable to:		
Owners of the parent	118.2	
Non-controlling interests		
Skip (49 W7 *25%) =12 (r)		
Jump (30 (W7) *20%) = 6	18	136.2
Total comprehensive income attributable to:		
Owners of the parent	118.2	
Non-controlling interests	18	
		136.2

* Statement of profit or loss = Income statement

Workings

(W1) Group structure and PURP

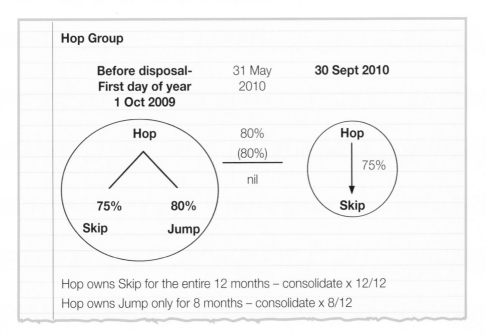

Hop Group

| Before disposal-
First day of year
1 Oct 2009 | 31 May
2010 | 30 Sept 2010 |

Hop owns Skip for the entire 12 months – consolidate x 12/12

Hop owns Jump only for 8 months – consolidate x 8/12

PURP

PURP – Parent sells to Subsidiary (adjust W5 retained earnings)

Inter-company sales between parent and subsidiary

Revenue – 48
Cost of sales – 48

PURP required for CSOFP

18 x 25/125= $3.6 – note CSOFP NOT asked for

ADJUST Retained earnings at W5 and Inventory on CSOFP

Impact on Cost of sales – NOTE opening balance on PURP

Opening PURP

9 x 25/125 = $1.8

As the PURP needs increasing by $1.8 an additional expense is needed in cost of sales of 1.8 (The opening PURP is 1.8m it needs to be 3.6m then additional 1.8 expense is needed in cost of sales).

(W2) Net Assets of subsidiary

Note – CSOFP not required, but disposal of Jump

Skip	At acquisition $m	
Equity share capital	60	
Retained earnings	60	
	120	
Jump	**At acquisition $m**	**At disposal $m**
Equity share capital	50	50
Retained earnings	75	195*
	125	245

*Retained earnings at date of disposal – 31 May 2010

	$m
Bal b/fwd at 1st October 2009	165
In year pro rata 45 x 8/12	30
No distribution made during 1 Oct 2009 - 31 May 2010	(nil)
Retained earnings at 31 May 2010	***195**

(W3) Goodwill (for Part B) - Skip

	$m
Cost of Investment	100
NCI value at acquisition	35
	135
Less:	
Fair value of net assets at acquisition (W2)	(120)
Goodwill on acquisition	15
Impairment up to 30 September 2009 (15 x 20%)	(3)
Further Impairment up to 30 September 2010 (15 x 20%)	
TAKE TO CONSOLIDATED STATEMENT OF PROFIT OR LOSS	**(3)**
Carrying value of Goodwill in CSOFP (FOR INFO ONLY)	9

The impairment that has occurred in the current year is the 3 that is added onto admin expenses in the CSOPL.

> **Note**
>
> *Remember any impairment on goodwill is taken to the consolidated statement of profit or loss. There is actually no rule as to which type of operating expense it is. It will be down to the parent company's accounting policies.*
>
> *Commonly you will see it treated as part of administrative expenses. Sometimes it will be presented as part of cost of sales and other times it is given its own separate presentation line. All are equally correct.*

(W3) Goodwill (for Part B) - Jump

	$m
Cost of Investment	120
NCI value at acquisition	30
	150
Less	
Fair value of net assets at acquisition (W2)	(125)
Goodwill on acquisition	25
Carrying value of Goodwill in CSOFP (NEEDED DUE TO DISPOSAL) (W6)	**25**

(W4) Non-controlling interest at date of disposal
(For disposal working - Jump only)

	$
NCI value at acquisition (as in W3)	30
NCI share of post-acquisition reserves up to date of disposal (W2)	
(245 - 125) *20%	24
NCI share of impairment (fair value method only)	(nil)
Non-controlling interest at date of disposal (W6)	**54**

(W5) Group retained earnings for CSOFP

NOT NEEDED AS NO CSOFP ASKED FOR

(W6) Profit/loss on disposal – entire disposal of Jump

	$m
Proceeds (fair value of consideration received)	245
Less all the net assets at disposal (W2)	(245)
Plus all the non controlling interest (W4)	54
Less the total goodwill remaining at disposal (W3)	(25)
Gain or loss on disposal to be recognised in income	29

Again not prescriptive where it goes but best practice is to give an exceptional presentation below profit from operations.

(W7) Profit attributable to:

	Profit/ TCI - Skip	Profit/TCI-Jump x 8/12
	$m	$m
Sub's profit as per Q	52	30
Adjustments:		
PURP - Parent to sub – no impact	nil	nil
Depreciation - no depn fv adj (W3)	nil	nil
Impairment (W3)	(3)	(nil)
	49	30

The NCI is calculated by taking the subsidiaries profit after tax and applying the NCI percentage to it.

> **Note** *TCI equals Total Comprehensive Income*

However if additional expenses have been created by the consolidation, such as creation of PURP, depreciation on fair value adjustments or goodwill being impaired in the period, the individual company profits will need adjusting as in (W7).

Transactions within equity

From the perspective of the group accounts, where there is a sale of shares but the parent still retains control then, in essence, this is an increase in the non-controlling interest.

For example if the parent holds 80% of the shares in a subsidiary and sells 5%, the relationship remains one of a parent and subsidiary and as such will remain consolidated in the group accounts in the normal way, but the NCI has risen from 20% to 25%.

Where there is such an increase in the non-controlling interest:

- no gain or loss on disposal is calculated
- no adjustment is made to the carrying value of goodwill
- The difference between the proceeds received and change in the non-controlling interest is accounted for in shareholders' equity as follows:

	$
Cash proceeds received	X
NCI% increase x (NAs at date of change plus unimpaired goodwill of subsidiary)	(X)
Difference to equity	X

Note

Unimpaired goodwill means the balance that remains on the goodwill account in the consolidated statement of financial position* after the impairment.

Transactional example

On 1 May 2008, Ashanti acquired 70% of the equity interests of Bochem, a public limited company. The purchase consideration comprised cash of $150 million and the fair value of the identifiable net assets was $160 million at that date.

The fair value of the non-controlling interest in Bochem was $54 million on 1 May 2008. Ashanti wishes to use the 'full goodwill' method for all acquisitions.

The share capital and retained earnings of Bochem were $55 million and $85 million respectively and other components of equity were $10 million at the date of acquisition.

The excess of the fair value of the identifiable net assets at acquisition is due to an increase in the value of plant, which is depreciated on the straight-line method and has a five year remaining life at the date of acquisition.

Ashanti disposed of a 10% equity interest to the non-controlling interests (NCI) of Bochem on 30 April 2010 for a cash consideration of $34 million.

The carrying value of the net assets of Bochem at 30 April 2010 was $210 million before any adjustments on consolidation.

Goodwill has been impairment tested annually and as at 30 April 2009 had reduced in value by 15% and as at 30 April 2010 had lost a further 5% of its original value before the sale of its equity interest to the NCI. The goodwill impairment should be allocated between group and NCI on the basis of equity shareholding.

Required

Calculate goodwill on acquisition, the transfer to the non-controlling interest and the adjustment to the parent's equity on disposal of the 10% holding on 30 April 2010.

(W1) Group structure

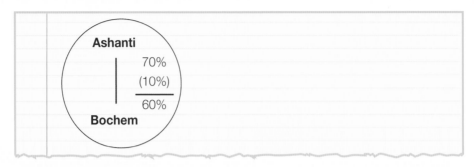

(W2) Net assets

Bochem	At acquisition $m	At disposal $m
Share Capital	55	55
Retained Earnings	85	145*
Other components of equity	10	10
Book value	150	210
Fair value Adjustment - Plant (balancing figure)	10	10
Less Depreciation (10 x 2/5)		(4)
	160	216

* Retained earnings at the date of the transaction within equity

	$m
Bal b/fwd at 1st May 2008	*85*
Increase in net assets (210 - 150)	*60*
Net assets increasing equals profit being earned	**145***

(W3) Goodwill

	$m
Parent holding (investment) at fair value	150
NCI value at acquisition	54
	204
Less	
100% Fair value of net assets at acquisition *(given)* (W2)	(160)
Goodwill on acquisition	44
Impairment – up to 30 April 2009 (44 x 15%)	(6.6)
Further Impairment – up to 30 April 2010 (44 x 5%)	(2.2)
Carrying value of Goodwill in CSOFP	**35.2**

Impact on equity	$m
Cash proceeds from disposal of shares	34
Impact on NCI account:	
Increase in NCI (216 + 35.2) x 10%	(25.12)
Increase in equity	8.88

In double entry terms:	$m	$m
DR Cash/Bank (this is the proceeds from the sale of the shares)	34	
CR NCI (this will increase as you sell shares)		25.12
CR Equity (the residual - difference between increase in liability occurring and increase in asset)		8.88

Conclusion

Once consolidated accounts are on your syllabus they tend be examined at every sitting. Once you are happy with identifying a subsidiary, you really need to get very familiar with IFRS 3, the companion standard which shows the method to be used for business combinations. You then need to make sure you don't underestimate how much practice this subject will take.

IAS 28 – Investments in associates

Introduction

> **"Goodness is the only investment that never fails."**
>
> **Henry David Thoreau (1817–1867)**

So ... what's it trying to achieve?

IAS 28 attempts to give guidance on when a parent has an associate and also the accounting treatments required in order to show a fair presentation when accounting for the interest in an associate.

 Transactional example

ACF Inc acquires 30% of the voting rights of Arden Inc on 8 March 20X7. It appoints three directors to the board, which consists of eight members. ACF is also the sole supplier of raw materials to Arden and has a contract to supply certain expertise regarding the maintenance of Arden's equipment.

ACF is likely to be exercising significant influence over Arden. As well as owning 30% of the vote and appointing three directors, it has influence as sole supplier and in the form of the maintenance contract. Arden will be treated as an associated company and should be accounted for using the equity method.

Note

A common error is to treat an associate as if it were a subsidiary and to add it into the parent company figures.

Sorry but you need to know ... DEFINITIONS

An **associate** is an entity, including an unincorporated entity such as a partnership, over which the investor has significant influence and that is neither a subsidiary nor an interest in a joint venture.

Significant influence is the power to participate in the financial and operating policy decisions of the investee but it is not control or joint control over those policies.

PURP for an associate

Although the associate is not in the group the equity method introduces part of the results and balances of the associate into the group. If there has been trading between the group and the associate, then inventory balances may mean adjustments are necessary.

However, it will only ever be the group's share of the associate that is introduced so the unrealised profit calculation is multiplied by the group share.

Examples:

Parent sells to the associate – the parent has recognised profits on inventory that will be brought back into the group within the share of net assets of the associate.

Consolidated Statement of Financial Position

Dr   Group retained earnings (cancel profit on goods still in the group)

   Cr   Investment in associate (reduce goods to cost to the group)

Associate sells to the parent – the associate has recognised profits on inventory that are still in the group, within the inventory of the parent.

Dr   Group retained earnings (cancel profit on goods still in the group)

   Cr   Group inventory (reduce goods to cost to the group).

Transactional example

Summarised Financial Statements for the year to 31 December 2008

Statements of financial position

	Percival $	Sid $	Arthur $
ASSETS			
Non Current Assets			
Tangibles	50,000	40,000	44,000
Investments	56,000	-	-
Current Assets			
Inventory	22,000	18,000	14,000
Receivables	14,000	26,000	22,000
Bank	10,000	18,000	24,000
	152,000	102,000	104,000
EQUITY AND LIABILITIES			
Equity Capital	60,000	20,000	50,000
Retained earnings	42,000	26,000	34,000
Current liabilities	50,000	56,000	20,000
	152,000	102,000	104,000

Statements of profit or loss

	Percival $	Sid $	Arthur $
Revenue	266,000	320,000	250,000
Cost of Sales	(162,000)	(184,000)	(132,000)
Gross Profit	104,000	136,000	118,000
Operating Expenses	(70,000)	(72,000)	(60,000)
Operating Profit	34,000	64,000	58,000
Investment Income	24,000	-	-
Profit Before Tax	58,000	64,000	58,000
Taxation	(26,000)	(34,000)	(34,000)
Profit for the year	32,000	30,000	24,000

1   Percival purchased 75% of Sid for $30,000 on 1 January 2006 when the retained earnings of Sid were $10,000. Goodwill has been impaired during the current year only by $500.

2   Percival also purchased 30% of Arthur for $26,000 two years ago when retained earnings were $12,000. Goodwill has been impaired by a total of $2,500 of which $1,000 relates to this year. The other 70% of Arthur's shares are owned by a number of small investors who hold no more than 5% each.

---

* Statement of financial position = Balance Sheet (see page 19)

3   During the year Percival sold goods to Sid to the value of $20,000 at a mark-up of 25% on cost. Percival also sold goods to Arthur to the value of $30,000 at the same mark-up. All of the goods sold to Sid were still in inventory at the year end but Arthur had sold half of his inventory by the year end.

4   Sid paid a dividend of $32,000 during the year.

Required

Prepare both the group statement of financial position* and statement of profit or loss** for the year to 31 December 2008 using the proportional method. Your answer should include a calculation for goodwill for Arthur.

Consolidated statement of financial position

Percival group statement of financial position
31 December 2008

	$
ASSETS	
Goodwill (W3)	7,000
Tangible (50,000+40,000)	90,000
Investment in Arthur (W6)	29,200
Current Assets	
Inventory (22,000+18,000-4,000 (W1))	36,000
Receivables (14,000+26,000)	40,000
Cash/Bank (10,000+18,000)	28,000
	230,200
EQUITY AND LIABILITIES	
$1 Equity Shares	60,000
Retained earnings (W5)	52,700
Non-controlling Interest (W4)	11,500
Current liabilities (50,000+56,000)	106,000
	230,200

---

* Statement of financial position = Balance Sheet (see page 19)

**Statement of profit or loss = Income statement

Consolidated statement of profit or loss

Percival group statement of profit or loss and other comprehensive income for the year ended 31 December 2008

	$	$
Revenue (266,000 + 320,000) - 20,000		566,000
Cost of sales (162,000 + 184,000) - 20,000 + 4,000 + 900 (W1)		(330,900)
Gross profit		235,100
Operating expenses (70,000 + 72,000 + 500 impairment)		(142,500)
Profit from operations		92,600
Share of profit of associate (24,000 x 30%) = 7,200		6,200
- 1,000 impairment (please note $24,000 is associates profit after tax)		
Finance income (24,000-24,000)		nil
Profit before tax		98,800
Tax (26,000+34,000)		(60,000)
Profit after tax		38,800
Attributable to:		
Equity shareholders of parent (38,800-7,500)	31,300	
Non-controlling interest (30,000 x 25%)	7,500	
Profit after tax		38,800

(W1) Group structure

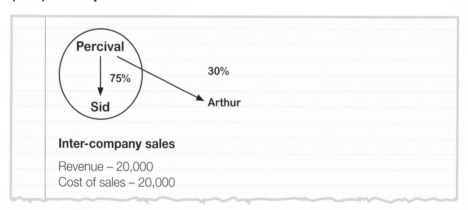

Inter-company sales

Revenue – 20,000
Cost of sales – 20,000

Note ⚠

Please note no adjustments are commonly made at the revenue line for sales between a group and associated companies. This however is only one interpretation of this standard and other examiners will adjust revenue. You will need to check if your examiner is following the standard approach I have used here or is adopting the alternative presentation. It is key you keep checking out past exam questions.

* Statement of profit or loss = Income statement

PURP
Sid

$$20,000 \times \frac{25}{125} \quad 4,000$$

Dr Group reserves (W5)   4,000
   Cr Inventory (face of CSOFP)   4,000

Parent to subsidiary so no NCI adjustment

CSOPL

Creating a provision for unrealised profit (PURP) of $4,000 means an additional expense is needed at the cost of sales line

Cost of sales + 4,000

Arthur

$30,000 \times 50\% = 15,000$

$$15,000 \times \frac{25}{125} = 3,000 \times 30\% = 900$$

	$	$
Dr Group reserves (W5)	900	
Cr Investment in Arthur account (W6)		900

CSOPL

In the Consolidated statement of profit and loss, the associate is considered outside the group and therefore no adjustments are generally made to sales .

PURP still needs calculating and as the parent is selling to the associate, it is an additional expense at the cost of sales line.

Cost of sales + 900

(W2) Net assets

	Sid		Arthur	
	At date of acquisition	At reporting date	At date of acquisition	At reporting date
	$	$	$	$
Equity Share Capital	20,000	20,000	50,000	50,000
Retained earnings	10,000	26,000	12,000	34,000
	30,000	46,000	62,000	84,000
	(W3)		(W3)	

(W3) Goodwill (proportionate policy)

	$
Cost of Investment	30,000
NCI value at acquisition (25% 30,000) (W2)	7,500
	37,500
Less 100% Fair value of net assets at acquisition (W2)	(30,000)
Goodwill on acquisition	7,500
Impairment (as per note 1)	(500)
Carrying value of Goodwill in CSOFP	7,000

!!!!!! Remember that $500 relates to this year only and should be added to operating expenses.

Remember any impairment on an associate's goodwill is deducted from share of profit in associate.

(W4) Non-controlling interest

Consolidated Statement of Financial Position*	**$**
NCI value at acquisition (W3)	7,500
NCI share of post acquisition reserves (W2) 25%	
(46,000 - 30,000)	4,000
NCI share of impairment (fair value only)	nil
NCI for CSOFP	**11,500**
Consolidated Statement of Profit or Loss**	**$**
25% Sid's profit after tax (25% x 30,000)	7,500

(W5) Group retained earnings

	$
100% Percival	42,000
75% Sid's post acquisition (46,000-30,000) (W2)	12,000
30% Arthur's post acquisition (84,000-62,000)	6,600
Less: PURP (W4) (4,000+900)	(4,900)
Less: impairment (W3) (500+2500) (W1)	(3,000)
	52,700

* Statement of financial position = Balance Sheet (see page 19)

** Statement of profit or loss = Income statement

(W6) Investment in associate Arthur

	$
Cost of investment	26,000
Add post acquisition profits	6,600
Less: impairment	(2,500)
Less: PURP (W1)	(900)
	29,200

And the really important stuff ... accounting practice

Consolidated accounts

A parent company must decide whether it has significant influence. The standard makes a presumption that significant influence exists where the parent has at least 20% of the voting rights.

If a parent company has significant influence it must use the equity method of accounting for its interest in the associate in the consolidated accounts unless the investment is held exclusively for resale.

The equity method requires that:

- the consolidated statement of profit or loss shows the parent's share of the profit or loss of the associate as a separate line
- the consolidated statement of financial position* shows the parent's share of the associate's net assets plus unamortised goodwill as a single entry in non-current assets. This can also be calculated by adding together the cost of the investment and any post-acquisition profits
- the consolidated statement of cash flow shows dividends from associates as either investing or operating activities.

It is not usual to recognise associates as negative amounts in the statement of financial position* of the parent company.

Conclusion

Although associates are not examined as frequently as subsidiaries, this is still a very important skill – you must be prepared to use the equity method of accounting.

* Statement of financial position = Balance Sheet (see page 19)

(27) IFRS 11 – Joint arrangements

Introduction

> **"Joint arrangements, like marriage, stand a better chance when they benefit both sides."**
>
> Anon

It is quite common for two parties to get together to undertake an activity. When the activity that is undertaken is subject to joint control, with both parties having to unanimously consent to the decisions relating to the activity, we have usually got a joint arrangement.

So ... both the parties are obtaining equal benefits?

Well, the key thing is that no one party (venturer) should be in a position to control the activities.

It is important that there is a contractual arrangement to establish this joint control. This could be by contract or via discussions (minuted) between the venturers, or they may be set out in the articles of the entity, but it should usually be in writing.

So ... what's it trying to achieve?

IFRS 11 defines joint control and requires an entity that is party to a joint arrangement to determine the type of joint arrangement in which it is involved by assessing its rights and obligations.

Interaction between IFRS 10, 11, 12 and IAS 28

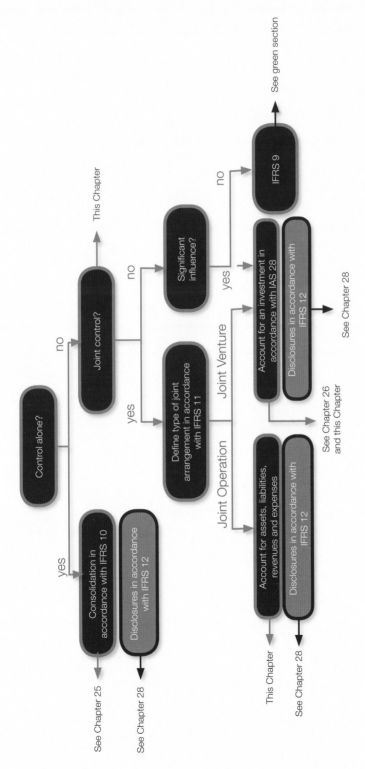

Joint venture

Transactional example

Golcar Inc and Longwood Inc decide to form a joint arrangement. Each company is to own 50% of the equity shares and provides equal numbers to the management board. There is an understanding that the shares in the joint venture cannot be sold unless first offered to the other shareholder. How will this venture be accounted for?

The structure of this arrangement means that joint control will exist, with each venturer having to consult the other before decisions can be made. Both will account for it as a joint entity, using the equity method of accounting.

Note ⚠

An equally common mistake is to treat an associate as a joint venture. This is not such a big deal now as both associates and joint ventures are accounted for in the same way - i.e. equity method applies.

Transactional example

Taylor entered into an agreement with Jorge, and Heavy, both public limited companies on 1 December 2011. Each of the companies holds one third of the equity in an entity, Wells, a public limited company, which operates offshore oilrigs. Any decisions regarding the operating and financial policies relating to Wells have to be approved by two thirds of the venturers. Taylor wants to account for the interest in the entity as a joint arrangement using the equity method and wishes advice on the matter.

To be treated as a joint arrangement per IFRS 11 joint control is needed. Joint control is identified as 'Contractually agreed sharing of control which….require…unanimous consent of the parties sharing control'.

We can see here that decision-making relating to Wells can be made by a majority of the three equity holders. Consequently it would appear that the investment in Wells cannot be regarded as being a joint arrangement within the definition of IFRS 11.

As Taylor, Jorge and Heavy have an interest in Wells which does not appear to meet the definition of a joint arrangement, it is likely IAS 28 will apply as they are all able to exercise significant influence.

Taylor should regard the investment in Wells as an associate. This will still mean equity method of accounting applies as associates are equity accounted per the IAS 28 Chapter.

Joint operation

When a joint arrangement does exist a decision will have to be made as to whether it is a joint venture (as in Golcar and Longwood above) or a joint operation (see definitions below).

Transactional example

Howey Inc owns a 10% interest in a pipeline, which is used to transport the oil from the offshore oilrig to a refinery on the land. Howey Inc has joint control over the pipeline and has to pay its share of the maintenance costs. Howey has the right to use 10% of the capacity of the pipeline. Howey wishes to show the pipeline as an investment in its financial statements to 30 November 2012.

This pipeline would be a good example of a joint operation whereby parties have joint control of the arrangement having rights to the assets (in this case the pipeline) and the obligations for the liabilities (in this case its share of the maintenance costs).

Howey would be wrong to show the asset as an investment, but should instead show 10% of the pipeline as Property, Plant and equipment. It should include its share of any outstanding liabilities in liabilities and its share of maintenance costs in its expenses.

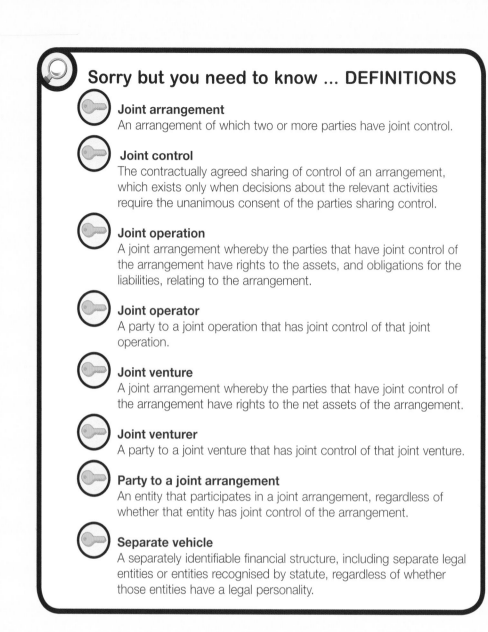

Sorry but you need to know ... DEFINITIONS

Joint arrangement
An arrangement of which two or more parties have joint control.

Joint control
The contractually agreed sharing of control of an arrangement, which exists only when decisions about the relevant activities require the unanimous consent of the parties sharing control.

Joint operation
A joint arrangement whereby the parties that have joint control of the arrangement have rights to the assets, and obligations for the liabilities, relating to the arrangement.

Joint operator
A party to a joint operation that has joint control of that joint operation.

Joint venture
A joint arrangement whereby the parties that have joint control of the arrangement have rights to the net assets of the arrangement.

Joint venturer
A party to a joint venture that has joint control of that joint venture.

Party to a joint arrangement
An entity that participates in a joint arrangement, regardless of whether that entity has joint control of the arrangement.

Separate vehicle
A separately identifiable financial structure, including separate legal entities or entities recognised by statute, regardless of whether those entities have a legal personality.

And the really important stuff... accounting practice

Joint operations

A jointly controlled operation occurs when each venturer uses its own assets and incurs its own expenses in contributing to a joint product. For example a number of venturers each might supply a part of a completed aircraft (engines, wings, etc) in return for a proportion of the proceeds from selling an aeroplane. Each venturer accounts for its own costs, assets and liabilities and takes a proportion of the sale proceeds, all line-by-line in the financial statements.

A joint operator shall recognise in relation to its interest in a joint operation:

(a) its assets, including its share of any assets held jointly

(b) its liabilities, including its share of any liabilities incurred jointly

(c) its revenue from the sale of its share of the output arising from the joint operation

(d) its share of the revenue from the sale of the output by the joint operation; and

(e) its expenses, including its share of any expenses incurred jointly.

Joint Ventures

A joint venturer shall recognise its interest in a joint venture as an investment and shall account for that investment using the equity method in accordance with IAS 28 Investments in Associates and Joint Ventures unless the entity is exempted from applying the equity method as specified in that standard.

> ## Note
> *Equity method is the same as we use for accounting for an associate – one line accounting.*

Conclusion

When you are doing group accounts, it is important that you can deal with subsidiaries and associates as they are examined so frequently. Remember that once you can tackle an associate question, the equity method you use is then a transferable skill for joint ventures also.

IFRS 12 - Disclosure of interests in other entities

Introduction

> **"If you always do what interests you, at least one person is pleased."**
>
> **Katharine Hepburn**

Users of financial statements have consistently requested improvements to the disclosure of a reporting entity's interests in other entities to help identify the profit or loss and cash flows available to the reporting entity and determine the value of a current or future investment in the reporting entity.

They highlighted the need for better information about the subsidiaries that are consolidated, as well as an entity's interests in joint arrangements and associates that are not consolidated but with which the entity has a special relationship

Global Financial Crisis

The global financial crisis that started in 2007 also highlighted a lack of transparency about the risks to which a reporting entity was exposed from its involvement with structured entities, including those that it had sponsored.

In response to input received from users and others, including the G20 leaders and the Financial Stability Board, the Board decided to address in IFRS 12 the need for improved disclosure of a reporting entity's interests in other entities when the reporting entity has a special relationship with those other entities.

The Board identified an opportunity to integrate and make consistent the disclosure requirements for subsidiaries, joint arrangements, associates and unconsolidated structured entities and present those requirements in a single IFRS. The Board observed that the disclosure requirements of IAS 27 Consolidated and Separate Financial Statements, IAS 28 Investments in Associates and IAS 31 Interests in Joint Ventures overlapped in many areas. In addition, many commented that the disclosure requirements for interests in unconsolidated structured entities should not be located in a consolidation standard. Therefore, the Board concluded that a combined disclosure standard for interests in other entities would make it easier to understand and apply the disclosure requirements for subsidiaries, joint ventures, associates and unconsolidated structured entities.

So ... what's it trying to achieve?

The objective of this IFRS is to require an entity to disclose information that enables users of its financial statements to evaluate:

(a) the nature of, and risks associated with, its interests in other entities; and

(b) the effects of those interests on its financial position, financial performance and cash flows.

And the really important stuff....accounting practice

Significant judgements and assumptions

An entity shall disclose information about significant judgements and assumptions it has made (and changes to those judgements and assumptions) in determining:

(a) that it has control of another entity, i.e. an investee as described in IFRS 10 Consolidated Financial Statements

(b) that it has joint control of an arrangement or significant influence over another entity; and

(c) the type of joint arrangement (i.e. joint operation or joint venture) when the arrangement has been structured through a separate vehicle.

Interests in subsidiaries

An entity shall disclose information that enables users of its consolidated financial statements:

(a) to understand:

   (i) the composition of the group; and

   (ii) the interest that non-controlling interests have in the group's activities and cash flows; and

(b) to evaluate:

   (i) the nature and extent of significant restrictions on its ability to access or use assets, and settle liabilities, of the group

   (ii) the nature of, and changes in, the risks associated with its interests in consolidated structured entities

   (iii) the consequences of changes in its ownership interest in a subsidiary that do not result in a loss of control; and

   (iv) the consequences of losing control of a subsidiary during the reporting period.

Interests in joint arrangements and associates

An entity shall disclose information that enables users of its financial statements to evaluate:

(a) the nature, extent and financial effects of its interests in joint arrangements and associates, including the nature and effects of its contractual relationship with the other investors with joint control of, or significant influence over, joint arrangements and associates; and

(b) the nature of, and changes in, the risks associated with its interests in joint ventures and associates.

Interests in unconsolidated structured entities

An entity shall disclose information that enables users of its financial statements:

(a) to understand the nature and extent of its interests in unconsolidated structured entities; and

(b) to evaluate the nature of, and changes in, the risks associated with its interests in unconsolidated structured entities.

Sorry but you need to know ... DEFINITIONS

Income from a structured entity

For the purpose of this IFRS, income from a structured entity includes, but is not limited to, recurring and non-recurring fees, interest, dividends, gains or losses on the remeasurement or derecognition of interests in structured entities and gains or losses from the transfer of assets and liabilities to the structured entity.

Interest in another entity

For the purpose of this IFRS, an interest in another entity refers to contractual and non-contractual involvement that exposes an entity to variability of returns from the performance of the other entity. An interest in another entity can be evidenced by, but is not limited to, the holding of equity or debt instruments as well as other forms of involvement such as the provision of funding, liquidity support, credit enhancement and guarantees. It includes the means by which an entity has control or joint control of, or significant influence over, another entity. An entity does not necessarily have an interest in another entity solely because of a typical customer supplier relationship.

Structured Entity

An entity that has been designed so that voting or similar rights are not the dominant factor in deciding who controls the entity, such as when any voting rights relate to administrative tasks only and the relevant activities are directed by means of contractual arrangements.

Conclusion

It makes sense to have a single point of reference on this issue.

IAS 7 – Group Statements of Cash Flow

Introduction

> "Laugh often, love much, live well."

The quote above is just one of my favourites and in my view a sign of a success in an individual. We discussed in Chapter 4 the quote about 'cash is king'. Well it is true that it is a lot easier to laugh often, love much and live well if cash is available, although it really doesn't guarantee any of these either, in fact the 'richest' people in the broader sense may have very little in terms of cash.

Anyway back to preparing a group statement of cash flows, it may be worth reworking Chapter 4 before you go any further with this Chapter. The ability to do an individual company cash flow statement is key to success for a group cash flow statement. Also the definitions are exactly the same as for basic statements of cash flow in Chapter 4.

Ready to move on to the group cash flow?

Like the other consolidated financial statements this should only include flows of cash external to the group.

Preparing a group statement of cash flows is going to involve exactly the same process as preparing an individual company statement of cash flows in that you will be expecting to be given two statements of financial position* (this years and last years) and also the statement of profit or loss and other comprehensive income that links the two dates (the current year one).

The difference between the individual company cash flow questions and the group cash flow questions is that these accounts will be consolidated statements of financial position and a consolidated statement of profit or loss and other comprehensive income.

Additional factors to consider when producing a group cash flow include:

- Cash flows to the non-controlling interests (NCI)
- Cash received from associates
- Payments to acquire subsidiaries
- Receipts from the disposal of subsidiaries.

* Statement of financial position = Balance Sheet (see page 19)

Cash flows to the Non-controlling interest (NCI)

When we prepare group accounts the Consolidated Statement of Financial Position (CSOFP) will include in the equity section a non-controlling Interest (NCI) account. This represents the NCI share of the net assets relating to any subsidiaries.

When we prepare the Consolidated Statement of Profit or Loss and Other Comprehensive Income (CSOPL) the total comprehensive income attributable to the NCI for the current year is calculated in the 'attributable to' section.

For the Consolidated Statement of Cash Flows we need to know if any cash was paid to the NCI in the accounting period. This will occur because if a subsidiary company pays a dividend, some of the dividend will stay within the group (as it is paid to the parent company), but some will be paid externally to the other shareholders, whom we call the non-controlling interest (NCI).

In the 'Financing' section of the group cash flow statement we therefore have an extra dividend line. We will still need to show 100% of any dividend paid by a parent as that always will be an external cash flow. In addition we need to calculate how much dividend was paid by a subsidiary to the NCI.

CSOFP*

Sheekey group statement of financial position* as at 31 December were as follows:

	31 March 2012	31 March 2011
	$000	$000
Equity and liabilities		
NCI	780	690

CSOPL

Sheekey group statement of profit or loss and other comprehensive income for the year ended 31 Dec 2012

	$000	$000
Total Comprehensive Income for the year		X
Attributable to :		
Equity Shareholders of the parent	X	
NCI	120	
		X

These new workings are not really new at all, but follow the same style and approach as the Chapter 4 ones.

Non-controlling Interest	
	$000
Balance (liability) on opening CSOFP	690
Add: Total Comprehensive Income attributable to NCI	120
Less: Balance (liability) remaining on closing CSOFP	(780)
= Dividends paid to Non-Controlling Interests in year (figure for the cash flow in the financing section)	**30**

---

* Statement of financial position = Balance Sheet (see page 19)

Alternatively you might prefer to use 'T' accounts for these workings - it is a personal preference so decide which you prefer and stick with it.

Non-controlling interests			
	$000		$000
= Dividend paid to NCI β	**30**	Balance b/fwd	690
		Total comprehensive income attributable to NCI	120
		(from the statement of profit or loss and other comprehensive income)	
Balance c/fwd	780		
	810		810

Cash flows from associated companies

Associates

Dividends received from associates should be shown as a separate line within "Cash flows from investing activities."

> ## ? Transactional example
>
> **CSOPL**
>
> **Wilton group statement of profit or loss and other comprehensive income for the year ended 31 December 2002 (extract)**
>
> | | $'000 | $'000 |
> |---|---|---|
> | Profit before interest and tax | | 60 |
> | Share of profit from associate | | 9 |
> | **Profit before tax** | | 69 |
> | Income tax expense | | (20) |
> | **Profit for the year** | | 49 |
> | **OTHER COMPREHENSIVE INCOME** | | |
> | Gain on revaluation | 15 | |
> | Share of other comprehensive income of associates | 3 | |
> | Income tax relating to OCI | (5) | |
> | OCI, net of tax | | 13 |
> | **TOTAL COMPREHENSIVE INCOME FOR THE YEAR** | | 62 |
>
> **CSOFF**
>
> **Wilton group statements of financial position as at 31 December (extracts)**
>
> | | 2002 | 2001 |
> |---|---|---|
> | **Non-current assets** | $'000 | $'000 |
> | Investment in associates | 94 | 88 |

With this information it is now possible to calculate the cash received from the associate, which will be any dividend income received.

Investment in associate	$000
Balance (asset) from opening CSOFP	88
Add: Share of profit from associate	9
Add: Share of other comprehensive income from associate	3
Less: Balance (asset) from closing COSFP	(94)
= Dividends received from associate **(figure for cash flow in the investing section)**	**6**

Again either a T account or a schedule will work here.

Investment in associate				
	$000			$000
Balance b/fwd	88	**= Dividends received**		
Share of profit from Associate	9	**from associate** β		**6**
Share of OCI from associate	3	Balance c/fwd		94
	100			100

Group cash flow statement with an acquisition of a subsidiary

Transactional example

On 1st October 2012 Mehaffey Inc acquired 90% of Prof Inc by issuing 100,000 shares at an agreed value of $1.60 per share and $140,000 in cash. Group policy is to value NCI at the date of acquisition at the proportionate share of the fair value of the acquiree's identifiable assets and liabilities assumed.

At that time the SOFP of Prof Inc (equivalent to the fair value of the assets and liabilities) was as follows:

	$'000
Property, plant and equipment	190
Inventories	70
Trade receivables	30
Cash and cash equivalents	10
Trade payables	(40)
	260

Mehaffey group statement of financial position* as at 31 December were as follows:

	2012	2011
	$'000	$'000
Non-current assets		
Property, plant and equipment	2,500	2,300
Goodwill	66	-
Current assets		
Inventories	1,450	1,200
Trade receivables	1,370	1,100
Cash and cash equivalents	16	50
Total assets	**5,402**	**4,650**
Equity and Liabilities		
Share capital ($1 ordinary shares)	1,150	1,000
Share premium	590	500
Retained earnings	1,791	1,530
Non-controlling interests	31	-
Current liabilities		
Trade payables	1,690	1,520
Income tax payable	150	100
	5,402	**4,650**

Mehaffey group statement of profit or loss** and other comprehensive income for the year ended 31 December 2012

	$000	$000
Revenue		10,000
Cost of sales		7,500
Gross Profit		2,500
Administrative expenses		(2,080)
Profit before tax		420
Income tax expense		(150)
Profit for the period		**270**
Other Comprehensive income (OCI)		nil
Total Comprehensive Income For The Year		**270**
Attributable to:		
Equity shareholders of Mehaffey (270 - 9)	261	
Non-controlling interests	9	
		270

* Statement of financial position = Balance Sheet (see page 19)

** Statement of profit or loss = Income statement

Additional information provided is as follows:

- all other subsidiaries are 100% owned
- depreciation charges amounted to $210,000
- there were no disposals of PPE during the year
- no dividends were paid by the parent
- the only gain for the year was profit.

It is now possible to prepare a cash flow statement for Mehaffey Inc. The Indirect method is the common approach and involves starting with calculating the cash flows from operating activities by using the profit before tax figure in the income statement.

Note

A note about 'profit'

IAS 7 is not precise about which profit figure should be adjusted, therefore some examiners start with Profit from operations as we did in Chapter 4, but some (particularly on higher level papers) start, as I am going to do here with Profit before taxation.

You need have a look at your past papers and see what your examiner prefers.

Once you have taken the profit figure from the question you will need to start adjusting for any items in this profit figure that are non-cash items, e.g. depreciation. This is exactly the same as we saw in Chapter 4 when we did individual company cash flow statements.

Impairment of goodwill

Because this is a **consolidated** statement of cash flow we need to consider whether when we did the annual impairment test on goodwill, the goodwill proved to be impaired, because if it did the expense will have been included in operating expenses. Like depreciation we will need to add this 'non-cash' expense back.

To find out whether the goodwill was impaired we consider the movement on the goodwill account between the two reporting dates.

(W1) Goodwill	$000
Balance (asset) on opening CSOFP	nil
Add: Goodwill on any acquired subsidiary in year (W2)	66
Less: Goodwill on any sold subsidiary in year	(nil)
(no subsidiaries were sold)	
Less: closing balance (asset) on closing CSOFP	(66)
= Impairment on goodwill during year (for the group statement of cash flow)	**Nil**

Alternatively if you prefer 'T' accounts

(W1)		Goodwill	
	$000		$000
Balance b/fwd	nil	Goodwill sold in year	nil
Goodwill acquired in year (W2)	66	**= Impairment on goodwill β**	**nil**
		Balance c/fwd	66
	66		66

When you acquire or sell a subsidiary you would normally expect to have to do the calculation of the goodwill at either the date of acquisition or date of disposal. Here it's an acquisition and the $66,000 can be calculated using the paragraph 1 information and the standard goodwill working. Note the accounting policy is proportionate.

(W2)	
Goodwill acquired with Prof Inc	
	$000
Cost of Investment Shares	160
100,000 x $1.60	
Cash *(given in the question)*	140
NCI at acquisition10%(260) *(net assets of Prof Inc at the date of acquisition)*	26
Less: 100% Net assets acquired	(260)
Goodwill	66

This can then be fed in to W1 to ascertain there was no impairment on goodwill.

So your first section starts just like an individual company cash flow from Chapter 4

CSOCF	**Cash flows from operating activities**	$000	$000
	Profit before taxation	420	
	Adjustments for:		
	Depreciation **(always an add back)**	210	
	Impairment on goodwill **(W1) (always an add back)**	nil	

Remember impairment is just like depreciation so it will always need adding back as well, we will be expecting to calculate it as we did in W1. Other adjustments as per individual company cash flow statements (Chapter 4) may also be needed.

Working capital movements

You will remember from Chapter 4 that to calculate the cash flow from operating activities adjustments are needed since the statement of profit or loss is prepared on the accruals basis, revenues are included whether or not you have received the cash from the sale by putting a receivable on the statement of financial position.

To work out the impact in an individual company is easy, in Chapter 4 we just compared the closing balance to the opening balance. If receivables had increased we needed to deduct the increase as a failure to collect debt promptly worsens cash flow. We made the same adjustment if we had increased inventory as this worsens cash flow (tying up cash in inventory) and the opposite adjustment if we increased trade payables, (delaying payment to our suppliers will improve cash flow) so needs adding back.

> ## Note
>
> *Remember working capital items can decrease instead of increasing*
>
> *Decreasing trade receivables improves cash flow - add it back*
>
> *Decreasing inventory improves cash flow - add it back*
>
> *Decreasing trade receivables worsens cash flow- deduct it.*

> **Note**   **Worsens = ( )**
>
> **Improves = no ( )**

Working capital movements with a change in group structure

We will not simply be able to take the closing balance and deduct the opening balance in these situations because the change in the group structure (whether a new subsidiary was bought or an old subsidiary was sold) will distort the movement.

If we consider the Mehaffey group inventory line as an example. Currently consolidated inventory is $1,450,000 compared to an opening balance of $1,200,000. An increase of $250,000. It looks like Mehaffey have spent a lot of cash buying additional inventory so may be tempted to think they have worsened their cash flow by $250,000 so we deduct $250,000 from the operating section.

This is wrong, as it is failing to take account of the acquisition of Prof Inc. We can see that Prof Inc had inventory of $70,000 when they were acquired. This is distorting the movement. Part of the reason the closing balances are higher than the opening balances is because the group is bigger at the year end than it was at the start. All the acquired balances will need adjusting.

The real underlying increase in inventory (effecting operating cash flow) is only $180,000 (250,000 - 70,000).

We will need to watch all the acquired balances at the date of acquisition and adjust as appropriate.

It is the same problem when we sell a subsidiary except in reverse - all the closing balances are smaller than expected because of the subsidiary removed from the accounts.

I would suggest therefore you get familiar with a standard working for the working capital movements in a group cash flow and stick to it.

Below is my suggestion, but you can use T accounts or order the schedule differently ... Find an approach that works for you and stick with it.

Note

The acquisition of Prof Inc itself is an investing activity. We will deal with this when we get to the investing section. For now we are just dealing with the distortions.

Working capital movements

(W3)	Inventory	Trade receivables	Trade payables
	$000	$000	$000
Closing balance	1,450	1,370	1,690
Less: Opening balance	(1,200)	(1,100)	(1,520)
Less: Balance acquired with new subsidiary	(70)	(30)	(40)
Add: Balance disposed of with old subsidiary	nil	nil	nil
	180	240	130

Note as this is positive on your calculator it indicates an increase in inventory (this will worsen your cash flow – transfer with a bracket on)

Note as this is a positive on your calculator it indicates an increase in receivables (this will worsen your cash flow transfer with a bracket on)

Note as this is a positive on your calculator it indicates an increase in payables (this will improve your cash flow by delaying payments to your suppliers, so transfer with no bracket on)

We can now calculate the cash generated from operations

Meheffey group statement of cash flows for the year ended 31 December 2012

	$000	$000
Cash flows from operating activities		
Profit before tax **(Plainly)**	*420*	
Adjustments for:		
Depreciation **(Dedicated)**	*210*	
Disposal of PPE (gain)/ (loss) **(Doctors)**	*nil*	
Goodwill impairment (W1)	*nil*	
Operating cash flows before working capital changes	*630*	
Inventories increase (W3) **(Inspire)**	*(180)*	
Receivables increase (W3) **(Real)**	*(240)*	
Payables increase (W3) **(People)**	*130*	
Cash generated from operations	*340*	

You may remember your mnemonic from chapter 4…it still applies

Plainly Dedicated Doctors Inspire Real People

However because you now have the Goodwill impairment to consider it needs extending

Plainly Dedicated Doctors Generally Inspire Real People

… might work for some

Interest paid and tax paid

(W4) Interest paid	$000
Balance (liability) due on opening CSOFP	nil
Add: Finance costs for the year from CSOPL	nil
Less: Balance (liability) due on closing CSOFP	(nil)
= Interest paid during year (figure for cash flow)	**nil**

Alternative as a T account:

(W4)	Interest paid		
	$000		$000
= Interest paid in year β	nil	Balance b/fwd	nil
Bal c/fwd	nil	Finance costs for year from CSOPL	nil
	nil		66

(W5)	Income tax	
		$000
Balance b/fwd (liability) on CSOFP		100
Add: Tax from CSPOL		150
Less: Balance c/fwd (liability) on CSOFP		(150)
= Tax paid (figure for cash flow)		100

or as a T account:

(W5)	Income tax payable		
	$000		$000
		Balance b/fwd	100
= Tax paid for the year β	100		
		Tax expense from CSOPL	150
Balance c/fwd	150		
	250		250

Remember you now deduct these two from 'cash generated from operations' to give Net cash from operating activities.

Meheffey group statement of cash flows for the year ended 31 December 2012

	$000	$000
Cash flows from operating activities		
Profit before tax **(Plainly)**	*420*	
Adjustments for:		
Depreciation **(Dedicated)**	*210*	
Disposal of PPE (gain)/loss **(Doctors)**	*nil*	
Goodwill impairment **(Generally) (W1)**	*nil*	
Operating cash flows before working capital changes	*630*	
Inventories increase **(Inspire) (W3)**	*(180)*	
Receivables increase **(Real) (W3)**	*(240)*	
Payables Increase **(People) (W3)**	*130*	
Cash generated from operations	*340*	
Interest paid **(W4)**	*nil*	
Tax paid **(W5)**	*(100)*	
Net cash from operating activities		**240**

Cash flows from investing activities

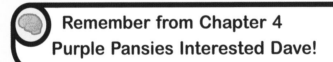

Remember from Chapter 4
Purple Pansies Interested Dave!

This mnemonic often helps when we start individual company statements of cash flow. I am going to suggest an extension for the group cash flow (see below) but really for the investing activities section we can move on from trying to rote learn what goes in here.

It is much easier to recognise that this middle section 'maps' to the statement of financial position, non-current asset section. You should start to look at the group balance sheet to identify a companies investing activities.

Looking at the Mehaffey CSOFP it only has two lines - PPE and goodwill.

We know for certain therefore the investing activities are restricted to buying and selling PPE and buying and selling companies.

So in a group statement of cash flows in addition to acquiring and selling property, plant and equipment (PPE) just like in Chapter 4, groups will also buy and sell subsidiaries.

Note

If Mehaffey had been investing in associates, intangibles or IFRS 9 investments it would be obvious from the non-current asset section of their statement of financial position.

We have seen that Mehaffey purchased Prof in the accounting period. Any cash flows relating to this acquisition need to be shown in the investing activities.

Remember it is perfectly possible to acquire a company with no cash implication, if for example you use a pure share for share exchange and the company has no bank balance at the date of acquisition the cash impact will be nil.

In this case Mehaffey did pay $140,000 cash for Prof Inc, so this does need to be included in the investing activities section.

Also, Prof did have cash and cash equivalents of $10,000 at the date of acquisition. This is a 'cash in' investing activity and needs to be reflected too.

If you do want a mnemonic for this section of the group statement of cash flows - this might work. Beware of relying though and start to check the non-current asset section. The investing activities will be obvious - honest!

 All Cute Purple Pansies Interested Dave!

Mehaffey group statement of cash flows for the year ended 31 December 2012

Cash flows from operating activities

	$'000	$'000
Profit before taxation	420	
Adjustment for:		
Depreciation	210	
	630	
Increase in trade and other receivables (1,370 - 1,100 - 30)	(240)	
Increase in inventories (1,450 - 1,200 - 70)	(180)	
Increase in trade payables (1,690 - 1,520 - 40)	130	
Cash generated from operation	340	
Interest paid		
Income taxes paid (W4)	(100)	
Net cash from operating activities		**240**

Cash flows from investing activities

Acquisition of subsidiary **(All)**	(140)	
Cash acquired with Prof inc **(Cute)**	10	
Purchase of property, plant and equipment (W6) **(Purple)**	(220)	
Proceeds from sale of equipment **(Pansies)**	nil	
Interest received **(Interested)**	nil	
Dividends received **(Dave)**	nil	
Net cash used in investing activities		**(350)**

(W6) Additions to PPE

(W6) Property, plant and equipment	$000
Balance b/fwd (from opening CSOFP)	2,300
Acquired with Prof (from question)	190
Less: Depreciation	(210)
Less: NBV/CV of asset sold	nil
Less: Balance c/fwd (from closing CSOFP)	2,500
= Additions in period	**220**

or as a T account:

Property, plant & equipment			
	$000		$000
Balance b/fwd (NBV/CV) (from opening CSOFP)	2,300	Depreciation *(given)*	210
Acquired with Prof	190		
Additions in the period β	**220**	Balance c/fwd (NBV/CV) (from closing CSOFP)	2,500
	2,710		2,710

Cash flows from financing activities

Finally you need to look at the two statements of financial position to see if the group have changed their financing arrangements in the current year. A company can only raise finance from one of two sources: debt (taking out loans) or equity (issuing shares). Any changes in shares or loans giving rise to either a cash inflow or cash outflow in the year are recorded in this section.

Also record the actual cash dividends paid by the group in the year.

You may remember the Chapter 4 mnemonic Purple Pansies Poison Dave.

You can reuse this but now remember you will have the additional Dividends paid to the NCI as this is a group cash flow

So… Purple Pansies Poison Dave's Dog… would do it!!

Remember finally

Purple Pansies Poison Dave's Dog

Cash flows from financing activities

	$'000	$'000
Proceeds from issuance of share capital **(W7) (Purple)**	80	
Proceeds from long-term borrowing **(Pansies)**	nil	
Payment of finance leases **(Poison)**	nil	
Dividends paid **(Daves)**	nil	
Dividend paid to NCI **(Dog)**	(4)	
Net cash used in financing activities		**76**

CSOCF

(W7) Proceeds from issuance of share capital

(W7) Proceeds from issuance of share capital	$000
Bal b/fwd on equity shares	1,000
Bal b/fwd on share premium	500
Shares issued to acquire Prof 100,000 x $1	100
Share premium on shares issued to acquire Prof 100,000 x $ 0.60	60
Less: Bal c/fwd on equity shares	(1,150)
Less: Bal c/fwd on share premium	(590)
= Proceeds from issuance of equity shares	**80**

(W8) Dividends paid to non-controlling interests

(W8)	Non-controlling interests		
	$000		$000
		Balance b/fwd (liability) from opening CSOFP	-
= Dividends paid to NCI β	**4**	Share of Total comprehensive income	9
		Share of NA's acquired	26
Balance c/fwd (liability) from closing CSOFP	31	(10% X $260 net assets at acquisition)	
	35		35

This should then reconcile to the movement on the cash and cash equivalents.

Remember, every exam question will vary slightly and there may be other non-standard cash flow items – however, these key elements will allow you to get a very high mark under exam conditions even if you miss something non-standard. Remember, the more past questions you practise the better you get at the standard things – AND – you start to meet and recognise non-standard stuff too.

Remember the key to numeric topics is practise, practise, practise

Mehaffey group statement of cash flows for the year ended 31 December 2012

Cash flows from operating activities

	$'000	$'000
Profit before taxation	420	
Adjustment for:		
Depreciation	210	
	630	
Increase in trade and other receivables (1,370 - 1,100 - 30)	(240)	
Increase in inventories (1,450 - 1,200 - 70)	(180)	
Increase in trade payables (1,690 - 1,520 - 40)	130	
Cash generated from operation	340	
Interest paid	nil	
Income taxes paid (W4)	(100)	
Net cash from operating activities		**240**

Cash flows from investing activities

Cash acquired with Prof Inc	10	
Acquisition of subsidiary	(140)	
Purchase of property, plant and equipment (W6)	(220)	
Proceeds from sale of equipment	nil	
Interest received	nil	
Dividends received	nil	
Net cash used in investing activities		**(350)**

Cash flows from financing activities

Proceeds from issue of share capital (240 - 160) (W7)	80	
Proceeds from long-term borrowings	nil	
Payments of finance lease liabilities	nil	
Dividend paid by parent	nil	
Dividends paid to NCI (W8)	(4)	
Net cash used in financing activities		**76**
Net increase in cash and cash equivalents		**(34)**
Cash and cash equivalents at beginning of period (per CSOFP)		**50**
Cash and cash equivalents at end of period (per CSOFP)		**16**

And the really important stuff ... accounting practice

IAS 7 believes all entities should prepare a cash flow statement that analyses the actual cash flows of an entity (i.e. cash in less cash out). The starting point is to learn the format. It takes the cash flows and divides them into three key sections:

- operating activities
- investing activities
- financing activities.

Conclusion

Statements of cash flow are a primary accounting statement, i.e. they are as important as the statement of financial position and the statement of profit or loss and other comprehensive income. They are common exam questions. If you hate the topic when you first meet it, it is essential to familiarise yourself with it – with practice you will love this topic – honest!!

(30) IAS 27 - Separate financial statements

Introduction

> **"Money is better than poverty, if only for financial reasons."**
>
> Woody Allen

The contents of IAS 27 were largely replaced with the advent of IFRS 10' Consolidated Financial Statements'. However the original IAS 27 covered both separate financial statements as well as consolidated financial statements.

What's the issue?

When a company purchases shares in another company there are two issues:

1 The impact on the consolidated accounts; i.e. should the company be treated as a subsidiary, as an associate, as a joint venture or as a simple IFRS 9 Investment. These aspects are covered by chapters 25 to chapter 29.

2 How to account for the investment in shares in the separate financial statements of a parent, subsidiary, associate or joint venture.

The accounting rules dealing with the separate financial statements are left in IAS 27.

Separate financial statements

In the separate financial statements of a parent company a subsidiary, associate or jointly controlled entity may be accounted for either:

- at cost; or
- in accordance with IFRS 9.

Transactional example

On 1 June 2010, Robby acquired 80% of the equity interests of Hail. The purchase consideration comprised cash of $50m. Robby has treated the investment in Hail at fair value through other comprehensive income (OCI). The statement of financial position shows:

Investment in Hail $55m

It is Robby's policy to measure the non-controlling interest at fair value and this was $15 million on 1 June 2010. On 1 June 2010, the fair value of the identifiable net assets of Hail were $60m.

Required
Calculate goodwill created on acquisition.

A common mistake made here, would be to use the $55m as many companies would have chosen to have left this investment at cost as per the IAS 27 choice above.

Robby, however, have chosen to use FVTOCI to measure the investment. The $55m is therefore irrelevant for the purpose of goodwill with the original cost being used.

Goodwill therefore calculates as follows:

	$m
Purchase consideration	50
NCI at acquisition	15
	65
Less: 100% Net assets acquired	(60)
Goodwill	5

Conclusion

The introduction of IFRS 10 has left IAS 27 as a very minor standard and a very quick learn!

Seriously advanced!!

"Only the little people pay taxes."

Leona Helmsley, hotel owner and prison inmate

Introduction

Once you start to get to final financial reporting/corporate reporting papers, you get to tackle companies that offer final salary pension schemes, foreign currency payment, share-based payment and the like.

For the seriously advanced!! – there are eleven 'red' standards:

- IAS 19   Employee benefits
- IAS 21   The effects of changes in foreign exchange rates
- IAS 24   Related party disclosures
- IAS 29   Financial reporting in hyper-inflationary economies
- IAS 34   Interim financial reporting
- IAS 41   Agriculture
- IFRS 1   First-time adoption of International Financial Reporting Standards
- IFRS 2   Share-based payment
- IFRS 4   Insurance contracts
- IFRS 6   Exploration for and evaluation of mineral assets
- IFRS 8   Operating segments

"The one serious conviction that a man should have is that nothing is to be taken too seriously."

Nicholas Butler (1862-1947)

31 IAS 19 – Employee benefits

Introduction

> **"Research indicates that employees have three prime needs: interesting work, recognition for doing a good job, and being let in on things that are going on in the company."**
>
> **Zig Ziglar – Employee**

Well it is true that employees want interesting work, recognition and to be 'in the know'… but as accountants we recognise they also expect to be paid! – not just salaries and wages but also other benefits such as pensions. If only it were so easy that they wanted merely the non-financial rewards of things like recognition!

It's four prime needs really then?

Absolutely – employees do expect remuneration. We need an accounting standard because employee remuneration is not only the simple stuff like salaries and wages, but also the not so simple stuff like post-retirement benefits – pensions. These schemes can be easy to account for (defined contribution) or they can be a complex accounting issue (defined benefit). This is the stuff covered by IAS 19.

Defined contribution plans

These are not a problem. They relate to post-employment benefit plans where the enterprise pays fixed amounts into a separate fund and has no legal or constructive obligation if the fund has insufficient assets to pay all employee benefits. (These are often referred to as 'money purchase schemes'.) As the company pays the contribution into the scheme we will debit the statement of profit or loss. Furthermore, as the company has made no further promises as to the level of pension that the employee will receive, there is no statement of financial position* impact – no further liability exists.

Statement of profit or loss = Income statement

Defined benefit plans

These are the problem – post-employment benefit plans other than defined contribution plans. (These are very variable but often relate to what is known as 'final salary schemes'.) These are difficult schemes to account for – the company is making promises to the employees about a level of pension which will be based on some pre-agreed formula. This is commonly based upon their final salary, the number of years they work for the employer and a pre-agreed fraction.

For example, it could be that, if you retire earning $60,000 after working for 30 years, you might be entitled to an annual pension of $30,000. This would be the case if your employer were offering you a scheme based on a fraction of 60, which is quite common. This would give you a pre-agreed formula – final salary × number of years worked/60.

($60,000 × 30/60 = $30,000) pension to be paid every year, between the date of retirement and the date you die. Note that even your death will often not cancel this liability completely as many schemes promise to pay a widow/widower benefit to your other half, when you die, until they die – the liability can be vast.

This sort of promise will therefore have a statement of financial position* implication. The company has now opened itself up to an obligation of an unknown amount – the level of liability will be dependent on factors like staff turnover and mortality rates. If your workforce tends to have a long life expectancy and to stay in employment with you for their entire career, this could clearly be a massive liability.

In order to account for such a promise, the company will use the services of an actuary who will model the expected liabilities, taking into account all factors including the time value of money. Note that the employees may not be due to retire for many years so the present value of the liability can be significantly different to the total estimate of the liability.

The actuary will then usually advise the company to contribute cash each year into a pension fund to buy assets, from which this future liability will be funded. This means we are accounting for a fund of assets as well as the projected liability. (We do occasionally see some companies that operate an 'unfunded' scheme – these companies only have a liability to account for; they pay the pensions directly out of current year income when employees retire.)

So ... what's it trying to achieve?

IAS 19 prescribes the accounting and disclosure requirements for employee benefits. The standard requires a liability to be recognised if employee benefits are to be paid in the future and an expense when the entity receives service from an employee in return for benefit, except those to which IFRS 2 share-based payment applies.

* Statement of financial position = Balance Sheet (see page 19)

Transactional example

Let us assume that Bowser makes up its financial statements to 31 December each year. The company offers its staff a defined benefit (final salary) pension scheme. It employs the services of an actuary to model the liability and advise upon contributions to an asset fund. To keep the computations simple, all transactions are assumed to occur at the year-end. The present value of the obligation and the market value of the plan assets were both $1,000 at 1 January 20X1. The following information is available from the actuary re the model.

	20X1	20X2
Discount rate at start of year	*10%*	*9%*
	$	*$*
Current service cost	*180*	*140*
Benefits paid	*150*	*180*
Contributions paid	*90*	*100*
Present value of obligations at 31 December	*1,100*	*1,380*
Market value of plan assets at 31 December	*1,190*	*1,372*

The statement of financial position*

The focus of IAS 19 is to ensure that the statement of financial position* reflects the position the company is in with regard to its promises to employees. If the obligation (liability) is the same as the fund of assets, there will be no impact on the statement of financial position* The liability and asset are presented net on the statement of financial position*. This would have been the case at the start of the year. Obligations are measured at $1,000 which is the same as the market value of the assets. As long as this continues to be the case there will no impact on the statement of financial position* (see below).

Statement of financial position*

Bowser Inc Statement of financial position* (extract) as at 31st December 20X0

	$
Pension fund assets	1,000
Pension fund liabilities	(1,000)
Net pension	nil

If there is a difference, however, the company will have to show either a net pension asset or a net pension liability on its statement of financial position*. This is the case at 31 December 20X1.

20X1 accounts

Bowser Inc Statement of financial position* (extract) as at 31st December 20X1

	$
Present value of obligation, 31 December	1,100
Fair value of assets, 31 December	1,190
Net pension fund asset	90

The statement of profit or loss and other comprehensive income

Note that none of the figures in the statement of profit or loss are the actual cash flows; we are using the information provided by the actuary, i.e. modelled figures.

The statement of profit or loss and other comprehensive income is affected in three places:

- operating expenses (service cost component)
- finance costs (net interest component)
- other comprehensive income (remeasurement component).

Service Cost Component

These relate to the two modelled costs that potentially hit operating costs

Current service cost is the increase in the present value of the scheme liabilities expected to arise from employee service in the current period. It is accounted for as:

Dr Statement of profit or loss
Cr Pension fund liability.

Past service cost is the increase in the present value of the scheme liabilities related to employee service in prior periods arising in the current period as a result of the introduction of, or improvement to, retirement benefits. It is accounted for as:

Dr Statement of profit or loss
Cr Pension fund liability.

Net interest component

Relates to the change in measurement in both the plan obligation (liability) and plan assets arising from the passage of time.

Plan Obligation (pension liability)

Because this is a liability that will not crystallise until employees retire at some point in the future, the time value of money can be significant. For this reason the pension fund liability (plan obligation) is measured by the actuary at present value. This means a discount factor is built into the model.

As staff get older and nearer to the date of retirement we would expect the liability to be building to nearer to the undiscounted figure. This 'passage of time' gives rise to what we (as accountants) call the 'unwinding of the discount'.

Statement of profit or loss = Income statement

It is the same principle that was applied in other long-term liabilities such as deferred consideration when a company is acquired or decommissioning provisions when legal obligations exist.

The 'unwinding of the discount' is usually computed by applying the discount rate used to measure the plan obligation at the start of the accounting period. It is accounted for as:

Dr Statement of profit or loss
Cr Pension fund liability.

Note

In practice this debit to the statement of profit or loss is presented netted with the credit on the plan assets as described below. Hence it is referred to as the ***'net interest component'***.

Plan Asset (pension assets) - if scheme is funded

If the scheme is funded, contributions are paid into a separate pension fund which are then invested by the trustees. Whether the investments are in shares, bonds, property or just a savings account (usually a mixed portfolio is held) the trustees should be getting some return from the assets (dividends, interest, rental income). The asset fund should therefore also be increasing as a result of the passage of time due to this expected return on the plan assets.

It is also computed by applying the discount rate used to the plan assets at the start of the accounting period. It is accounted for as:

Dr Pension fund assets
Cr Statement of profit or loss

Note

As stated above, this credit to the statement of profit or loss is actually presented netted with the unwinding of the discount above. In reality the figure for the statement of profit or loss can be calculated by applying the discount used at the start of the accounting period to the opening net liability (or asset). This will automatically give you the net interest expense (or interest income).

Net interest is charged (or credited) as a separate component to profit or loss for the year. In practical terms, the discount rate will be used when reconciling the movements in the plan obligation and plan assets for the year, whether this is done separately, or on a combined net basis. This is because the principal issue when accounting for defined benefit schemes is how to account for what is effectively a long- term liability and how it is funded.

The two statement of profit or loss entries are shown net as either a charge or a credit.

The impact on profit (the statement of profit or loss) is made up of the current service cost and past service cost being included in operating expenses and the net interest component which is included in finance costs or finance income as appropriate.

There may also be curtailments, settlements and capping to take account of in the statement of profit or loss. These along with the remeasurement component (actuarial gains and losses) we will consider in a little while.

First we have to learn the key impact on the statement of profit or loss* – as illustrated below for Bowser.

Bowser Inc Statement of profit or loss (extract) for the year ended 31 Dec 20X1

	$
Operating expense	
Current service cost (a debit)	180
Past service cost	nil
Finance cost	
Interest cost (1,000 × 10%) (a debit)	100
Expected return on plan assets (1,000 × 10%) (a credit)	(100)
Net interest component	nil
(interest cost on liabilities (1,000 x 10%) being netted against expected return on plan assets (1,000 x 10%))	

Please note in practice we would just see the one figure - here it nets to nil

---

Remember, none of the figures in the statement of profit or loss are the actual cash flows; we are using the modelled figures.

Note

Contributions

Please be aware that the cash the company contributes to the pension fund asset is not an expense for the statement of profit or loss, it simply increases the pension fund assets. It is accounted for as:*

Dr Pension fund asset
Cr Bank (cash)

Note

Benefits paid out

When a pension fund is mature and employees reach the age of retirement, benefits will need to be paid out. Please note these are not expenses in the statement of profit or loss (that would be double-counting as the current service costs have been expensed in the years you benefit from the staff being in employment) nor are they cash flows for the employing company (again that would be double-counting if it's a funded scheme as the company have been contributing to the fund). The pension fund itself will prepare accounts and write the cheques. For the employing company this is a reduction to the asset fund but also a reduction to the pension liabilities (a contra). It is accounted for as:

Dr Pension fund liabilities
Cr Pension fund assets

---

* Statement of profit or loss = Income statement

Remeasurement component

This comprises what are called actuarial gains and losses arising because the model as determined by the actuary is based on assumptions that are different to the actual outcomes.

This is the bit that will end up as 'Other Comprehensive Income'.

We now need to calculate how the model worked compared to actuals to determine what, if any, actuarial gains and losses have arisen. These calculations can be done by comparing the expected obligations and asset values at the end of each period with the actual obligations or asset values.

Let us explore the change in the liability – we usually expect it to increase. This is because of two reasons; firstly we have benefited from the employees for an additional year, and secondly, as staff get older and we get nearer to the liability being paid, we would expect the present value to be increasing (i.e. as we 'unwind the discount').

Remember the debits in the statement of profit or loss* are not credited to cash but to the liability account (a statement of financial position** account) as shown below.

Pension fund liability a/c (skeleton)

	$		$
		Bal b/fwd *(per 20X0 SOFP*)*	1,000
		Current service cost *(per 20X1 SOPL)*	180
		Interest cost (1,000x10%) *(per 20X1 SOPL)*	100
			1,280

If the scheme is mature, i.e. if people have reached the age of retirement, this account will need to reflect the benefits paid out in the year. NB. A common error made by students is to make the benefits paid out a cash flow of the company. The company accounts will only show one cash flow – the contribution to the fund each year. If the company contributes cash to the fund each year and was then to pay the pensions directly too, you will be double counting. The benefits are being paid out of the pension fund assets – therefore you will have a contra entry for benefits paid out:

Dr Pension fund liability
Cr Pension fund assets

A separate set of accounts is maintained by the pension fund, which holds the assets in trust.

* Statement of profit or loss = Income statement

** Statement of financial position = Balance Sheet (see page 19)

Pension fund liability a/c (skeleton continued)

	$		$
Benefits paid out *(from example)*	150	Bal b/fwd *(per 20X0 SOFP*)*	1,000
		Current service cost *(per 20X1 SOPL*	180
		Interest cost (1,000 × 10%) *(per 20X1 SOPL)*	100
			1,280

The figure that we take to the statement of financial position* is not the balance on the account (Bowser Inc) but the actual present value of the liability as recalculated by the actuary – in our example it is now $1,100. If you look at our 'T' account, it is showing a balance of 1,130 (1,000 + 180 + 100 − 150 = 1,130). As the liability is actually lower than we had anticipated, we have made an actuarial gain of $30 (1,130 − 1,100). Actuarial gains or losses are taken to reserves and therefore recognised in *other comprehensive income* with the $1,100 carried to the statement of financial position* as below:

Pension fund liability a/c (complete)

	$		$
Benefits paid out *(from example)*	150	Bal b/fwd *(from 20X0)*	1,000
		Current service cost *(from 20X1 SOPL)*	180
		Interest cost	100
Actuarial gain on liabilities *(goes to other comprehensive income)*	30	(1000 × 10%) *(from 20X1 SOPL)*	
Bal c/fwd *(from 20X1 SOFP*)*	1,100		
	1,280		1,280
		Bal b/fwd	1,100

As we are also accounting for a fund of assets we will need a second ledger to show the movement on the asset account.

---

* Statement of financial position = Balance Sheet (see page 19)

Pension fund assets (skeleton)

	$		$
Balance b/fwd *(per the 20X0 SOFP*)*	1,000	Benefits paid out *(per the liability account)*	150
Expected return on the assets *(per the 20X1 SOPL)*	100		

The contributions paid into the fund by the company are then debited to the asset account and credited to cash (the only cash flow for the company).

Pension fund assets (skeleton continued)

	$		$
Balance b/fwd *(per the 20X0 SOFP*)*	1,000	Benefits paid out *(per the liability account)*	150
Expected return on the assets100 *(per the 20X1 SOPL)*			
Contributions *(cash paid)*	90		

Again the actual outcome on the asset account can be different to what we had planned. If we get a stock market or property boom, our assets invested in shares or buildings may have a higher fair value than we had planned – an actuarial gain will arise. If the stock market or property values fall we can make an actuarial loss. These actuarial gains and losses are accounted for in reserves. Here we can see we are expecting the asset balance to be 1,000 + 100 + 90 – 150 = $1,040. The actual fair value of the assets at 31 December 20X1 is measured at $1,190. We again have made an actuarial gain, this time of 150 (1,190 – 1,040 = 150). This is again taken to reserves and therefore reported in 'other comprehensive income' (see below). This enables us to carry the 1,190 to the statement of financial position*.

Pension fund assets a/c (complete)

	$		$
Balance b/fwd *(per the 20X0 SOFP*)*	1,000	Benefits paid out *(per the liability account)*	150
Expected return on the assets *(per the 20X1 SOPL)*	100		
Contributions *(cash paid)*	90		
Actuarial gain on pension fund assets *(goes to Other Comprehensive Income)*	150	Bal c/fwd *(figure from 20X1 SOFP)*	1,190
	1,340		1,340
Bal b/fwd	1,190		

We can see with both the assets and liabilities the actual outcome can be different to the model – in respect of the liabilities, if retired employees start to live longer than the actuaries model had estimated, our liabilities will be bigger than expected and an actuarial loss will arise. If we get a stock market boom, our assets invested in shares may have a higher fair value than we had planned – an actuarial gain will arise.

Bowser Inc

Statement of profit or loss and other comprehensive income

Statement of profit or loss* and other comprehensive income for the year ended 31 December 20X1 (extract)

	$	$
Operating expenses		
Current service cost (a debit)		(180)
Past Service cost (a debit)		nil
Finance Cost		
Unwinding the discount (1,000 x 10) (a debit)	(100)	
Expected return on plan assets (1,000 x 10%) (a credit)	100	
Net interest Component		(nil)
Profit for the period		X
OTHER COMPREHENSIVE INCOME		
Actuarial gain on defined benefit pension scheme (30 + 150)		180
TOTAL COMPREHENSIVE INCOME		X

Bowser continues with the 20X2 accounts

The 20X1 accounts for Bowser Inc have been shown using T accounts and full double entry bookkeeping in order to facilitate the understanding of the underpinning transactions. However once you are happy with the principles it will be quicker and more usual to work with the pension fund assets and pension fund liabilities on a net basis and to use a schedule working rather than a T account working.

Let us now look at the 20X2 accounts for Bowser Inc but now using the net approach.

By the time Bowser Inc gets to 31st December 20X2 the pension liabilities are in excess of the pension assets. The net pension liability will either be presented in non-current liabilities or neither as non-current or current but separately presented on the face of the statement of financial position.

<table>
<tr><td rowspan="4" style="writing-mode:vertical-rl">Statement of financial position</td><td colspan="2">**Bowser Inc Statement of financial position* (extract) as at 31st December 20X2**</td></tr>
<tr><td></td><td>$</td></tr>
<tr><td></td><td></td></tr>
<tr><td>Net pension liability (1,380 - 1,372)</td><td>8</td></tr>
</table>

<table>
<tr><td rowspan="9" style="writing-mode:vertical-rl">Statement of profit or loss and other comprehensive income</td><td colspan="2">**Statement of profit or loss and other comprehensive income for the year ended 31 December 20X2 (extract)**</td></tr>
<tr><td></td><td>$</td></tr>
<tr><td>**Operating expenses**</td><td></td></tr>
<tr><td>Current service cost (a debit)</td><td>(140)</td></tr>
<tr><td>Past Service cost (a debit)</td><td>nil</td></tr>
<tr><td>Net interest component
90 (from last year's SOFP) x 9% (a credit)</td><td>8</td></tr>
<tr><td>Profit for the period</td><td>X</td></tr>
<tr><td>**OTHER COMPREHENSIVE INCOME**</td><td></td></tr>
<tr><td>**Actuarial loss on defined benefit pension scheme (W1)**</td><td></td></tr>
</table>

(W1) Actuarial gain or loss

	$
Net pension b/fwd 1st January 20X2 (a net asset)	90
Net interest	8
Current and past service cost	(140)
Contributions into plan	100
Net pension c/fwd (now a net liability)	8
Actuarial loss	66

Curtailments and settlements

A curtailment occurs when there is a significant reduction in the number of employees covered by a defined benefit plan. This may occur when there is closure of a plant or discontinuance of an operation. A curtailment gives rise to a past service cost which is recognised at the earlier of three possible dates:

- when the related restructuring costs are recognised, if it is part of a restructuring, or
- when the related termination benefits are recognised, if it is linked to termination, or
- when the curtailment occurs.

A settlement is a transaction that eliminates all further legal or constructive obligations for part or all of the benefits provided under a defined benefit plan.

For example, an employee leaves the entity for a new job elsewhere, and a payment is made on behalf of the employee into the defined benefit plan of the new employer.

The gain or loss arising on a curtailment or settlement should be recognised when the curtailment or settlement occurs.

The gain or loss comprises the difference between the fair value of the plan assets paid out and the reduction in the present value of the defined benefit obligation.

Curtailments and settlements do not affect profit or loss if they have already been allowed for in the actuarial assumptions; any impact would be considered part of the remeasurement component.

Transactional example

AB decides to close a business segment. The segment's employees will be made redundant and will earn no further pension benefits after being made redundant. Their plan assets will remain in the scheme so that the employees will be paid a pension when they reach retirement age (i.e. this is a curtailment without settlement).

Before the curtailment, the scheme assets had a fair value of $500,000, and the defined benefit obligation had a present value of $600,000. It is estimated that the curtailment will reduce the present value of the future obligation by 10%, which reflects the fact that employees will have fewer years of work and service with AB before retirement, and therefore be entitled to a smaller pension than previously estimated or accounted for.

The obligation is to be reduced by 10% x $600,000 = $60,000, with no change in the fair value of the assets as they remain in the plan. The reduction in the obligation represents a gain on curtailment which should be included as part of the service cost component and taken to profit or loss for the year. The net position of the plan following curtailment will be:

	Before $000	On curtailment $000	After $000
Present value of obligation	600	(60)	540
Fair value of plan assets	(500)	–	(500)
Net obligation in SOFP	100	(60)	40

The gain on curtailment is $60,000 and this will be included as part of the service cost component in profit or loss for the year.

The asset ceiling

Sometimes the deduction of plan assets from the pension obligation results in a negative amount: i.e. an asset. IAS 19 states that pension plan assets (surpluses) are measured at the lower of:

- the amount calculated as normal per earlier examples and illustrations, or
- the total of the present value of any economic benefits available in the form of refunds from the plan or reductions in future contributions to the plan.

Applying the 'asset ceiling' means that a surplus can only be recognised to the extent that it will be recoverable in the form of refunds or reduced contributions in future. This would make it compatible with the definition of an asset as included within the Conceptual Framework for Financial Reporting.

Statement of profit or loss = Income statement

Transactional example

The following information relates to a defined benefit plan:

	$000
Fair value of plan assets	950
Present value of pension liability	800
Present value of future refunds and reductions in future contributions	70

Required

What is the value of the asset that is recognised in the financial statements?

The amount that can be recognised is the lower of:

	$000
Present value of plan obligation	800
Fair value of plan asset	(950)
	(150)

	$000
PV of future refunds and/or reductions in future contributions	(70)

Therefore the amount of the asset recognised is restricted to $70,000.
This ceiling needs to be applied as otherwise we may end up with an asset in the books at more than its recoverable amount.

As we know that is an accounting no no!!

Sorry but you need to know ... DEFINITIONS

Employee benefits are all forms of consideration given by an entity in exchange for services rendered by employees. Four types of employee benefit are identified

- post-employment benefits, other than termination benefits (pensions etc)
- short-term benefits (wages, salaries and bonus etc)
- termination benefits (redundancy payments etc)
- other long-term employee benefits (long service awards etc).

Defined contribution plans are post-employment benefit plans where the entity pays fixed amounts into a separate fund and has no legal or constructive obligation if the fund has insufficient assets to pay all employee benefits. (These are often referred to as 'money purchase schemes'.)

Defined benefit plans are post-employment benefit plans other than defined contribution plans. (These are very variable but often relate to what is known as 'final salary schemes'.)

Current service cost is the increase in the present value of the defined obligation resulting from employee service in the current period.

Net interest component relates to the change in measurement in both the plan obligation and plan assets arising from the passage of time. It is computed by applying the discount rate used to measure the plan obligation to the net liability (or asset) at the start of the reporting period, irrespective of whether this results in net interest expense (or interest income) for the year. Net interest is charged (or credited) as a separate component to profit or loss for the year. In practical terms, the discount rate will be used when reconciling the movements in the plan obligation and plan assets for the year, whether this is done separately, or on a combined net basis. This is because the principal issue when accounting for defined benefit schemes is how to account for what is effectively a long-term liability and how it is funded.

Past service cost is the change in the present value of the defined benefit obligation related to employee service in prior periods arising in the current period as a result of the introduction of, or improvement to, retirement benefits.

Remeasurement/actuarial gains/losses are changes in actuarial deficits or surpluses that have arisen because (a) events have not coincided with actuarial assumptions made for the last valuation or (b) the actuarial assumptions have changed.

And the really important stuff ... accounting practice

Short-term benefits

An entity should recognise all short-term benefits at undiscounted amounts as liabilities (reduced by anything paid in the period) and as expenses. This generally means salaries and wages are debited to the statement of profit or loss and credited to cash, with an accrual being made for anything outstanding at the statement of financial position* date.

Post-employment benefits

Defined contribution schemes

Defined contribution schemes are accounted for by recognising a cost (the accruals concept is applied) in the statement of profit or loss equal to the contributions payable to the scheme for the period. Again we make a debit in the statement of profit or loss* and a credit to cash with an accrual if anything is outstanding at the statement of financial position* date.

Defined benefit schemes

The scheme assets are valued at fair value (usually market value).

The scheme liabilities are measured using the projected unit credit method, discounted at the current rate of return on high quality corporate bonds.
The statement of financial position** recognises the total of:

Market value of scheme assets	x
Less: present value of the obligations of the fund	(x)
Statement of financial position** asset (liability)	x(x)

The statement of profit or loss* charge for the period is made up from the current service cost, the net interest component, any actuarial gains and losses recognised, and past service costs recognised and the effect of curtailments and settlements.

Past service costs are recognised in the statement of profit or loss* as part of the service cost component and are recognised at the earlier of:

- when the related restructuring costs are recognised, where it is part of a restructuring, or
- when the related termination benefits are recognised, where it is linked to termination benefits, or
- when the curtailment occurs; this is a matter of judgement – it could be, for example, when the change is announced, or when it is implemented.

Disclosures

Significant disclosures are required. An entity should disclose the following information about defined benefit plans:

- explanation of the regulatory framework within which the plan operates, together with explanation of the nature of benefits provided by the plan
- explanation of the nature of the risks the entity is exposed to as a consequence of operating the plan, together with explanation of any plan amendments, settlements or curtailments in the year
- the entity's accounting policy for recognising actuarial gains and losses, together with disclosure of the significant actuarial assumptions used to determine the net defined benefit obligation or assets. Although there is no longer a choice of accounting policy for actuarial gains and losses, it may still be helpful to users to explain how they have been accounted for within the financial statements.

---

* Statement of profit or loss = Income statement

** Statement of financial position = Balance Sheet (see page 19)

- a general description of the type of plan operated
- a reconciliation of the assets and liabilities recognised in the statement of financial position
- a reconciliation showing the movements during the period in the net liability (or asset) recognised in the statement of financial position
- the charge to total comprehensive income for the year, separated into the appropriate components
- analysis of the remeasurement component to identify returns on plan assets, together with actuarial gains and losses arising on the net plan obligation
- sensitivity analysis and narrative description of how the defined benefit plan may affect the nature, timing and uncertainty of the entity's future cash flows.

Termination benefits

The definition of what constitutes termination benefits, and how they should be accounted for, was included in the revised edition of IAS 19 issued in June 2011. Termination benefits may be defined as benefits payable as a result of employment being terminated, either by the employer, or by the employee accepting voluntary redundancy. Such payments are normally in the form of a lump sum; entitlement to such payments is not accrued over time, and only become available in a relatively short period prior to any such payment being agreed and paid to the employee. The obligation to pay such benefits is recognised either when the employer can no longer withdraw the offer of such benefits (i.e. they are committed to paying them), or when it recognises related restructuring costs (normally in accordance with IAS 37). A termination benefit to be settled wholly within twelve months after the end of the reporting period is treated as a short-term termination. Payments which are due to be paid more than twelve months after the reporting date should be discounted to their present value.

Other long-term employee benefits

This comprises other items not within the above classifications and will include long-service leave, long-term disability benefits and other long-service benefits. These employee benefits are accounted for in a similar manner to accounting for post-employment benefits, typically using the projected unit credit method, as benefits are payable more than twelve months after the period in which services are provided by an employee.

Conclusion

Accounting for employee benefits can be very easy. If all the company offers in addition to salaries and wages is a defined contribution pension scheme, then it is basically a case of Dr Statement of profit or loss, Cr Cash.

However, if the company offers a defined benefit pension scheme, it is a different thing altogether. There is a complete divorce between what goes in the statement of profit or loss* and the statement of cash flow. The emphasis is on the statement of financial position**. The accruals concept is still bedrock though – the scheme **IS** being expensed in appropriate periods. It takes a while to adjust to the entries required, but once you are familiar with 'the model' these are nice questions to answer.

* Statement of profit or loss = Income statement

** Statement of financial position = Balance Sheet (see page 9)

IAS 21 – The effects of changes in foreign exchange rates

Introduction

> "To the optimist the glass is half full,
> to the pessimist the glass is half empty,
> to the accountant the glass is twice as big as it
> needs to be."
>
> **Traditional**

Even the smallest of companies will find themselves having to account for changing foreign exchange (forex) rates. Companies will export their goods, import their inventory, source plant from overseas, for example. Inevitably this will mean they have to record a transaction in their books, which is in a different currency to their own accounting currency. An accounting standard is essential in this area if we are going to record these transactions in a consistent manner.

It's about importing and exporting stuff then?

Well … hmmm … yes … BUT it also covers the issue of foreign subsidiaries as well as your basic individual company transactions. It is therefore relevant to some group accounting questions – it's really a standard of two halves!!

Individual company issues

This section gives guidance to companies that enter into a transaction where the currency is not that of their primary economic environment e.g. an Australian company that buys plant from Europe, a UK company that imports inventory from China, or a French company exporting its cars to Africa. These transactions will all need translating into the 'functional currency' – i.e. the accounting currency.

So ... what's it trying to achieve?

IAS 21 explains the standard accounting practice for translating foreign transactions (and foreign operations) and for presenting the exchange differences that arise. This standard does not apply to hedge accounting for foreign currency items, including the hedging of a net investment in foreign operation.

 ## Transactional example

Let us assume Aston plc has a year end of 31 December 20X1.
On 25 October 20X1 Aston plc buys goods from a Swedish supplier for SwK 286,000.

On 16 November 20X1 Aston plc pays the Swedish supplier in full.

The goods remain in inventory at the year end.

Exchange rates

25 October 20X1	*$1 = SwK 11.16*
16 November 20X1	*$1 = SwK 10.87*
31 December 20X1	*$1 = SwK 11.02*

This illustrates the issue – what rate of exchange do we use to record this transaction? Well initially we record it at the 'spot rate' – the rate of exchange as at the date we entered into the transaction. At 25 October 20X1 the spot rate is $1= Swk 11.16. We will therefore record the initial purchases/payables as at that rate.

Journal entries			$	$
25 October 20X1	Dr Purchases (W1)		25,627	
	Cr Payables			25,627

Workings
(W1) SwK 286,000 ÷ 11.16 = $25,627

When we come to pay for the goods on 16 November the forex rate has moved – inevitably we make a gain or a loss. Forex gains and losses are taken through the statement of profit or loss* as shown below.

---

* Statement of profit or loss = Income statement

			$	$
16 Nov 20X1	Dr	Payables	25,627	
	Dr	Statement of profit or loss – other operating expense	684	
	Cr	Cash (W2)		26,311
Workings				
(W2)		SwK 286,000 ÷ 10.87 = $26,311		

(It is actually costing us $26,311. We recorded the liability originally at $25,627 and this is now cleared to zero.) The difference is taken as an expense through the statement of profit or loss – a forex loss has occurred.

Reporting date

At the year-end, closing balances should be translated as follows:

- monetary items (cash, bank, receivables, payables, loans) at closing rate, i.e the rate of exchange as at the statement of financial position* date

- non-monetary items at historic rate, i.e. do not retranslate but leave on statement of financial position* at original translation as at date we entered into the transaction. Therefore no exchange difference arises.

Here the inventory is unused as at the statement of financial position* date. The goods will remain in stock at the year end at $25,627.

Unsettled items

However If the payable had been outstanding at the statement of financial position* date, this would have been retranslated to the closing rate and the forex gain/loss arising would be routed through the statement of profit or loss.

Sorry but you need to know ... DEFINITIONS

Closing rate is the spot rate at the statement of financial position* (reporting date).

Foreign operation is an entity that is a subsidiary, associate, joint venture or branch of a reporting entity, the activities of which are based or conducted in a country or currency other than those of the reporting entity.

Functional currency is the currency of the primary economic environment in which the entity operates.

Presentation currency is the currency in which the financial statements are presented.

Spot exchange rate is the exchange rate for immediate delivery.

The company you are preparing group accounts for may have a foreign operation. This is when an entity that is a subsidiary, associate, joint venture or branch of a reporting entity, prepares its accounts in a currency other than those of the reporting entity. Again we will have a translation issue.

* Statement of financial position = Balance Sheet (see page 19)

Group accounting issues

If the financial statements of the operation are in a different currency to the functional currency of the parent then they must be translated prior to consolidation. They will be translated to the presentation currency using the following rules:

Assets and Liabilities	Use the closing rate at the SOFP date for each set presented.
Income and Expenses	Use the average rate.
Exchange differences	Recognised in equity in either a separate translation reserve or in retained earnings.

Any goodwill and fair value adjustments are treated as assets and liabilities of the foreign operation and are translated at the closing rate.

Consolidation approach – the CSOFP

We are going to use the same core workings for a consolidated statement of financial position that we learnt in the blue section (IFRS 3 revised chapter). You may wish to go back to that chapter and refresh yourself on the 5 core workings.

However when a subsidiary prepares its accounts in a foreign currency, once we have calculated, say goodwill or non-controlling interest, we will have to apply the IAS 21 rules to translate it into the dollar.

For example goodwill calculated in a foreign currency will need to be translated using the closing rate at each reporting date, (goodwill being an asset).

We will still use the core workings for the consolidated statement of financial position*.

Transactional example

Gobbo Plc bought 80% of Sly Inc on 31 December 20X2 for Krams 6,000 when the exchange rate was Krams 4 = $1. The retained earnings of Sly Inc at that date were Krams 2,000.

Gobbo Plc does not trade.

On 31 December 20X3 the statements of financial position were as follows:*

	Gobbo Plc $	Sly Co Krams
Investment in Sly	1,500	–
Other assets	500	9,300
	2,000	9,300
Equity share capital	2,000	4,000
Retained earnings	–	5,300
	2,000	9,300

---

* Statement of financial position = Balance Sheet (see page 19)

> The rate of exchange on 31 December 20X3 was Krams 2.5 = $1.
> Group policy is to measure non-controlling interests at acquisition date
> at their proportionate share of the net fair value of the identifiable assets
> and liabilities assumed. The goodwill was tested for impairment and is
> not impaired.
>
> **Required**
>
> Prepare the consolidated statement of financial position as at 31st
> December 20X3

WORKINGS

(W1) Group structure and PURP

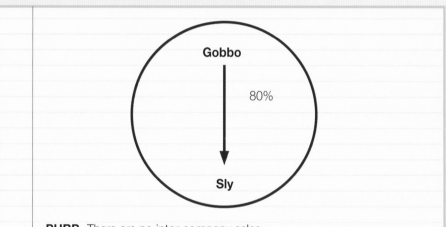

PURP -There are no inter-company sales

(W2) Net assets

(NOTE - keep in foreign currency)

	At date of acquisition	At reporting date
	Krams	Krams
Share capital	4,000	4,000
Retained earnings	2,000	5,300
Net assets	6,000	9,300

(W3) Goodwill

(NOTE – initially calculate in foreign currency)

	Krams
Parent holding (investment) at fair value	6,000
NCI value at acquisition (6,000 x 20%)	1,200
Less Fair value of net assets at acquisition (W2)	(6,000)
Goodwill on acquisition	1,200

All assets, including goodwill are translated for the CSOFP using the closing rate

Krams 1,200/2.5 = $480

(W4) Non-controlling interest

(NOTE – initially calculate in foreign currency)

	Krams
NCI value at acquisition (W3) -	1,200
NCI share of post-acquisition reserves (W2) - (9,300-6,000) *20%	660
Non-controlling interest in Krams	**1,860**

All liabilities including NCI are translated for the CSOFP using the closing rate

Krams 1,860/2.5 = $744

* Statement of profit or loss = Income statement

(W5) Group reserves

(NOTE – as this includes parent you need to work in $ and translate as appropriate)

	$
100% Parent retained earnings	nil
Forex diff on cost of investment Krams 6,000/4 = $1,500 Krams 6,000/2.5 = $2,400 Forex gain	900
Parents share of Sly's post acquisition retained earnings (9,300-6,000) *80%= Krams 3,300/2.5	1,056
Total Group reserves for CSOFP	**1,956**

Remember all SOFP figures are translated on the closing rate.

Gobbo group statement of financial position* at 31 December 2013.

	$
Intangible assets: goodwill (W3)	480
Other assets (500+3,720) (9,300/2.5= 3,720)	4,220
	4,700
Equity share capital	2,000
Group reserves (W5)	1,956
	3,956
Shareholders' funds	3,956
Non-controlling interests (W4)	744
	4,700

Consolidated statement of financial position*

IAS 21 – The effects of changes in foreign exchange rates

---

* Statement of financial position = Balance Sheet (see page 19)

Transactional example

Gobbo (1 year later)

Moving on from earlier transactional example, on 31 December 20X4 the statements of financial position of Gobbo and Sly were as follows.

	Gobbo plc	Sly Inc
	$	*Krams*
Investment in Sly	*1,500*	*–*
Other assets	*500*	*12,900*
	2,000	*12,900*
Equity share capital	*2,000*	*4,000*
Retained earnings	*–*	*8,900*
	2,000	*12,900*

The rate of exchange on 31 December 20X4 was Krams 3.0 = $1.

Required

Prepare a consolidated statement of financial position* at 31 December 20X4. Goodwill has been impairment tested and is not impaired.

WORKINGS

(W1) Group structure and PURP

PURP -There are no inter-company sales

---

* Statement of financial position = Balance Sheet (see page 19)

(W2) Net assets

(NOTE – it is kept in Krams)

	At date of acquisition	At reporting date
	Krams	Krams
Equity share capital	4,000	4,000
Retained earnings	2,000	8,900
Net assets	6,000	12,900

(W3) Goodwill

(NOTE – initially calculate in foreign currency)

	Krams
Parent holding (investment) at fair value	6,000
NCI value at acquisition (6,000 x 20%)	1,200
Less Fair value of net assets at acquisition (W2)	(6,000)
Goodwill on acquisition	1,200

All assets, including goodwill are translated for the CSOFP using the closing rate Krams 1,200/3 = $400

(W4) Non-controlling interest

(NOTE – initially calculate in foreign currency)

	Krams
NCI value at acquisition (W3)	1,200
NCI share of post-acquisition reserves (W2) - (12,900- 6,000) *20%	1,380
Non-controlling interest in Krams	**2,580**

All liabilities including NCI are translated for the CSOFP using the closing rate

Krams 2,580/3 = $860

(W5) Group Reserves

(NOTE – as this includes parent you need to work in $ and translate as appropriate)

	$
100% Parent retained earnings	nil
Forex diff on cost of investment Krams 6,000/4 = $1,500 Krams 6,000/3 = $2,000 Forex gain	500
Parents share of Sly's post acquisition retained earnings (12,900-6,000) = 6,900/3 = 2,300 *80%	1,840
Total Group reserves for CSOFP	**2,340**

Remember all SOFP figures are translated on the closing rate.

Gobbo group statement of financial position* at 31 December 20X4	$
Intangible assets (goodwill) (W3)	400
Other assets (500+4,300)	4,800
	5,200
Equity share capital	2,000
Group reserves (W5)	2,340
	4,340
Non-controlling interest (W4)	860
	5,200

Note

Group reserves

With a foreign subsidiary in the group this now includes:

Group retained earnings and Forex gain or loss on retranslation of foreign subsidiary.

These can be presented separately as two different reserves.

---

* Statement of financial position = Balance Sheet (see page 19)

Transactional example continued – the statement of profit or loss and other comprehensive income

The statement of profit or loss* of Sly for the year ended 31 December 20X4 was as follows.

	Sly Inc Krams
Profit before tax	7,200
Tax	(3,600)
Profit for the year	3,600

The average rate of exchange for the year (which should be used to translate the statement of profit or loss) was $2.85 = £1.

NOTE: Gobbo (the parent) did not trade in the period.

Required

Prepare a consolidated statement of profit or loss and other comprehensive income for the year ended 31 December 20X4.

REMEMBER IT IS A STANDARD CONSOLIDATION EXCEPT FOR NEEDING TO TRANSLATE INTO THE $ (USE THE AVERAGE RATE FOR THE WHOLE INCOME STATEMENT)

Gobbo group statement of profit or loss and other comprehensive income for the year ended 31 December 20X4

	$	$
Profit before tax (parent + 7,200/2.85)		2,526
Tax (parent + 3,600/2.85)		(1,263)
Profit for the year		1,263
Other comprehensive income		
Forex difference on translation of foreign operation (W1)		763
Total comprehensive income		2,026
Profit Attributable to:		
Equity shareholders of the parent (1263 - 253)	1,010	
Non-controlling interest (1263 x 20%)	253	1,263
Total Comprehensive income attributable to: Equity shareholders of the parent (2,026 -137 (W1))	1,889	
Non-controlling interest (W1)	137	
		2,026

---

* Statement of profit or loss = Income statement

WORKINGS

(W1) Forex difference

Forex arising on

Goodwill

	Total $	NCI $	Group $
Goodwill (W3) (note proportionate policy)			
Krams 1,200/2.5 (opening rate)	480		
Krams 1,200/3 (closing rate)	400		
Forex loss	(80)	Nil	(80)

Opening net assets (W2)

Krams 9,300/2.5 (opening rate) = 3,720			
Krams 9,300/3 (closing rate) = 3,100			
Forex loss	(620)	(124)	(496)

Profit

Krams 3,600/2.85 (average rate) = 1,263			
Krams 3,600/ 3 (closing rate)	(63)	(13)	(50)
Total FOREX LOSS TO OCI	(763)		
Attributable to :			
NCI		(137)	
Group			(626)

Reconciliation of group reserves

Retained earnings on 1 January 20X4 (opening balance)	1,956
Retained profit (from the CSOPL)	1,010
Exchange difference (763 - 137)	(626)
Retained earnings on 31 December 20X4	2,340

> **Note**
>
> *A separate translation reserve can also be maintained.*

And the really important stuff ... accounting practice

Translation of transactions into functional currency

Translation rules	Exchange difference treatment
(1) All transactions in the period should be translated at the rate in force on the date of the transaction (actual rate). (2) At the year-end closing balances should be translated: • monetary items at closing rate • non-monetary items using the exchange rate at the date of the transaction (historic rate) • non-monetary items that are measured at fair value in foreign currency shall be translated using the exchange rates at the date when the fair value was measured. (3) It is not acceptable to use forward contract rates.	(1) All exchange differences are to be recognised in the statement of profit or loss* in the period in which they arise.

Foreign operations

(a) The following rules apply to foreign operations with a different functional and presentation currency.

Translation rules	Exchange differences
(1) All net assets should be translated at the closing rate. (2) Goodwill and fair value adjustments must be made in the local currency and shall be translated at closing rate. (3) The statement of profit or loss must be translated at average rate.	(1) Arise on the restatement of opening net assets from opening to closing rate, and retained profit from average rate to closing rate. (2) The parent's percentage of the total exchange difference is shown as a movement in a separate item in equity (exchange difference reserve).

(b) If the functional currency of the subsidiary is not the same as its local currency the transactions must be translated into functional currency following the rules for translating individual transactions.

(c) On disposal of a foreign operation any exchange differences recorded in the separate item of equity should be recycled and made part of the profit or loss on disposal.

---

* Statement of profit or loss = Income statement

Disclosure

- Exchange differences recognised in the statement of profit or loss*.
- Exchange differences recognised in equity and disclose it in other comprehensive income.
- Differences in presentation and functional currency with reasons explaining those differences.
- Changes in functional currency.

Conclusion

Even the smallest companies enter into foreign currency transactions. Many lower level accountancy exam papers are very unreal as they ignore IAS 21 altogether. In the real world, this is a vital standard. Higher level exam papers will therefore commonly include foreign transactions somewhere. It is vital that you learn the rules for both individual and group transactions.

* Statement of profit or loss = Income statement

33 IAS 24 – Related party disclosures

Introduction

> "Ah … this is the one that always makes me think about birthdays – relations and parties."
>
> **Accountancy student**

Well unfortunately it's not about 'party parties', with or without your relations! When readers of accounts are trying to analyse the performance of a company, one of the big dangers is the presence of related party transactions. These transactions can have a completely distorting effect on the accounts. This topic is not just important in so far as you may get a written question on related party transactions, but you have to watch for the issue in interpretation of accounts questions.

Why the big fuss?

The presence of related party transactions in a set of accounts can seriously undermine the fair presentation of the company's results. If you ignore the issue you can make a seriously bad investment decision!! ... For example …

You decide that you want to buy a coffee/sandwich shop in the city centre. Your target businesses are those in tower blocks with many different office workers employed in the building. You identify two businesses close to each other, both up for sale, and you obtain their accounts. On comparison, one is clearly more profitable than the other, despite the sale price being the same. It seems like a no brainer … you offer for the more profitable shop and the deal is done.

However, what the owner didn't tell you was that her dad owned the office block and she paid no rent. It was not surprising that she made profit – she was benefiting from a related party transaction. When we look at accounts we assume that transactions are 'arms-length', unless the accounts tell us differently. We need to have 'non-arms' length transactions spelt out clearly. That is all IAS 24 requires – it's a disclosure standard.

So ... what's it trying to achieve?

IAS 24 tries to ensure that attention is drawn to the possibility that the financial position and performance of the enterprise may have been affected by the existence of related parties and transactions and balances with those related parties.

Transactional example

Smudge Inc is a manufacturer of pet accessories and has provided an interest-free loan to a company owned by the finance director of Smudge Inc. Would this need to be disclosed as a related party transaction?

Yes, this loan would need to be disclosed in the accounts because the finance director is a member of the key management personnel of the entity and is therefore a related party.

The loan is a related party transaction and would need disclosure. The fact that it is interest free will warrant disclosure since Smudge would not normally provide unrelated parties with interest-free loans.

Sorry but you need to know ... DEFINITIONS

A **related party** is a person or entity that is related to the entity that is preparing its financial statements.

(a) A person or a close member of that person's family is related to a reporting entity if that person:

  (i) has control or joint control of the reporting entity

  (ii) has significant influence over the reporting entity; or

  (iii) is a member of the key management personnel of the reporting entity or of a parent of the reporting entity.

(b) An entity is related to a reporting entity if any of the following conditions applies.

  (i) The entity and the reporting entity are members of the same group (which means that each parent, subsidiary and fellow subsidiary is related to the others).

  (ii) One entity is an associate or joint venture of the other entity (or an associate or joint venture of a member of a group of which the other entity is a member).

  (iii) Both entities are joint ventures of the same third party.

(iv) One entity is a joint venture of a third entity and the other entity is an associate of the third entity.

(v) The entity is a post-employment benefit plan for the benefit of employees of either the reporting entity or an entity related to the reporting entity. If the reporting entity is itself such a plan, the sponsoring employers are also related to the reporting entity.

(vi) The entity is controlled or jointly controlled by a person identified in (a).

(vii) A person identified in (a)(i) has significant influence over the entity or is a member of the key management personnel of the entity (or of a parent of the entity).

A **related party transaction** is a transfer of resources, services or obligations between a reporting entity and a related party, regardless of whether a price is charged.

Close members of the family of a person are those family members who may be expected to influence, or be influenced by, that person in their dealings with the entity and include:

(a) that person's children and spouse or domestic partner

(b) children of that person's spouse or domestic partner; and

(c) dependants of that person or that person's spouse or domestic partner.

Compensation includes all employee benefits (as defined in IAS 19 Employee Benefits) including employee benefits to which IFRS 2 Share-based Payment applies. Employee benefits are all forms of consideration paid, payable or provided by the entity, or on behalf of the entity, in exchange for services rendered to the entity. It also includes such consideration paid on behalf of a parent of the entity in respect of the entity.

Compensation includes:

(a) short-term employee benefits, such as wages, salaries and social security contributions, paid annual leave and paid sick leave, profit-sharing and bonuses (if payable within twelve months of the end of the period) and non-monetary benefits (such as medical care, housing, cars and free or subsidised goods or services) for current employees

(b) post-employment benefits such as pensions, other retirement benefits, post-employment life insurance and post-employment medical care

(c) other long-term employee benefits, including long-service leave or sabbatical leave, jubilee or other long-service benefits, long-term disability benefits and, if they are not payable wholly within twelve months after the end of the period, profit-sharing, bonuses and deferred compensation

(d) termination benefits; and

(e) share-based payment.

Key management personnel are those persons having authority and responsibility for planning, directing and controlling the activities of the entity, directly or indirectly, including any director (whether executive or otherwise) of that entity.

Government refers to government, government agencies and similar bodies whether local, national or international.

A **government-related entity** is an entity that is controlled, jointly controlled or significantly influenced by a government.

Note

In considering each possible related party relationship, attention is directed to the substance of the relationship and not merely the legal form.

An associate includes subsidiaries of the associate and a joint venture includes subsidiaries of the joint venture. Therefore, for example, an associate's subsidiary and the investor that has significant influence over the associate are related to each other.

The following are not related parties

(a) Two entities simply because they have a director or other member of key management personnel in common or because a member of key management personnel of one entity has significant influence over the other entity.

(b) Two joint venturers simply because they share joint control of a joint venture.

(c) (i) Providers of finance,
   (ii) Trade unions,
   (iii) Public utilities.
   (iv) Departments and agencies of a government that does not control, jointly control or significantly influence the reporting entity, simply by virtue of their normal dealings with an entity (even though they may affect the freedom of action of an entity or participate in its decision making process).

(d) a customer, supplier, franchisor, distributor or general agent with whom an entity transacts a significant volume of business, simply by virtue of the resulting economic dependence.

Required disclosures

Relationships between a parent and its subsidiaries shall be disclosed irrespective of whether there have been transactions between them. An entity shall disclose the name of its parent and, if different, the ultimate controlling party. If neither the entity's parent nor the ultimate controlling party produces consolidated financial statements available for public use, the name of the next most senior parent that does so shall also be disclosed.

An entity shall disclose key management personnel compensation in total and for each of the following categories:

(a) short-term employee benefits

(b) post-employment benefits

(c) other long-term benefits

(d) termination benefits; and

(e) share-based payments.

If an entity has had related party transactions during the periods covered by the financial statements, it shall disclose the nature of the related party relationship as well as information about those transactions and outstanding balances, including commitments necessary for users to understand the potential effect of the relationship on the financial statements.

At a minimum:

(a) the amount of the transactions

(b) the amount of outstanding balances, including commitments, and:

(i) their terms and conditions, including whether they are secured, and the nature of the consideration to be provided in settlement; and

(ii) details of any guarantees given or received

(c) provisions for doubtful debts related to the amount of outstanding balances; and

(d) the expense recognised during the period in respect of bad or doubtful debts due from related parties.

Government-related entities

A reporting entity is exempt from the disclosure requirements in relation to related party transactions and outstanding balances, including commitments, with:

(a) a government that has control or joint control of, or significant influence over, the reporting entity; and

(b) another entity that is a related party because the same government has control or joint control of, or significant influence over, both the reporting entity and the other entity.

Note

If a reporting entity applies this exemption it shall disclose the following about the transactions and related outstanding balances:

(a) the name of the government and the nature of its relationship with the reporting entity (i.e. control, joint control or significant influence)

(b) the following information in sufficient detail to enable users of the entity's financial statements to understand the effect of related party transactions on its financial statements:

(i) the nature and amount of each individually significant transaction; and

(ii) for other transactions that are collectively, but not individually, significant, a qualitative or quantitative indication of their extent.

Conclusion

 Although IAS 24 is nobody's favourite accounting standard, it is really essential. Miss the issue of related party transactions at your peril – it is a good way of messing up a ratios question!!

34 IAS 29 – Financial reporting in hyperinflationary economies

Introduction

> "Bankers know that history is inflationary and that money is the last thing a wise man will hoard."
>
> **William J Durant**

Historic cost accounting has little value if a country is experiencing what we term 'hyperinflation'. Hyperinflation is not actually defined by IAS 29. When a country suffers from the general characteristics of a hyperinflationary economy, presenting financial information in historic cost terms presents a distorted picture.

There are many examples of countries who have suffered this problem:

- 1922 Germany 5,000%
- 1985 Bolivia 10,000%
- 1989 Argentina 3,100%
- 1990 Peru 7,500%
- 1993 Brazil 2,100%
- 1993 Ukraine 5,000%
- 2007 Zimbabwe 11,000%.

So – we are going to have to do something other than report historical terms?

Absolutely, adjustments to the financial statements will be necessary.

So ... what's it trying to achieve?

IAS 29 prescribes the rules about restating the financial statements of companies for the effects of hyperinflation. This ensures that the users of the financial statements get better information as the financial statements can be influenced by very high levels of inflation.

Transactional example

Holland Inc operates in an hyperinflationary economy. The accounts are prepared to 31 December and for the year ended 31 December 20X5 its statement of financial position* is as follows:

Statement of financial position* at 31 December 20X5

	Krams (m)
Property, plant and equipment	450
Inventory	1,350
Cash	175
	1,975
Share capital (issued 20X1)	200
Retained earnings	1,175
Non-current liabilities	250
Current liabilities	350
	1,975

The movement of the general price index (GPI) has been as follows:-

	31 December
20X1	100
20X2	130
20X3	150
20X4	240
20X5	300

The property, plant and equipment was purchased on 3 December 20X3 and there is six months' inventory held. The non-current liability was a loan raised on 31 March 20X5.

---

* Statement of financial position = Balance Sheet (see page 19)

Holland will need to restate the property, plant and equipment, the inventory and the share capital. Retained earnings become a balancing figure. The monetary items do not need restating.

Restated statement of financial position at 31 December 20X5*

	Krams (m)
Property, plant and equipment (450 × 300/150) current GPI/GPI in year of purchase	900
Inventory (1,350 × 300/270) *(note bought six months)* (300 + 240/2 =270)	1,500
Cash (monetary item)	175
	2,575
Share capital (200 × 300/100) (current GPI/GPI in year of issue)	600
Retained earnings (balance)	1,375
Non-current liabilities (monetary item)	250
Current liabilities (monetary item)	350
	2,575

Note

The inventory has been restated on the assumption that the index has increased proportionately over time.

And the really important stuff ... accounting practice

There is no prescriptive definition in the standard about what constitutes hyperinflation, but typical characteristics are:

(a) the general population prefers to keep its wealth in non-monetary assets

(b) the general population regards monetary amounts in terms of a relatively stable foreign currency

(c) sales and purchases on credit are at prices compensating for inflation

(d) interest rates, wages and prices are linked to a price index

(e) the cumulative inflation rate over three years is approaching or exceeds 100%.

The financial statements of companies in hyperinflationary economies should be stated in terms of the measuring unit current at the end of reporting period. The comparative amounts should also be restated to the measuring unit current at the end of reporting period.

The gain or loss on the net monetary position should be included in profit or loss and separately disclosed.

The restatement should be done using a general price index.

The above rules apply to both individual company financial statements and consolidated financial statements.

Disclosures

(a) The fact that the financial statements and comparatives have been restated.
(b) Whether the financial statements are based on a historical cost or current cost approach.
(c) The identity and level of the price index at the end of the reporting period, and the movement in the index in the current and previous period.

Conclusion

Financial Reporting in hyperinflationary economies is quite a rare problem, for both the real world and in the exam hall – however, IAS 29 exists to give guidance should you need it.

Statement of profit or loss = Income statement

IAS 34 – Interim financial reporting

Introduction

> **"Maybe it should, but IAS 34 does not detail which entities should publish interim financial reports or how frequently they should be published."**
>
> **Anon**

Before you go any further with this chapter, just stop and check that you do actually need to know this standard. Even at the higher levels many accounting syllabuses exclude this accounting standard. Check with your tutor or list of examinable documents. There is a good chance you can miss this one out!! ... yippee! (or maybe not ...)

So ... what's it trying to achieve?

IAS 34 prescribes the minimum content of an interim financial report and the principles for recognition and measurement in complete or condensed financial statements for an interim period. The standard does not prescribe the companies that should produce interim financial reports.

Sorry but you need to know ... DEFINITIONS

Interim period is a financial reporting period shorter than a full financial year.

Interim financial report means a financial report containing either a complete set of financial statements or a set of condensed financial statements for an interim period.

And the really important stuff ... accounting practice

Contents of an interim report

The minimum contents prescribed by the standard are:

- a condensed statement of financial position*
- a condensed statement of profit or loss and other comprehensive income
- a condensed cash flow statement
- a condensed statement of changes in equity; and
- selected explanatory notes.

The condensed information must at least have the same headings and subtotals as were in the latest annual financial statements.

Basic and diluted EPS should be presented in the interim report.

Periods covered

The interim statements should cover the following periods:

- a statement of financial position* as of the end of the current interim period and a comparative statement of financial position* as of the end of the immediately preceding financial year
- the statement of profit or loss** for the current period and cumulatively for the current financial year to date, with comparative the statement of profit or loss for the comparable interim periods (current and year-to-date) of the immediately preceding financial year
- a statement of changes in equity cumulatively for the current financial year to date, with a comparative statement for the comparable year-to-date period of the immediately preceding financial year; and
- statement of cash flow cumulatively for the current financial year to date, with a comparative statement for the comparable year-to-date period of the immediately preceding financial year.

The type of notes to be disclosed include changes in accounting policy, changes in outstanding debt or equity, dividends, segment information, subsequent events and changes in contingencies.

Special disclosure is also required regarding unusual events and transactions in the interim period.

Conclusion

For most accounting syllabuses this is not even planned for examination. If it is on your syllabus though, it does become a current issue following debate about corporate collapses. However, note that an entity that does not comply with IAS 34 does not compromise its compliance with International Financial Reporting Standards (IFRS) in its annual financial statements.

---

* Statement of financial position = Balance Sheet (see page 19)

** Statement of profit or loss = Income statement

IAS 41 – Agriculture

Introduction

> ## "You mean we have an accounting standard on 'accounting for cows'?"
>
> **Accountancy student**

Well, it's a bit broader than that, but essentially – 'yes'.

> ## So ... what's it trying to achieve?
>
> IAS 41 prescribes the accounting treatments and disclosures for agricultural activity.

When an agricultural business has biological assets such as a dairy herd to account for, using IAS 2 Accounting for inventory does not give relevant information. Instead IAS 41 would apply, which would require the herd to be measured at each statement of financial position* date at fair value less estimated point of sale costs except where fair value cannot be measured reliably.

---

* Statement of financial position = Balance Sheet (see page 19)

Transactional example

The Smart Dairy has an inventory of 70,000 milk-producing cows and 35,000 heifers which are being raised to produce milk.

The herds comprise at 31 May 20X6:

50,000 – 3-year-old cows (all purchased on or before 1 June 20X5)
25,000 – Heifers (average age 1.5 years old – purchased 1 December 20X5)

No animals were born or sold in the year.

The per unit values less estimated point of sales costs were as follows:
20X5 data

2-year-old animal at 1 June 20X5	*$50*
1-year-old animal at 1 June 2005 and 1 December 20X5	*$40*

20X6 data

3-year-old animal at 31 May 20X6	*$60*
1.5-year-old animal at 1 May 20X6	*$46*
2-year-old animal at 31 May 20X6	*$55*
1-year-old animal at 31 May 20X6	*$42*

For the year to 31 May 20X6, let us consider how the herd would be accounted for.

First of all we need the fair value of the herd at the start of the year:

	$000
Fair value at 1 June 20X5 50,000 × $50	2,500
Then consider any purchases:	
1 December purchases 25,000 × $40	1,000
Then add on increase due to price fluctuation (fair value)	
50,000 × $(55 - 5-0)	250
25,000 × $(40 - 42)	50
Then add on increase due to physical change	
50,000 × $(60 - 55)	250
25,000 × $(46 - 42)	100
	4,150
Made up value less point of sale costs at 31 May 20X6	
50,000 × 60	3,000
25,000 × 46	1,150
	4,150

Sorry but you need to know ... DEFINITIONS

Agricultural activity is the management by an entity of the biological transformation of biological assets for sale, into agricultural produce, or into additional biological assets.

A biological asset is a living animal or plant.

Harvest is the detachment of produce from a biological asset or the cessation of a biological asset's life processes.

Biological transformation comprises the processes of growth, degeneration, production or procreation that cause qualitative or quantitative changes in a biological asset.

Agricultural produce is the harvested product of the enterprise's biological assets.

Any gains or losses should be included in net profit or loss in the period in which it arises. The standard encourages companies to separate the changes in fair value less estimated point of sale costs between that due to physical changes and the portion attributable to price changes.

And the really important stuff ... accounting practice

An enterprise should recognise a biological asset or agricultural produce when, and only when:

- the entity controls the asset as a result of past events
- it is probable that future economic benefits will flow to the entity; and
- the fair value or cost of the asset can be measured reliably.

Biological assets should be measured initially and at each reporting period at fair value less estimated point of sale costs.

Harvested produce should also be measured at fair value less point of sale costs at the point it is harvested.

Any gains or losses generated by measuring at fair value should be recognised in the statement of profit or loss* immediately.

Biological assets should be separately presented on the face of the statement of financial position**.

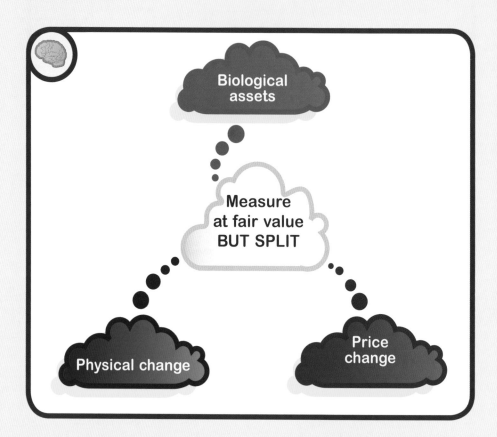

Disclosures

Significant disclosures are required for biological assets including reconciliations of the changes in biological assets over the period.

Conclusion

IAS 41 is very specific to a certain industry and as such is not examined very frequently. However, when faced with biological assets, students will need to know the difference between using IAS 2 – value at lower of cost or NRV – and the very different answer you get with IAS 41.

* Statement of profit or loss = Income statement

** Statement of financial position = Balance Sheet (see page 19)

IFRS 1 – First-time adoption of International Financial Reporting Standards

Introduction

> **"In terms of the largest companies included in the Fortune 500 list, 176 prepare their accounts under US GAAP and 200 under IFRS, 81 under Japanese GAAP."**
>
> **Michael Prada, Chair of the Technical Committee of IOSCO, February 2006**

So ... what's it trying to achieve?

IFRS 1 aims to ensure that an entity's first IFRS financial statements and its interim reports during its first period provide high quality and transparent information where the costs of producing the information do not outweigh the benefits the information provides.

Transactional example

Sardinia Inc presented its financial statements, under its local GAAP annually as at 31 December each year. The most recent financial statements were presented to 31 December 20X6. Sardinia Inc decided to adopt IFRS as of 31 December 20X7 and to present one-year comparative information for the year 20X6. Sardinia needs to consider when it should prepare its first statement of financial position* to IFRS.

** Statement of financial position = Balance Sheet (see page 19)

Well, Sardinia Inc will need an 'opening statement of financial position*', prepared as at 1 January 2006. Note that the more comparative periods it wants to give, the earlier will be the date of the opening statement of financial position*.

Sorry but you need to know ... DEFINITIONS

First IFRS reporting period

The latest reporting period covered by an entity's **first IFRS financial statements.**

Opening IFRS statement of financial position

An entity shall prepare and present an opening IFRS statement of financial position* at the date of transition to IFRSs. This is the starting point for its accounting in accordance with IFRSs.

Accounting policies

An entity shall use the same accounting policies in its opening IFRS statement of financial position* and throughout all periods presented in its first IFRS financial statements. Those accounting policies shall comply with each IFRS effective at the end of its first IFRS reporting period, except as specified below.

Estimates

An entity's estimates in accordance with IFRSs at the date of transition to IFRSs shall be consistent with estimates made for the same date in accordance with previous GAAP (after adjustments to reflect any difference in accounting policies), unless there is objective evidence that those estimates were in error.

Exceptions to the retrospective application of other IFRSs

An entity shall apply the following exceptions:

(a) derecognition of financial assets and financial liabilities

(b) hedge accounting

(c) non-controlling interests

(d) classification and measurement of financial assets; and

(e) embedded derivatives.

---

* Statement of financial position = Balance Sheet (see page 19)

Exemptions for business combinations

A first-time adopter may elect not to apply IFRS 3 (revised) retrospectively to past business combinations (business combinations that occurred before the date of transition to IFRSs). However, if a first-time adopter restates any business combination to comply with IFRS 3, it shall restate all later business combinations and shall also apply IFRS 10 from that same date. For example, if a first-time adopter elects to restate a business combination that occurred on 30 June 20X6, it shall restate all business combinations that occurred between 30 June 20X6 and the date of transition to IFRSs, and it shall also apply IFRS 10 from 30 June 20X6.

An entity need not apply IAS 21 The effects of changes in foreign exchange rates retrospectively to fair value adjustments and goodwill arising in business combinations that occurred before the date of transition to IFRSs. If the entity does not apply IAS 21 retrospectively to those fair value adjustments and goodwill, it shall treat them as assets and liabilities of the entity rather than as assets and liabilities of the acquiree. Therefore, those goodwill and fair value adjustments either are already expressed in the entity's functional currency or are non-monetary foreign currency items, which are reported using the exchange rate applied in accordance with previous GAAP.

Exemptions from other IFRSs

An entity may elect to use one or more of the following exemptions:

(a) share-based payment transactions

(b) insurance contracts

(c) deemed cost

(d) leases

(e) cumulative translation differences

(g) investments in subsidiaries, joint ventures and associates

(h) assets and liabilities of subsidiaries, associates and joint ventures

(i) compound financial instruments

(j) designation of previously recognised financial instruments

(k) fair value measurement of financial assets or financial liabilities at initial recognition

(l) decommissioning liabilities included in the cost of property, plant and equipment

(m) financial assets or intangible assets accounted for in accordance with IFRIC 12 Service Concession Arrangements;

(n) borrowing cost

(o) transfers of assets from customers

(p) extinguishing financial liabilities with equity instruments

(q) severe hyperinflation

(r) joint arrangements; and

(s) stripping costs in the production phase of a surface mine.

Transactional example

Lockfine, a public limited company, operates in the fishing industry and has recently made the transition to International Financial Reporting Standards (IFRS). Lockfine's reporting date is 30 April 20X1.

Lockfine was unsure as to whether it could elect to apply IFRS 3 Business combinations retrospectively to past business combinations on a selective basis, because there was no purchase price allocation available for certain business combinations in its opening IFRS statement of financial position*.

As a result of a major business combination, fishing rights of that combination were included as part of goodwill. The rights could not be recognised as a separately identifiable intangible asset at acquisition under the local GAAP because a reliable value was unobtainable for the rights. The fishing rights operated for a specified period of time.

On transition from local GAAP to IFRS, the fishing rights were included in goodwill and not separately identified because they did not meet the qualifying criteria set out in IFRS 1, even though it was known that the fishing rights had a finite life and would be fully impaired or amortised over the period specified by the rights.

Lockfine wished to amortise the fishing rights over their useful life and calculate any impairment of goodwill as two separate calculations.

In accordance with IFRS 1, an entity which, during the transition process to IFRS, decides to retrospectively apply IFRS 3 to a certain business combination must apply that decision consistently to all business combinations occurring between the date on which it decides to adopt IFRS 3 and the date of transition. The decision to apply IFRS 3 cannot be made selectively. The entity must consider all similar transactions carried out in that period; and when allocating values to the various assets (including intangibles) and liabilities of the entity acquired in a business combination to which IFRS 3 is applied, an entity must necessarily have documentation to support its purchase price allocation. If there is no such basis, alternative or intuitive methods of price allocation cannot be used unless they are based on the strict application of the standards. The requirements of IFRS 1 apply in respect of an entity's first IFRS financial statements and cannot be extended or applied to other similar situations.

Lockfine was unable to obtain a reliable value for the fishing rights, and thus it was not possible to separate the intangible asset within goodwill. IAS 38 requires an entity to recognise an intangible asset, whether purchased or self-created (at cost) if, and only if:

- it is probable that the future economic benefits that are attributable to the asset will flow to the entity; and
- the cost of the asset can be measured reliably.

As Lockfine was unable to satisfy the second recognition criteria of IAS 38, the company was also not able to elect to use the fair value of the fishing rights as its deemed cost as permitted by IFRS 1. As a result the goodwill presented in the first financial statements under IFRS, insofar as it did not require a write-down due to impairment at the date of transition to IFRS, will be the same as its net carrying amount at the date of transition. The intangible asset with a finite useful life, subsumed within goodwill, cannot be separately identified, amortised and presented as another item. Goodwill which includes a subsumed intangible asset with a finite life, should be subject to annual impairment testing in accordance with IAS 36 and no part of the goodwill balance should be systematically amortised through the income statement. The impairment of goodwill should be accounted for in accordance with IAS 36 which requires an annual impairment test.

Disclosures

In the first IFRS financial statements the following extra disclosures are required:

- full statement of financial position* reconciliations from previous GAAP to IFRS for the beginning of the first reporting period and at the date of transition to IFRS
- full statement of profit or loss reconciliation for the comparative period statement of profit or loss
- full explanations of the adjustments made in the above reconciliations.

Conclusion

This was a very important standard for students around 2005 when many countries adopted IFRS for the first time. It is now less important as IFRS is becoming established. However, from time to time questions still crop up involving first time adoption.

---

* Statement of financial position = Balance Sheet (see page 19)

IFRS 2 – Share-based payments

Introduction

> **"… demand for greater transparency …
> particularly in regard to employee share options."**
>
> **Sir David Tweedie, IASB Chair**

When senior staff negotiate an employment package, it is not usually just salary and pension, but often includes share options. Traditional accounting methods did not expense this part of employee remuneration as there was no associated cash flow. IFRS 2 has brought in a radical new approach.

So … what's it trying to achieve?

IFRS 2 prescribes the accounting treatment when enterprises undertake share-based payment transactions. It requires an entity to reflect the effect of share-based payments in its profit or loss* and financial position**. IFRS 2 requires the recognition of all share based payment transactions measured at fair value.

Transactional example

Bonofi granted 2,000 share options to each of its three directors on 1 January 20X7 subject to the directors being employed on 31 December 20X9. The options vest on 31 December 20X9. The fair value of each option on 1 January 20X7 is $10 and it is anticipated that all of the share options will vest on 31 December 20X9.The options will only vest if the company's share price reaches $14 per share. It is anticipated that there will only be two directors employed on 31 December 20X9. The directors are unsure as to how the share options will be accounted for in the accounts for the year ended 31 December 20X7.

---

* Statement of profit or loss = Income statement

** Statement of financial position = Balance Sheet (see page 19)

Directors' share options

IFRS 2 requires that, when a company grants share options to its employees, an expense is arising. The employees are benefiting from a form of remuneration and the company is benefiting from their labour. The expense will have to be calculated based on the fair value of the directors' share options at the date they were granted – 1 January 20X7. The fair value will need to be used. Share option pricing models such as Black-Scholes are available. The market-based condition, i.e. the increase in the share price, can be ignored for the purpose of the calculation. However, the employment condition must be taken into account.

Expense arising

The options will be treated as follows:

2,000 options $\times$ 2 Directors $\times$ \$10 $\times$ 1year/3 years = \$13,333. Equity will be increased by this amount and an expense shown in the statement of profit or loss for the year ended 31 December 2007.

Dr Statement of profit or loss
Cr Other equity

Sorry but you need to know ... DEFINITIONS

Vesting conditions are conditions that must be satisfied for the counterparty to become entitled to receive cash, other assets or equity instruments under a share-based payment arrangement.

Vesting period is the period during which all the specified vesting conditions of a share-based arrangement are to be satisfied.

Share-based payment arrangements are agreements between the entity and a third party (including an employee) to enter into a share-based payment transaction.

And the really important stuff... accounting practice

Equity-settled (company will issue shares in the future/has issued shares now)

For goods and services (other than employee service) the fair value in the statement of profit or loss is the fair value of the goods or services received. For employee service it is the fair value of the equity instruments issued at their grant date.

The fair value of options at the grant date will usually be measured by using a pricing model (such as Black-Scholes), and must take into account:

- exercise price of the option
- life of the option
- current price of the underlying shares
- expected volatility of the share price
- dividends expected on the shares; and
- risk-free interest rate.

The charge must be recognised over the vesting period using the 'truing-up' method from US GAAP (SFAS 123). This method bases the charge on the number of options that vest. (Options vest even if they are not subsequently exercised.)

The credit entry is recognised as a separate item of equity.

Cash-settled (company will pay cash based on the share price)

The charge is the fair value of the expected cash payment spread over the period to which the liability is settled.

The fair value must be remeasured at each statement of financial position* date.

The credit entry is made as a liability.

Transactional example

On 1 June 2009, William granted 500 share appreciation rights to each of its 20 managers. All of the rights vest after two years service and they can be exercised during the following two years up to 31 May 2013. The fair value of the right at the grant date was $20. It was thought that three managers would leave over the initial two-year period and they did so. The fair value of each right was as follows:

Year	31 May 2010	31 May 2011	31 May 2012
	$	$	$
Fair value at year end	*23*	*14*	*24*

On 31 May 2012, seven managers exercised their rights when the intrinsic value of the right was $21. William wishes to know what the liability and expense will be at 31 May 2012.

Expenses in respect of cash-settled share based payment transactions should be recognised over the period to which goods are received or services rendered, and measured at the fair value of the liability. The fair value of the liability should be remeasured at each reporting date until settled.

** Statement of financial position = Balance Sheet (see page 19)

Changes in fair value are recognised in the statement of profit or loss.

The credit entry in respect of Williams share appreciation rights (SAR's) is presented as a liability in the SOFP.

The fair value of each SAR is made up of an intrinsic value and its time value. The time value reflects the fact that the holders of each SAR have the right to participate in future gain.

Statement of financial position* (extract) as at 31 May 2012

	$
Liability	120,000
(10 x 500 x $24)	

In order to work out the expense for the year ended 31 May 2012 you would need to know what the balance was on the opening statement of financial position

Statement of financial position* (extract) as at 31 May 2011

	$
Liability	119,000
(17 x 500 x $14)	

You also need to know about the cash paid on 31 May 2012, which has settled the liability with 7 managers.

Cash paid (7 x 500 x $21) = $73,500

Share Appreciation Rights (SAR's) Liability

	$		$
Cash paid (7 X 500 X $21)	73,500	Bal b/fwd	119,000
Bal c/fwd	120,000	Expense for SOPL	74,500
	193,500		**193,500**

Therefore, the expense for the year is $74,500 and the liability at the year end is $120,000.

* Statement of financial position = Balance Sheet (see page 19)

IFRS 2 – Share-based payments

Cash or equity settled

If the supplier has the choice of settlement the company treats the charge as the issue of a compound instrument. This means that it is recognised as a liability and an equity option.

If the entity has the choice the instrument is either treated as equity-settled or cash-settled dependent on the likelihood of settlement method. For cash settled transactions, the goods or services acquired and the liability incurred are measured at the fair value of the liability. In contrast with equity settled there is no re-measurement.

Disclosures

An entity must disclose information that enables users of the financial statements to understand the nature and extent of share-based payment arrangements that existed during the period.

- How the fair value of the goods or services received or the fair value of the equity instruments granted during the period was determined.
- The effect of the expenses arising from the share based payment on the entity's statement of profit or loss and financial position.

Conclusion

IFRS 2 is a frequently examined topic for the more advanced student. Consequently it is very much a transaction that it is worth getting familiar with.

IFRS 4 – Insurance contracts

Introduction

> **"There are worse things in life than death. Have you ever spent the evening with an insurance salesman?"**
>
> **Woody Allen**

Before you read on you need to check whether this is actually examinable – it often isn't as it is so specific. Please check with your tutor or list of examinable documents.

So ... what's it trying to achieve?

IFRS 4 provides guidance on accounting for insurance contracts issued by companies. In particular the standard requires:

(a) limited improvements to accounting by insurers for insurance contracts

(b) improved disclosures for insurance contracts in the financial statements of insurers.

Sorry but you need to know ... DEFINITIONS

An **insurance contract** is a contract under which one party (the insurer) accepts significant insurance risk from another party (the policyholder) by agreeing to compensate the policyholder if a specified uncertain future event (the insured event) adversely affects the policyholder.

Insurance liability is an insurer's net contractual obligations under an insurance contract.

Insurance assets are an insurer's net contractual rights under an insurance contract.

Scope

(a) The IFRS applies to:

- insurance contracts; and
- financial instruments with a discretionary participation feature.

(b) This IFRS does not address other aspects of accounting by insurers, such as accounting for financial assets held by insurers and financial liabilities issued by insurers.

(c) An entity shall not apply this IFRS to:

- product warranties issued directly by a manufacturer, dealer or retailer (see IAS 18 Revenue and IAS 37 Provisions, contingent liabilities and contingent assets).
- employers' assets and liabilities under employee benefit plans (see IAS 19 Employee Benefits and IFRS 2 Share-based payment)
- contractual rights or contractual obligations that are contingent on the future use of, or right to use, a non-financial item (for example, some licence fees, royalties, contingent lease payments and similar items), as well as a lessee's residual value guarantee embedded in a finance lease (see IAS 17 Leases, IAS 18 Revenue and IAS 38 Intangible assets)
- financial guarantee contracts unless the issuer has previously asserted explicitly that it regards such contracts as insurance contracts and has used accounting applicable to insurance contracts, in which case the issuer may elect to apply either IAS 32, IFRS 7 and IFRS 9 or this IFRS to such financial guarantee contracts. The issuer may make that election contract by contract, but the election for each contract is irrevocable
- contingent consideration payable or receivable in a business combination (see IFRS 3 (revised) Business combinations)
- direct insurance contracts that the entity holds (i.e. direct insurance contracts in which the entity is the policyholder). However, a cedant shall apply this IFRS to reinsurance contracts that it holds.

And the really important stuff ... accounting practice

The standard exempts an insurer from the normal accounting policy requirements in IAS 8 for both insurance contracts that it issues and reinsurance contracts that it holds.

The standard does not exempt insurers from some requirements:

- insurers shall not recognise as a liability any provisions for possible future claims, if those claims arise under insurance contracts that are not in existence at the end of reporting period
- insurers must carry out a liability adequacy test
- insurers shall remove a liability only when it is extinguished
- no offsetting of insurance liabilities and reinsurance assets, or income and expenses from insurance and reinsurance contracts
- impairment tests are required for reinsurance assets
- no changes in accounting policy are required but if policies are changed some restrictions on new policies are enforced

Discretionary participation features (such as with-profits elements in policies) can be separated out from the guaranteed element of policies, but it is not compulsory. Discretionary features can be treated as a liability or a separate component of equity.

Disclosures

An insurer should disclose information about the following:

- information that identifies and explains the amounts in its financial statements arising from insurance contracts
- the amount, timing and uncertainty of cash flows that arise under insurance contracts. The nature and extent of risks arising from insurance contracts.

There is detail in the standard about the necessary disclosures under each of these main sections.

Conclusion

This one you may be able to ignore – don't forget to check – it is commonly not examinable!!

40

IFRS 6 – Exploration for and evaluation of mineral resources

Introduction

> "We shall never cease from exploration
> And the end of all our exploring
> Will be to arrive where we started
> And know the place for the first time."
>
> **TS Eliot (1888-1965)**

IFRS 6 is another standard that is often excluded from a syllabus. Please check with your tutor or examinable document list before reading any further.

The exploration industry (particularly the oil and gas industry) has faced serious issues as a result of the move to International Financial Reporting Standards (IFRS). In particular the impact of IAS 36 Impairment of assets, with its requirement to consider cash-generating units at the lowest possible level. For this industry it can mean an individual petrol station is a separate cash-generating unit.

Also, with regards to the costs involved in exploration, evaluation and extraction of mineral resource assets, prior to IFRS 6 there was a complete lack of consistency in their treatment. Some countries had a GAAP that failed to deal with the issue at all and, where national standards did exist, the allowed accounting practices were diverse. Some countries required capitalisation of these expenses, others required immediate write-off to income and others were allowed a choice.

So what was the norm?

Most of the major companies in this sector use the 'successful efforts' method. This means the costs incurred in finding, acquiring and developing reserves are capitalised on a 'field by field' basis. What this means is that, when a commercially-viable mineral reserve is discovered, the capitalised costs are allocated to the discovery. If a discovery is not made, the expenditure is charged as an expense.

So what was the other method called?

Well some companies have used the 'full cost' approach, where all costs are capitalised. Prior to IFRS 6, on a move to IFRS companies would have to default to the IASB 'Framework' which would have forced a change in practice. IFRS 6 has therefore been issued as an interim standard and is intended to be a short-term solution to the problem.

So ... what's it trying to achieve?

IFRS 6 is designed to provide some limited guidance to companies but does not aim to harmonise accounting practice in these areas.

Transactional example

Emily Inc is adopting IFRS. It has always applied an accounting policy of capitalisation of exploration costs. Will the move to IFRS affect this policy?

IFRS 6 permits entities to continue to use their existing accounting policies, provided they comply with paragraph 10 of IAS 8 Accounting policies, changes in accounting estimates and errors. What this means is that the information provided must be relevant and reliable, although it is not in full compliance with the definition of an asset in the IASB Framework. IFRS 6 therefore is allowing an exemption from the Framework.

Criteria to be used

IAS 8 paragraph 10 sets out the criteria for determining whether a policy is relevant and reliable. You need to learn this.

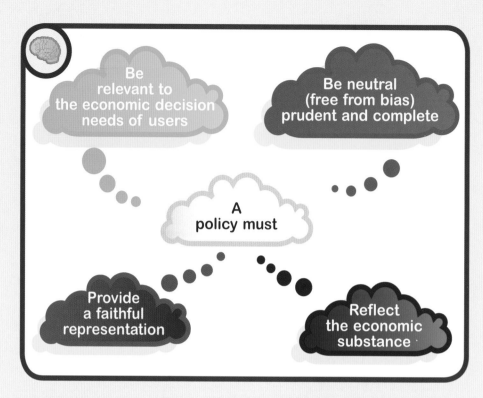

Emily Inc can change its accounting policy for exploration and extraction assets but only if the result brings it closer to the principles of the IASB Framework. The change must result in a policy that is more reliable and no less relevant or more relevant and no less reliable than the previous policy. Emily may, therefore, have an asset on the statement of financial position* that does not meet the IASB Framework definition of an asset. The capitalisation criteria may not require the demonstration of future economic benefits. Following IFRS 6, therefore, may result in earlier capitalisation than would be the case under the IASB Framework.

Tangible or intangible?

Recognised exploration and evaluation assets can be classified as either tangible or intangible assets under IFRS 6. Assets recognised in respect of licences and surveys should be classified as intangible assets. Subsequent costs incurred during the exploration and evaluation phase should be capitalised in accordance with this same policy. Basically the entity can retain the accumulated cost as an exploration asset until there is sufficient information to determine whether there will be commercial cash flows or not.

Application of IAS 16 and IAS 38

These standards will apply to these assets. Initially the assets are recognised using the cost model as normal. Subsequently Emily Inc will have a choice of using the cost model or adopting the revaluation model as described in IAS 16 and IAS 38. Depreciation and amortisation is not calculated for the assets because the economic benefits that the assets represent are not consumed until the production phase.

The trigger for an impairment test on these assets

IFRS 6 is very clear with regards to the impairment testing of these assets. Emily will have to test for impairment if the carrying value (Net Book Value) of the asset may not be recoverable.

You must learn the circumstances and facts that indicate a possible impairment and will trigger an impairment test:

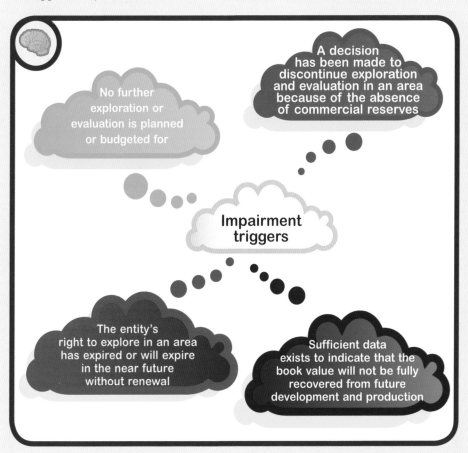

A decision has been made to discontinue exploration and evaluation in an area because of the absence of commercial reserves

No further exploration or evaluation is planned or budgeted for

Impairment triggers

The entity's right to explore in an area has expired or will expire in the near future without renewal

Sufficient data exists to indicate that the book value will not be fully recovered from future development and production

---

 Note

A common error is to read the information – the company has a lack of sufficient data to determine whether the carrying amount of the exploration and evaluation asset is likely to be recovered in full from successful development or by sale – **as meaning an impairment test must be performed. This would actually <u>NOT</u> trigger an impairment test**.

The impairment test

As this type of asset does not generate cash inflows it will have to be tested for impairment as part of a 'cash-generating unit' – a larger group of assets. Emily will need an accounting policy for allocating these assets to groups of cash-generating units (CGUs). **Note that a CGU is also referred to as an IGU – 'income-generating unit' – it means the same thing**. The policy will need to be applied consistently. IAS 36 will then apply in testing the CGU for impairment, subject to certain special requirements.

Special requirements?

The limitation specified in IFRS 6 is that the CGU to which the assets are allocated should not be larger than a segment of the entity. You may remember that IAS 36 specifies that an CGU is the smallest unit for which independent cash flows can be identified. Without this special exemption, it could mean that each individual extraction unit (such as an oil rig) would be classified as a CGU. IFRS 6 is therefore allowing some flexibility for these companies when defining a CGU.

At what point does IFRS 6 stop being relevant to the asset?

If Emily Inc has demonstrated the technical and commercial feasibility of extracting a mineral resource, the assets fall outside IFRS 6 and are reclassified according to other appropriate standards. An impairment test must be performed at this point, i.e. before reclassification.

Sorry but you need to know ... DEFINITIONS

Exploration for and evaluation of mineral resources

The search for mineral resources, including minerals, oils, natural gas and similar non-regenerative resources after the entity has obtained legal rights to explore in a specific area, as well as the determination of the technical feasibility and commercial viability of extracting the mineral resource.

And the really important stuff ... accounting practice

The standard permits a company to continue with its existing accounting policies for mineral resources, and exempts them therefore from the normal requirements for setting accounting policies of IAS 8.

Impairment tests must be performed on exploration and evaluation assets if circumstances suggest the asset may have impaired.

Disclosure

Exploration and development costs that are capitalised are classified as non-current assets in the statement of financial position*, and should be separately disclosed on the face, distinguished from production assets where material.

The classification as tangible or intangible, income and expenses and operating and investing cash flow arising from the exploration for and evaluation of mineral resources.

Details of the amounts recognised in the financial statements, including:

- accounting policies; and
- the amounts of assets, liabilities, income, expenditure and cash flows.

Conclusion

IFRS 6 is not aiming to or achieving consistency of accounting treatment in this area. In fact it allows companies using very different accounting policies to claim adherence to IFRS GAAP. It is exempting such companies from applying the Framework in a similar way to IFRS 4 Insurance contracts. It was argued that it was too harsh to force those entities that use capitalisation in their accounts to switch to expensing, even though IAS 38 requires that they treat these costs as costs not assets. There was also a problem with those companies that exist solely to carry out exploration. Once the exploration is complete they then sell the rights to the minerals found. Prior to IFRS 6, with an application of the Framework and IAS 36 to their transactions, they would only ever have costs and no substantial assets would appear on their statement of financial position*. The IASB accepted these arguments and issued IFRS 6.

IFRS 6 is a very likely exam question where it is on your syllabus as it presents examiners with a useful industry-based scenario, is very current and allows discussion of the conflict between the Framework and some standards.

** Statement of financial position = Balance Sheet (see page 19)

IFRS 8 – Operating segments

Introduction

> **"You might be an accountant if … you have no idea that GAP is also a clothing store!"**
>
> **Traditional**

Well we are nearly at the end of IFRS GAAP now (feel free to cheer!). So what is IFRS 8 about? Well, when a business operates in a variety of different types (classes) of business or in different geographical locations, the external reporting (per IAS 1) of just totals for stuff like profit and revenue is not actually that useful to investors. If meaningful comparisons are to be made, the informed investor would require further detail on performance and sales within specific businesses.

So it's like taking the revenue line, etc and doing a pie chart – segmenting it?

Yep, you've got it – it's just for listed companies and it requires disclosures of certain totals, broken down and reconciled (sort of like a pie chart, i.e. segmented by type of operation). Only then is the reader of the accounts getting a complete and understandable picture of the company's operations.

Sorry but you need to know … DEFINITIONS

An operating segment is a component of an entity:

(a) that engages in business activities from which it may earn revenues and incur expenses (including revenues and expenses relating to transactions with other components of the same entity)

(b) whose operating results are regularly reviewed by the entity's chief operating decision maker to make decisions about resources to be allocated to the segment and assess its performance, and

(c) for which discrete financial information is available.

Transactional example

Berkeley, a public limited company are considering adopting IFRS. Berkeley has three business segments which are currently reported in its financial statements. Berkeley is an international hotel group which reports to management on the basis of region. It does not currently report segmental information under IFRS 8 Operating segments. The results of the regional segments for the year ended 31 May 2008 are as follows:

Region	Revenue		Segment results Profit/(loss)	Segment assets	Segment liabilities
	External	Internal			
	$m	$m	$m	$m	$m
European	200	3	(10)	300	200
South East Asia	300	2	60	800	300
Other regions	500	5	105	2,000	1,400

There were no significant inter-company balances in the segment assets and liabilities. The hotels are located in capital cities in the various regions, and the company sets individual performance indicators for each hotel based on its city location.

Upon adoption of IFRS 8, Operating segments, the identification of Berkeley's segments may or may not change depending on how segments were identified previously. IFRS 8 requires operating segments to be identified on the basis of internal reports about the components of the entity that are regularly reviewed by the chief operating decision maker in order to allocate resources to the segment and to assess its performance.

Transparency

A company adopting IFRS for the first time may find IFRS 8 a bit hard to take, especially if they are from a part of the world that has a culture of secrecy. Whilst Berkeley may have prepared this sort of segmental information for internal use and for review by the board, it may not be prepared for the news that this sort of information may need to be made available to competitors via the notes to the accounts.

Application of the definition

Berkeley will need to consider each part of the IFRS 8 definition to determine what its required disclosures will need to be. There are also quantitative thresholds that need to be considered in order to decide if the operating segment is actually reportable.

Quantitative thresholds

IFRS 8 requires an entity to report separately information about an operating segment that meets any of the following:

- the reported revenue, from both external customers and intersegment sales or transfers, is 10% or more of the combined revenue, internal and external, of all operating segments; or
- the absolute measure of its reported profit or loss is 10% or more of the greater, in absolute amount, of (i) the combined reported profit of all operating segments that did not report a loss, and (ii) the combined reported loss of all operating segments that reported a loss; or
- its assets are 10% or more of the combined assets of all operating segments.

75% rule

If the total external revenue reported by operating segments constitutes less than 75% of the entity's revenue, additional operating segments must be identified as reportable segments (even if they do not meet the quantitative thresholds set out above) until at least 75% of the entity's revenue is included in reportable segments. There is no precise limit to the number of segments that can be disclosed.

Application of quantitative thresholds to Berkeley

As the key performance indicators are set on a city by city basis, there may be information within the internal reports about the components of the entity which has been disaggregated further. Also the company is likely to make decisions about the allocation of resources and about the nature of performance on a city basis because of the individual key performance indicators.

In the case of the existing segments, the European segment meets the criteria for a segment as its reported revenue from external and inter segment sales ($203 million) is more than 10% of the combined revenue ($1,010 million). However, it fails the profit/loss and assets tests. Its results are a loss of $10 million which is less than 10% of the greater of the reported profit or reported loss which is $165 million. Similarly its segment assets of $300 million are less than 10% of the combined segment assets ($3,100 million). The South East Asia segment passes all of the threshold tests. If the company changes its business segments then the above tests will have to be reperformed. A further issue is that the current reported segments constitute less than 75% of the company's external revenue (50%), thus additional operating segments must be identified until 75% of the entity's revenue is included in reportable segments.

Berkeley may have to change the basis of reporting its operating segments. Although the group reports to management on the basis of three geographical regions, it is likely that management will have information which has been further disaggregated in order to make business decisions. Therefore, the internal reports of Berkeley will need to be examined before it is possible to determine the nature of the operating segments.

Statement of profit or loss = Income statement

So ... what's it trying to achieve?

IFRS 8 requires an entity to report financial and descriptive information about its reportable segments. It requires an entity to adopt the 'management approach' to reporting on the financial performance of its operating segments. Generally this means that, the information to be reported would be what management uses internally for evaluating segment performance, and for deciding how to allocate resources to operating segments. IFRS 8 also applies to the consolidated financial statements of a group.

And the really important stuff ... accounting practice

Financial information is required to be reported on the basis that it is used internally for evaluating operating segment performance and deciding how to allocate resources to operating segments.

The definition of an operating segment includes a component of an entity that sells primarily or exclusively to other operating segments of the entity, if the entity is managed that way.

The standard requires reconciliations of total reportable segment revenues, total profit or loss, total assets, total liabilities and other amounts disclosed for reportable segments to corresponding amounts in the entity's financial statements.

Disclosures

An entity shall disclose information to enable users of its financial statements to evaluate the nature and financial effects of the business activities in which it engages and the economic environments in which it operates. Reconciliations of total reportable segment:

- revenues
- profit or loss
- assets
- liabilities
- other amounts.

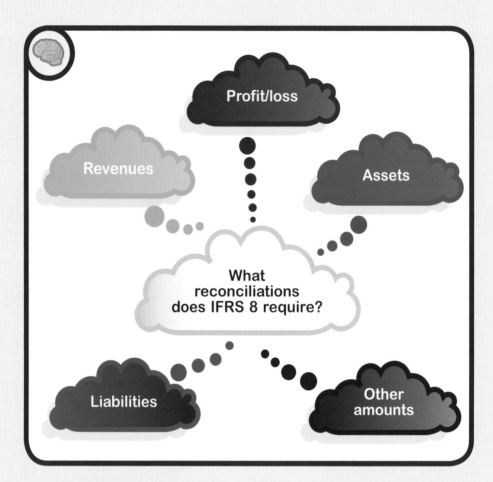

Further Disclosures

- An explanation of how segment profit or loss and segment assets and liabilities are measured for each reportable segment.
- Information about the revenues derived from its products or services (or groups of similar products and services), about the countries in which it earns revenues and holds assets, and about major customers, regardless of whether the information is used by management in making operating decisions.
- Descriptive information is required about the way the operating segments were determined, the products and services provided by the segments, differences between the measurements used in reporting segment information and those used in an entity's financial statements, and changes in the measurement of segment amounts from period to period.

A summary of the disclosures required

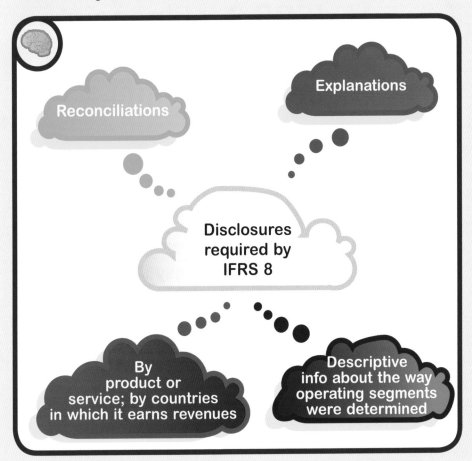

Conclusion

IFRS 8 is merely about providing extra analysis and disclosure. As such questions on this topic are usually 'gifts' – particularly for somebody who likes numbers – practise a few and enjoy.

42 IFRS 9 – Financial instruments - more complex issues

Introduction

> **" Old accountants never die... they simply get derecognised'**
>
> **Anon**

The full IFRS 9: Financial instruments is a very detailed standard it covers:

- recognition of financial instruments
- classification and measurement of financial instruments
- derecognition of financial instruments.

The basics of IFRS 9 have been covered back in Chapter 22 (the green section). It may be worth going back to this and making sure you are happy with the basics. Remember also that IAS 21 Financial instruments: presentation was covered in the green section. It is worth making sure you are happy with this chapter too before going any further.

However if you are sitting an more advanced 'Corporate Reporting' style paper, you probably need a bit more than the basics...you will have to read on:

Recognition of financial instruments

Good news here - nothing new to learn. The initial recognition rule is:

An entity shall recognise a financial asset or a financial liability in its statement of financial position when, and only when, the entity becomes party to the contractual provisions of the instrument.

This was applied throughout Chapter 22, in the green section.

Classification and measurement of financial assets

Again, good news. If you were happy with Chapter 22, there is nothing new to learn.

Classification and measurement of financial liabilities

You will note from Chapter 22 that IFRS 9 recognises two classes of financial liabilities:

- financial liabilities measured at amortised cost using the effective interest method.
- financial liabilities at fair value through profit or loss*.

Most financial liabilities are measured on the statement of financial position** using the standard amortised cost method, and Chapter 22 concentrated on this method. However there may be circumstances when amortised cost is not appropriate and therefore exceptions do exist.

So although Chapter 22 covered the main class of financial liability (amortised cost), for more advanced papers you may need to know the exceptions and the reasons why the fair value classification may be used.

Criticism of the amortised cost method for financial liabilities

Two financial liabilities with identical cash flow obligations can give rise to different measurements using the amortised cost method.

Transactional example

Reeves Inc borrowed $47million on 1st December 2008 when the effective and market interest rate was 5%.

It is repayable on 30 November 2013 and is a single payment note with both interest and capital being repaid on that date.

The same company took out a second loan on 30 November 2009 of $45m when the current market and effective interest rate was 7.4%.

It is repayable on 30 November 2013 and is a single payment note with both interest and capital being repaid on that date.

The first loan of $47m was taken out on 1st December 2008 and is repayable on 30 November 2013. (5 years later.)

The second loan of $45 was taken out on 1st December 2009 and is repayable on 30 November 2013. (4 years later.)

Using amortised cost to measure these liabilities at 30 November 2009 will give materially different answers for each loan.

---

* Statement of profit or loss = Income statement

** Statement of financial position = Balance Sheet (see page 19)

Loan 1 - Initial recognition

(taken out 1 yr earlier)

Dr Bank (cash) $47m
  Cr Loan a/c $47m

> This is the 'normal' style of the amortised cost table with no 'rolled up interest' column. You can continue to put in the 'rolled-up' interest column per Chapter 22, if you prefer.

Subsequent measurement

Date	Balance b/fwd	Finance cost 5%	Cash	Balance c/fwd
	$m	$m	$m	$m
1st December 20X8	47	2.35	(nil)	49.35

So this loan a/c will show a liability in the SOFP of $49.35

Statement of financial position* (extract) as at 30 November 2009

Non-current liabilities	$m
Loan a/c	49.35

The second loan has just been taken out and will show a liability of $45m as you are still at the date of initial recognition

Loan 2- Initial recognition

Dr Cash $45
  Cr Loan a/c $45

Statement of financial position* (extract) as at 30 November 2009

Non-current liabilities	$m
Loan a/c	45

Loan 1 is reported as a liability of $49.35m

Loan 2 is reported as a liability of $45m

It can be argued that fair value would be more informative to the user. On a fair value basis at each reporting date you would present the present value of the future cash flows. Each of these loans as at 30 November 2009 is committing the company to identical future cash flows on 30 November 2013.

*Statement of profit or loss = Income statement

Commitment to future cash flows

Loan 1 for $47m has to be paid back along with 5 years interest of 5% i.e $47m x 1.05 for 5 years = 59.9m on 30 November 2013.

Loan 2 for $45m has to be paid back along with 4 years interest of 7.4% i.e $45m x 1.074 for 4 years = 59.9m on 30 November 2013.

As they have the same future cash flow to the organisation it is argued fair value measurement would be a fairer presentation.

Loan 1- Under fair value measurement

Initial recognition

Dr Bank (cash) $47m
   Cr Loan a/c $47m

i.e no change

Subsequent measurement

1   Identify future cash flows $59.9m
2   Discount to present value based on current interest rates $59.9 x $1/1.074^4$= $45m

The difference between the initial recording of £47m and the subsequent measurement of $45m is a gain that goes to profit of $2m (a reduction in a liability is a gain).

The statement of profit or loss* will still need to show the 2.35m interest expense so will need to show an unrealised gain of $4.35m.

Loan a/c

	$		$
Gain to SOPL	4.35	*1st Dec 2008* Cash	47
Balance c/fwd	45	Finance cost (SOPL)	2.35
		(47 x 5%)	
	49.35		49.35

Reeves Inc actually has identical commitments under these two loans and using fair value i.e. present value of future cash flows, can be argued to be giving a fairer presentation.

So...amortised cost is not always the best answer, so exceptions do exist...

*Statement of profit or loss = Income statement

Exception 1 - Option to designate a financial liability at fair value through profit or loss

An entity may, at initial recognition, irrevocably designate a financial liability as measured at **fair value** through profit or loss when permitted, or when doing so results in more relevant information, because either:

(a) it eliminates or significantly reduces a measurement or recognition inconsistency (sometimes referred to as 'an accounting mismatch') that would otherwise arise from measuring assets or liabilities or recognising the gains and losses on them on different bases; or

(b) a group of financial liabilities or financial assets and financial liabilities is managed and its performance is evaluated on a fair value basis, in accordance with a documented risk management or investment strategy, and information about the group is provided internally on that basis to the entity's key management personnel (as defined in IAS 24 Related party disclosures), for example the entity's board of directors and chief executive officer.

Transactional example - FVTPL

Ethan wishes to apply the fair value option rules of IFRS 9 Financial Instruments to debt issued to finance its investment properties. Ethan's argument for applying the fair value option is based upon the fact that the recognition of gains and losses on its investment properties and the related debt would otherwise be inconsistent. Ethan argued that there is a specific financial correlation between the factors, such as interest rates, that form the basis for determining the fair value of both Ethan's investment properties and the related debt.

Normally debt issued to finance Ethan's investment properties would be accounted for using the amortised cost model. However, Ethan may apply the fair value option in IFRS 9 Financial instruments as such application would eliminate or significantly reduce a measurement or recognition inconsistency between the debt liabilities and the investment properties to which they are related. The provision requires there to be a measurement or recognition inconsistency that would otherwise arise from measuring assets or liabilities or recognising the gains and losses on them on different bases. The option is not restricted to financial assets and financial liabilities.

Accounting mismatch

The IASB concludes that accounting mismatches may occur in a wide variety of circumstances and that financial reporting is best served by providing entities with the opportunity of eliminating such mismatches where that results in more relevant information. Ethan supported the application of the fair value option with the argument that there is a specific financial correlation between the factors that form the basis of the measurement of the fair value of the investment properties and the related debt.

Particular importance was placed on the role played by interest rates, although it is acknowledged that the value of investment properties will also depend, to some extent, on rent, location and maintenance and other factors. For some investment properties, however, the value of the properties will be dependent on the movement in interest rates.

Under IFRS 9, entities with financial liabilities designated as FVTPL recognise changes in the fair value due to changes in the liability's credit risk directly in other comprehensive income (OCI). There is no subsequent recycling of the amounts in OCI to profit or loss*, but accumulated gains or losses may be transferred within equity. The movement in fair value due to other factors would be recognised within profit or loss.

However, if presenting the change in fair value attributable to the credit risk of the liability in OCI would create or enlarge an accounting mismatch in profit or loss*, all fair value movements are recognised in profit or loss. An entity is required to determine whether an accounting mismatch is created when the financial liability is first recognised, and this determination is not reassessed. The mismatch must arise due to an economic relationship between the financial liability and the associated asset that results in the liability's credit risk being offset by a change in the fair value of the asset.

Exception 2 - If the financial liability is a derivative

Note

Note how broad the definition is of a financial instrument ...

'Any contract that gives rise to both a financial asset of one enterprise and a financial liability or equity instrument of another enterprise.'

This means that if the question you are looking at has a company that has taken out any of the following derivative contracts:

- forwards
- futures
- options
- swaps

then IFRS 9 will apply to these contracts as well as stuff like issuing loan notes.

A derivative contract is simply any contract that derives its value from the movement in an underlying financial market.

The underlying financial market could be the foreign exchange rate (like a foreign forward contract) or the interest rate (like an interest rate swap). Other underlying markets could be commodity prices or share prices.

*Statement of profit or loss = Income statement

Derivative contracts will need to be measured at the statement of financial position*. As at the reporting date the contract could be in a favourable position – a derivative asset may exist, or indeed it may be in an unfavourable positive – a derivative liability may exist. Basic accounting rule is to classify derivative contracts as 'Fair Value through P&L' (FVTPL). However there is a possibility that the company might employ an alternative mechanism we call 'hedge accounting'.

 Transactional example

Margie, a public limited company, is a manufacturer of aluminium products. The finance director has entered into a contract with a producer to purchase 350 tonnes of wheat. The purchase price will be settled in cash at an amount equal to the value of 2,500 of Margie shares.

Margie may settle the contract at any time by paying the producer an amount equal to the current market value of 2,500 of Margie shares, less the market value of 350 tonnes of wheat.

Margie has no intention of taking physical delivery of this wheat.

This is not a purchase of wheat, but a financial contract to pay or receive a cash amount.

The contract will be accounted for as a derivative contract and should be valued at fair value..

Initially the fair value of such a contract is nil as under the terms of a commercial contract the value of 2,500 shares should equate to the value of 350 tonnes of wheat.

At each period end the contract would be revalued and it would be expected that differences will arise between the values of wheat and Margie shares as their respective market values will be dependent on a number of differing factors.

The net difference is taken to profit or loss.

This is known as a speculative derivative.

Sometimes a company only has a derivative instrument as part of a 'hedging strategy'. If this is the case basic accounting may not give the fairest presentation.

Hedge accounting will eventually be covered by IFRS 9 but for now it continues to be part of IAS 39.

If hedge accounting is examinable for you please read the section elsewhere in this book. The rest of IAS 39 has been superseded by IFRS 9. Eventually hedge accounting will be incorporated too.

* Statement of financial position = Balance Sheet (see page 19)

Exception 3 - Financial liabilities that arise when a transfer of a financial asset does not qualify for derecognition or when the continuing involvement approach applies.

If a transfer does not result in derecognition because the entity has retained substantially all the risks and rewards of ownership of the transferred asset, the entity shall continue to recognise the transferred asset in its entirety and shall recognise a financial liability for the consideration received. In subsequent periods, the entity shall recognise any income on the transferred asset and any expense incurred on the financial liability.

This was actually what we did in Chapter 22 when we factored the receivables.

Exception 4 - Financial guarantee contracts

A contract that requires the issuer to make specified payments to reimburse the holder for a loss it incurs because a specified debtor fails to make payment when due in accordance with the original or modified terms of a debt instrument.

An issuer of such a contract shall subsequently measure it at the higher of:

(i) the amount determined in accordance with IAS 37 Provisions, Contingent Liabilities and Contingent Assets and

(ii) the amount initially recognised less, when appropriate, cumulative amortisation recognised in accordance with IAS 18 Revenue.

Exception 5 - Providing a loan at below-market interest

After initial recognition, an issuer of such a commitment shall subsequently measure it at the higher of:

(i) the amount determined in accordance with IAS 37 and

(ii) the amount initially recognised less, when appropriate, cumulative amortisation recognised in accordance with IAS 18.

Some companies grant interest free loans to their employees. This is a transaction, which would need you to refer to IFRS 9 Financial Instruments and IAS 19 Employee Benefits.

You would also need to know the market rate of interest if a similar loan had been provided in an arms length transaction.

When a financial asset is recognised initially, IFRS 9 requires it to be measured at fair value, plus transaction costs in certain situations. Normally the fair value is the fair value of the consideration given. However the fair value of an interest free loan may not necessarily be its face amount. The fair value may be estimated as the discounted present value of the future receipts using the market interest rate.

If the financial asset is to be measured at amortised cost, it must comply with both tests i.e. the asset is held to collect the cash flows associated with the asset with those cash flows consisting solely of interest and capital. It this is not the case the financial asset would need to be valued at fair value through profit or loss.

Transactional example - interest free loans

Lucy granted interest free loans to its employees on 1st June 2011 of $10million. The loans will be paid back on 31 May 2012 as a single payment by the employees: The market rate of interest for both of the above dates is 6% per annum. The company is unsure how to account for the loan but wishes to classify the loans as being accounted for at amortised cost under IFRS 9 Financial instruments.

Required

Discuss, with relevant computations, how this financial instrument should be accounted for in the financial statements for the year ended 31 May 2011.

When a financial asset is recognised initially, IFRS 9 requires it to be measured at fair value, plus transaction costs in certain situations. Normally the fair value is the fair value of the consideration given. However the fair value of an interest free loan may not necessarily be its face amount.

In this case the fair value may be estimated as the discounted present value of the future receipts using the market interest rate.

If the financial asset is to be measured at amortised cost, it must comply with both tests i.e. the asset is held to collect the cash flows associated with the asset with those cash flows consisting solely of interest and capital. If this is not the case the financial asset would need to be valued at fair value through profit or loss.

In this case the tests appear to be met. The fair value of the loan can be measured at 1st June 2010 as the present value of the future cash flows. 10m x 1/1.062 = 8.9 million.

The difference between the 8.9m and the 10 million repayment will be debited to the statement of profit or loss over the two year period.

*Statement of profit or loss = Income statement

Initial recognition

At 1st June 2010	$	$
Dr Financial asset –	8.9m	
Dr Employee compensation	1.1m	
Cr Bank (cash)		10m

Subsequent measurement

At 31 May 2011 Amortised cost	$	$
Dr Financial asset	0.53	
Cr Statement of profit or loss		0.53

	Bal b/fwd	Finance income 6%	Cash received	Bal c/fwd
1st June 2010	8.9	0.53	nil	9.43
1st June 2011	9.43	0.57	nil	10.0

Derecognition

Derecognition is the removal of a previously recognised financial asset or financial liability from an entity's statement of financial position.

In Chapter 22 the concept of derecognition was introduced along with the basic application of the need to have transferred substantially all risks and rewards of ownership. The Chapter 22 transactional example of debt factoring is a very common transaction and one all students need to be familiar with.

The standard however has more to it than the basic application of 'risk and reward transfer'. In more advanced papers, you may need to be able to advise on more complex transactions.

Derecognition - more complex transactions

In consolidated financial statements, an entity first consolidates all subsidiaries in accordance with IFRS 10 Consolidated financial statements and then applies IFRS 9 to the resulting group.

Before evaluating whether, and to what extent, derecognition is appropriate an entity determines whether derecognition should be applied to a part of a financial asset (or a part of a group of similar financial assets) or a financial asset (or a group of similar financial assets) in its entirety, as follows.

Derecognition - full or partial

Derecognition is applied to a part of a financial asset (or a part of a group of similar financial assets) if, and only if, the part being considered for derecognition meets one of the following three conditions.

(i) The part comprises only specifically identified cash flows from a financial asset (or a group of similar financial assets).

 Transactional example

Glasshouse purchased a debt instrument but now enters into an 'interest rate strip' with Watermarque Inc.

This gives Watermarque Inc the right to the interest cash flows but not the principal cash flow, which will still go to Glasshouse.

> Glasshouse still holds a financial asset for the present value of the expected future cash flow (principal only).
> The interest element of the asset may be derecognised.

(ii) The part comprises only a fully proportionate (pro rata) share of the cash flows from a financial asset (or a group of similar financial assets).

(iii) The part comprises only a fully proportionate (pro rata) share of specifically identified cash flows from a financial asset (or a group of similar financial assets).

In all other cases, the financial asset is derecognised in its entirety (or to the group of similar financial assets in their entirety).

Derecognition of a financial asset

Derecognition occurs when the contractual rights to the cash flows expire (e.g. a receivable would be derecognised when the customer pays their debt) or when a financial asset is transferred/sold (based on whether substantially all of the risks and rewards of ownership have been transferred).

Risks and rewards of ownership

For example, if a company sells an investment in shares, but retains the right to repurchase the shares at any time at a price equal to their current fair value then it should derecognise the asset.

If the company sells an investment in shares and enters into an agreement whereby the buyer will return any increases in value to the company and the company will pay the buyer interest plus compensation for any decrease in the value of the investment, then the company should not derecognise the asset as it has retained substantially all the risks and rewards.

Transactional example

Liberty Inc purchased a portfolio of debt instruments, whose coupon and effective interest rate is 10% for $10,000. Liberty now enters into a transaction with Juju Inc. Juju Inc agrees to pay $9,115 to Liberty.

Juju now has the right to $9,000 of any collections of principal plus interest thereon at 9.5%.

Liberty retains the right to $1,000 of any collections of principal plus interest thereon of 10% plus the excess spread of 0.5% on the remaining $9,000 of principal.

Collections from the portfolio are allocated between Liberty and Juju proportionately in the ratio of 1:9, but any defaults are deducted from Liberty's interest of $1,000 until that interest is exhausted.

The fair value of the debt instrument at the date of the transaction is $10,000 and the fair value of the excess spread is $40.

Liberty determines it has transferred some significant risks and rewards of ownership but has retained some significant risks and reward of ownership (defaults are deducted from them first).

To apply this IFRS, the entity analyses the transaction as (a) a retention of a fully proportionate retained interest of $1,000, plus (b) the subordination of that retained interest to provide credit enhancement to the transferee for credit losses.

The entity calculates that $9,090 (90 per cent x $10,100) of the consideration received of $9,115 represents the consideration for a fully proportionate 90 per cent share. The remainder of the consideration received ($25) represents consideration received for subordinating its retained interest to provide credit enhancement to the transferee for credit losses. In addition, the excess spread of 0.5 per cent represents consideration received for the credit enhancement. Accordingly, the total consideration received for the credit enhancement is $65 ($25 + $40).

The entity calculates the gain or loss on the sale of the 90 per cent share of cash flows. Assuming that separate fair values of the 90 per cent part transferred and the 10 per cent part retained are not available at the date of the transfer, the entity allocates the carrying amount of the asset as follows:

	Fair value	Percentage	Allocated carrying amount
Portion transferred	9,090	90%	9,000
Portion retained	1,010	10%	1,000
	10,100		10,000

Liberty Inc computes its gain or loss on the sale of the 90 per cent share of the cash flows by deducting the allocated carrying amount of the portion transferred from the consideration received, i.e. $90 ($9,090 – $9,000). The carrying amount of the portion retained by the entity is $1,000.

In addition, Liberty Inc recognises the continuing involvement that results from the subordination of its retained interest for credit losses. Accordingly, it recognises an asset of $1,000 (the maximum amount of the cash flows it would not receive under the subordination), and an associated liability of $1,065 (which is the maximum amount of the cash flows it would not receive under the subordination, i.e. $1,000 plus the fair value of the subordination of $65).

The entity uses all of the above information to account for the transaction as follows:

	$	$
Bank (cash)	9,115	
Asset recognised for subordination or the residual interest	1,000	
Asset for the consideration received in the form of excess spread	40	
Cr Original asset		9,000
Cr Liability		1,065
Cr Profit or loss...		90

Immediately following the transaction, the carrying amount of the asset is $2,040 comprising $1,000, representing the allocated cost of the portion retained, and $1,040, representing the entity's additional continuing involvement from the subordination of its retained interest for credit losses (which includes the excess spread of $40).

In subsequent periods, the entity recognises the consideration received for the credit enhancement ($65) on a time proportion basis, accrues interest on the recognised asset using the effective interest method and recognises any credit impairment on the recognised assets. As an example of the latter, assume that in the following year there is a credit impairment loss on the underlying loans of $300. The entity reduces its recognised asset by $600 ($300 relating to its retained interest and $300 relating to the additional continuing involvement that arises from the subordination of its retained interest for credit losses), and reduces its recognised liability by $300.

The net result is a charge to profit or loss for credit impairment of $300.

Derecognition of a financial liability

An entity shall remove a financial liability (or a part of a financial liability) from its statement of financial position* when, and only when, it is extinguished - i.e. when the obligation specified in the contract is discharged or cancelled or expires.

An exchange between an existing borrower and lender of debt instruments with substantially different terms shall be accounted for as an extinguishment of the original financial liability and the recognition of a new financial liability. Similarly, a substantial

---

* Statement of financial position = Balance Sheet (see page 19)

modification of the terms of an existing financial liability or a part of it (whether or not attributable to the financial difficulty of the debtor) shall be accounted for as an extinguishment of the original financial liability and the recognition of a new financial liability.

The difference between the carrying amount of a financial liability (or part of a financial liability) extinguished or transferred to another party and the consideration paid, including any non-cash assets transferred or liabilities assumed, shall be recognised in profit or loss.

Transactional example - derecognition

Rona held a 3% holding in the shares of Marts, a public limited company. The investment was designated upon recognition as fair value through other comprehensive income. At 31 May 2010 the fair value was $5 million. The cumulative gain recognised in equity relating to the investment was $400,000. On the same day, the whole of the share capital of Marts was acquired by Given, a public limited company, and as a result Rona received shares in Given with a fair value of $5.5 million in exchange for its holding in Marts. The company wishes to know how the exchange of shares in Marts for the shares in Given should be accounted for in its financial records.

Required

Discuss, with relevant computations, how the above financial instruments should be accounted for in the financial statements for the year ended 31 May 2010.

Shares in Marts

Rona first of all has to determine if the transfer of shares in Marts qualifies for derecognition. The criteria are firstly to determine that the asset has been transferred, and then to determine whether or not the entity has transferred substantially all the risks and rewards of ownership of the asset. If substantially all the risks and rewards have been transferred, the asset is derecognised. If substantially all risks and rewards have been retained, derecognition of the asset is not allowed.

In this case derecognition is allowed as Rona no longer retains any risks and rewards of ownership. The proceeds in the asset exchange will be the fair value of the shares received in Given

Carrying amount of the 3% holding in Marts	$5
Proceeds - FV of asset gained	$5.5
Profit on disposal to statement of profit or loss*	$0.5

*Statement of profit or loss = Income statement

In addition Rona can choose to make a transfer with equity of the cumulative gain arising at the disposal date of $400,000.

The shares in Rona are now recognised at their fair value of $5.5 million.

In addition Rona obtains a new financial asset which is the shares in Given.

Recognition of the shares in Given

The shares in Given should be recognised at fair value of $5.5m.

Conclusion

IFRS 9 is probably the most complex of all the accounting standards. If you have conquered the green section, you are actually going to be fine for the majority of exam questions.

It is possible though that you may occasionally come across a more complex transaction, so you do need to be aware that exceptions to the basic rules do exist.

IAS 39 – Financial instruments: recognition and measurement

Introduction

> "Two accountants are in a bank, when armed robbers burst in. While several of the robbers take the money from the tellers, others line the customers, including the accountants, up against a wall, and proceed to take their wallets, watches, etc. While this is going on accountant number one jams something in accountant number two's hand. Without looking down, accountant number two whispers, "What is this?" to which accountant number one replies, "It's that $50 I owe you."
>
> **Traditional**

Financial instruments are in a period of transition. IFRS 9 supersedes most of IAS 39. However two areas remain:

- hedge accounting
- impairment of financial assets.

Eventually Hedge accounting will be incorporated with IFRS 9 and Impairment of financial assets will get its own standard.

For now, however, these bits of IFRS 9 live on

So ... what's it trying to achieve?
The standard provides rules and treatments for hedge accounting.

Hedge accounting

To be allowed to hedge account an entity must formally designate a hedging relationship between a hedged item (the asset/liability, future transaction or foreign subsidiary) being protected and the hedging instrument (always a derivative unless protecting foreign exchange risk where it may be a primary instrument, a loan).

The hedge can be one of three types.

- Fair value   Hedged item is an asset or liability or a firm commitment.
- Cash flow   Hedged item is a forecast future transaction (or a firm commitment for foreign exchange transactions).
- Net investment   Hedged item is a foreign subsidiary.

To hedge account (see below) the following criteria must be met:

- formal documentation at the inception of the hedge
- designation between the hedged item and the hedging instrument is documented
- hedge is expected to be highly effective at inception and on-going
- effectiveness can be measured
- for cash flow hedges – transaction must be highly probable
- the hedge is assessed on an on-going basis, and effective throughout the period.

An effective hedge is when the gain or loss on the hedged item is offset by an opposite gain or loss on a hedging instrument between 80% and 125%.

A mnemonic **(DEAD)** works well here – remember it if you are asked the criteria for hedge accounting in the exam:

D Document the hedge formally at its inception

E Effectiveness of the hedge must be expected

A Assessment of the hedge is assessed on an on-going basis (80–125%)

D Designation between the hedged item and hedging instrument at the outset

The hedge accounting treatment is as follows.

Fair value hedge

Both the hedged item and the hedging instrument are revalued to fair value, and the opposite gains and losses are recognised directly in the statement of profit or loss.

Cash flow hedge

The hedging instrument is revalued to fair value and the gain or loss is taken to a separate reserve. When the hedged item is recognised the separate reserve is recycled to the income statement, or if it is a non-monetary asset or liability the recycling can be to the cost of the hedged item.

Net investment hedge

The hedging instrument (usually a loan) is revalued to fair value with any gain or loss recognised in reserves to offset against the gain or loss on the foreign subsidiary. The offset is limited to the gain or loss recognised on the subsidiary.

Impairment of financial assets

Financial assets that are measured at fair value through profit or loss are not subject to an impairment review. Remeasurement of fair value at each reporting date will automatically take account of any impairment.

Similarly, financial assets measured at fair value through other comprehensive income are not subject to an impairment review. Any changes in fair value, including those, which may relate to impairment, are recognised in other comprehensive income. There is no recognition or recycling of impairment to profit or loss.

For financial assets measured at amortised cost, IAS 39 requires that an assessment be made, at every reporting date, as to whether there is any objective evidence that a financial asset is impaired, i.e. whether an event has occurred that has had a negative impact on the expected future cash flows of the asset.

The event causing the negative impact must have already happened. An event causing impairment in the future shall not be anticipated. For example, on the last day of its financial year a bank lends a customer $100,000. The bank has consistently experienced a default rate of 5% across all its loans. The bank is not permitted immediately to write this loan down to $95,000 based on its past experience, because no default has occurred at the reporting date.

Transactional example

A company makes a 5-year loan of $15,000 at an effective and original interest rate of 7% received at the end of the year. The loan will be repaid at a value of $15,000. One year before maturity, there is evidence of impairment due to the financial difficulties of the borrower and it is estimated the company will only receive $7,500 in the future.

The loan is measured at the present value of the estimated future cash flows discounted using the original effective interest rate i.e. $7,500 discounted for one year at 7% (£7,009). The impairment loss recognised would be $(15,000 – 7,009) i.e. $7,991.

IAS 39 requires accrual of interest on impaired loans and receivables using the effective interest rate. Thus interest of $491 ($7,009 * 7%) would be accrued.

If the amount of £7,500 is eventually received then the entry would be:

	$	$
Dr Cash	7,500	
Cr Interest Income		491
Cr Loans and receivables		7,009

Conclusion

IAS 39 is still an important standards as the global economic crisis has led to a lot of exam questions involving impairment testing of financial assets. Do not ignore this one!

The area of accounting standards is subject to frequent change. If you would like to check up on whether the position has changed, or is about to, have a look at www.kaplanpublishing.co.uk/ifrs.

* Statement of financial position = Balance Sheet (see page 19)

Index

Index

G

H

I

O

P

Q

R

S